20010124

A COUNTRY HELD HOSTAGE

HOW THE WORLD FINANCES CANADA'S DEBT

MIVILLE TREMBLAY

Translated by Fred A. Reed

Stoddart

Published in 1996 by
Stoddart Publishing Co. Limited
34 Lesmill Road
Toronto, Canada
M3B 2T6
Tel. (416) 445-3333
Fax (416) 445-5967

Stoddart Books are available for bulk purchase for sales promotions,
premiums, fundraising, and seminars. For details, contact the
Special Sales Department at the above address.

Canadian Cataloguing in Publication Data

Tremblay, Miville, 1955–
A country held hostage: how the world finances Canada's debt

Translation of: Le pays en otage: le financement de la dette publique.

ISBN 0-7737-2985-2

1. Debts, Public – Canada. 2. Debts, External – Canada.
3. Deficit financing – Canada. 4. Investments, Foreign – Canada.
I. Title.

HJ8513.T7313 1996   336.3'6'0971   C96-931255-5

Cover Design: Bill Douglas @ The Bang
Text Design: Andrew Smith

Printed and bound in Canada

*Stoddart Publishing gratefully acknowledges the support of the
Canada Council and the Ontario Arts Council in the development
of writing and publishing in Canada.*

For my children, Maxime and Laurence,
in the hope that the thirst for learning
will be their lifelong companion.

CONTENTS

ACKNOWLEDGMENTS

If I believed in astrology, I would have pointed to the favourable alignment of the planets. In like manner, my research depended for its success on the favourable alignment of many individuals and organizations. Their cooperation was, from the beginning, exemplary.

The impetus for this book came from the Atkinson Fellowship in Public Policy, awarded each year to a Canadian journalist for a one-year research project on a topical issue of public policy. The fellowship is sponsored by the Atkinson Charitable Foundation, the *Toronto Star*, and the Beland Honderich Family, and includes a stipend of $85,000. I want to thank all members of the jury, especially Abe Rotstein and John Honderich. I must also express my appreciation to my employers at *La Presse*, who granted me a one-year leave of absence, and who published, beginning on October 7, 1995, simultaneously with the *Toronto Star*, an extended series of articles based on my research.

I was also able to call upon the financial and logistical support of the Asia Pacific Foundation of Canada and of the Foreign Press Center, Japan, which generously covered the expenses of my two-week visit to Japan. In Tokyo, Ms. Chise Takahashi devoted several days to organizing meetings for me. While in London and Edinburgh, I was the guest of the United Kingdom Foreign Office, which was of inestimable assistance in establishing contacts.

In Montreal, my physical and intellectual home port for this year of study and research was the Centre for International Business Studies of the École des Hautes Études Commerciales, where André Poirier opened all doors to me, and where I was able to draw upon a wealth of incomparable expertise and vital material assistance.

On my return from my globe-trotting, I found myself alone before the blank page. Several people placed their skills and rich experience at my disposal, to read, criticize, and encourage me in my efforts: Mark Auger, Jean Biron, André Charbonneau, Marie-Éva De Villers, François Leroux, Lise Nadon-Tremblay, Claude Picher, and Rayond Théoret. Their support proved invaluable.

Another group of people assisted me in ways as diverse as they were precious, difficult to explain, and unforgettable: Diane Bellemare, Bernard Bonin, Houri Bosnoyan, Yvan Bourdeau, Rick Boychuck, Ann Brockle-hurst, Wallid Daoudi, Alain Dubuc, Pierre Fortin, and Serge Godin.

I am also grateful to Fred Reed, who faithfully translated this book, and to the staff of Stoddart Publishing, for their invaluable assistance.

Thanks also to those people who, both in Montreal and Toronto, put me in contact with their own international networks; for fear of not naming each one, my gratitude to all. Finally, my warmest thanks to all who spent hours, sometimes days, explaining their professional activities in the smallest detail. Without their patience and remarkable confidence, this book would simply not exist.

INTRODUCTION

IT HAD ALL the makings of a scoop. The dust from the October 1993 federal election, which saw the Bloc Québécois become the official opposition, had hardly settled when my phone rang. The breathless voice on the line, a bond dealer I knew, was telling me that an American institutional investor had just unloaded $1.3 billion of Quebec government securities. The principal buyer was none other than the province's powerful Caisse de dépôt et placement, the public body that manages many funds, including the Quebec Pension Plan and the provincial employees' pension plan. It was the heftiest transaction ever registered on the secondary provincial bond market, said my source.

The details were hard to pin down — deals of this kind are confidential — but it looked suspiciously as though a major foreign creditor had decided to bail out. Curiosity cranked up, I got on the phone, and after four hours of probing I finally tracked down the mystery investor: Retirement Systems of Alabama (RSA), the state employees' pension fund.[1]

The story took another twist when I reached Tom Milne, the RSA official who had made the decision to sell the bonds. The sale, he explained, covered $700 million (CA) of long-term Government of Quebec and Hydro-Québec bonds, plus $250 million of Government of Ontario bonds. But there was more: the transaction had been completed several days before the election; it had nothing to do with politics or provincial debt levels. RSA simply wanted to trim the average maturity of its bond portfolio, reasoning that long-term bonds were unlikely to realize additional capital gains. "We sold the Quebec bonds because they were easier to sell than several small blocks of American bonds" of the same maturity, he said. There went my scoop.

Milne was actually paying the province a compliment! Hard-nosed investors prize the liquidity of an issue. Not to mention that RSA had

1

already rung up more than $100 million in capital gains and interest since buying the Quebec bonds eight months before. The State of Alabama has been buying Quebec bonds since the mid 1970s, he added, and will buy them again at the next favourable opportunity.

By then I knew there was no scandal to expose. But I had stumbled onto a fascinating subject for investigation. I'd also learned two important lessons. First, that a lone foreign institutional investor can single-handedly move a huge block of bonds. The $950-million total represented almost one-third of Quebec's net borrowing for 1993. If other investors had followed suit, the impact would have sent shock waves rippling through Canadian financial markets, driving down the dollar and sending interest rates sky-high.

Lesson two was a touchier one. Imputing motives to foreign investors can be risky. Better ask them their reasons — and check the facts, even if it means taking a trip to Montgomery, Alabama.

This book will take you to Montgomery, and to the financial capitals of the world. It will be your tour guide into the labyrinth of public debt financing, your key to the doors of powerful financial institutions. We will spend whole days in trading rooms never before visited by outsiders. Together we will observe and listen to the key players: government borrowers, middlemen, and creditors. Most of the people we will be meeting have agreed to speak on the record for the first time. Over a glass of Perrier, a demitasse of espresso, a mug of watery coffee, a milky cup of British tea, or a bowl of the Japanese green variety, we will get to know some of the foreign investors we hear so much, but know so little, about.

We can argue the pros and cons of the deficit until the cows come home. But as long as Canadians are not saving enough to meet the country's capital needs, including the financing of our public debt, as long as trade surpluses cannot offset our anemic savings, we have no alternative: we must turn to foreign investors. Will they continue to lend us the money we need, when we need it? Assuming they do, what will be their conditions?

Canada's indebtedness is cause for general concern in the investment community. Constitutional uncertainty magnifies this concern. No one can predict how the debt will be apportioned in the event that Quebec decides to separate. Not surprisingly, fund managers have serious questions about the budget situation in a sovereign Quebec — and in a Canada without

Quebec. So far, these concerns remain unaddressed.

Our investigation begins with the election of the Parti Québécois on September 12, 1994, and ends after the referendum of October 30, 1995. Not a single one of the investors we encountered believed that the Yes side would win. The No's hair's breadth victory shook more than a few assumptions. Until Quebeckers and Canadians devise a long-lasting solution to their political problems, foreign investors can be expected to be wary.

The situation in a nutshell

Before setting out on our whirlwind, round-the-world tour, let's take a quick look at the situation as it stood at the end of 1994.

The national debt represents the total of the country's annual deficits, and it can be computed in two principal ways. Finance departments use the budgetary accounts method, which covers the government's fiscal year, from April 1 to March 31.[2] Economists prefer the national accounts budgeting method, which they claim is more thorough and better adapted for international comparison. Using this approach, net public debt can be defined as debt incurred by all levels of government, less financial assets. In 1974, the debt so defined represented 5 percent of Gross Domestic Product (GDP), the value of all goods and services produced in Canada that year. Twenty years later it had reached 97 percent of GDP. Average debt level for the principal OECD countries stands at 42 percent of GDP.

These figures suggest three propositions:

- First: theoretically speaking, in order to repay the debt all individuals and corporations would have to contribute their full salaries, profits, and other income for an entire year. That would mean forcing Canadians to live on bread and water — an unlikely prospect.
- Second: we cannot continue on as we have for the last twenty years and hope to keep up our membership in the club of wealthy countries. Debate on public finance should lead to a compromise between the two extremes, and consensus on how we reach it.

3

- Third: we should bear in mind that the debt level in Canada is twice as high as the average for developed countries.

THE DEBT: PRIMARILY A FEDERAL MATTER
Net public debt breakdown at the end of 1994 using the national accounting method

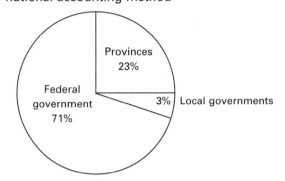

Provinces
23%

Federal
government
71%

3% Local governments

Total: $691 billion (CA)

Source: Statistics Canada, nº 68-212, March 1995

Canada's net debt of $691 billion, as a percentage of GDP, can be broken down among the different levels of government as follows: federal, 71 percent; provincial, 23 percent; local governments, 3 percent; for a total of 97 percent. Indebtedness is a crushing burden for public administration as a whole, but its greatest impact is on Ottawa and the provinces.

Who finances the debt? Canadians themselves, for up to 60 percent of the total. They do this when they purchase Canada Savings Bonds, but most of all when they place their savings in institutions that then invest a portion in negotiable bonds and Treasury bills issued by the federal and provincial governments. Canadians who invest in these securities are motivated less by patriotism than by profit considerations and low risk levels. The same can be said for foreigners, though their perspective on Canadian bonds is quite different.

How extensive is foreign ownership of Canadian financial assets? When they make the decision to invest in Canadian securities, non-residents, as defined by Statistics Canada, prefer bonds over stocks by fourteen to one, and public over corporate paper by eight to one. Over the last ten years, lending by foreigners to Canadian governments has nearly doubled. Non-Canadians now hold $278 billion in government securities, evenly divided between the federal government and provincial

4

governments and their crown corporations. Municipal bonds account for only 3 percent of the total.

Foreign-held securities represent a quarter of federal and two-thirds of provincial debt financed on the open market.[3] A portion of the debt, particularly accounting entries that set the amounts governments owe their employees' pension funds, need not be financed on the market. This is what is called an unfunded actuarial liability. Applying the broader concept of net debt, which includes accounting entries, 40 percent of Canadian net government debt is held by foreigners.

As a rule, the federal government borrows only in Canadian dollars, issuing Treasury bills and bonds on the Canadian market. Foreigners may then purchase or sell through Canadian-based investment dealers or banks. But to replenish its international exchange reserves, Ottawa occasionally floats securities denominated in U.S. dollars on American and European markets, borrowings which account for no more than 4 percent of total debt. Federal agencies like the Canada Development Bank (formerly the Federal Business Development Bank) or the Export Development Corporation (EDC) regularly issue bonds in foreign currencies on foreign markets. The provinces, and provincial electric utilities, borrow massively abroad, offering bonds sometimes denominated in Canadian funds but principally in foreign currencies on the London, New York, and Tokyo financial markets.[4] Of the $142.5 billion in provincial securities in foreign hands, only 18 percent are repayable in Canadian

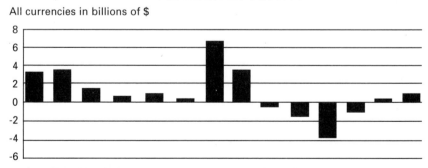

FOREIGNERS BUYING CANADIAN BONDS: THE SEESAW EFFECT

All currencies in billions of $

Jan. Feb. March April May June July Aug. Sept. Oct. Nov. Dec. Jan. Feb.
1994 1995

Source: ScotiaMcLeod

5

AMERICANS: OUR LARGEST CREDITORS

Breakdown of government securities held by foreign investors
at the end of 1994

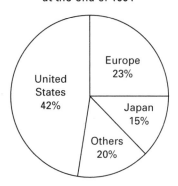

Total: $278 billion (CA)

Source: Statistics Canada, nº 67-202, March 1995

dollars, a shrinking portion. Nearly 65 percent are repayable in U.S. dollars, 12 percent in Japanese yen, and 14 percent in European currencies.

Of Canadian public securities in foreign hands, 42 percent are held by Americans. European Union investors hold 23 percent, the Japanese 15 percent, and other countries (including Switzerland) the remaining 20 percent. Proportions are fluid, with monthly figures revealing wide fluctuations in purchases and sales from different parts of the world. Borrowing instrument preferences also vary widely. For example, 1994 saw foreigners buying provincial bonds denominated in foreign currencies; they decreased their proportion of federal government bonds, selling slightly more than they bought; and they increased their proportion of Treasury bills. The number of securities held by foreigners reflects an erratic buying pattern, the net result of millions of buy and sell transactions. Irregular capital flows fuel uncertainty, not only where current deficit financing is concerned but also with respect to the ongoing process of accumulated debt renewal. With borrowing comes high economic costs: in 1994, governments paid foreigners $18 billion in interest, double Canada's trade surplus for the same year.

We are trapped between a rock and a hard place. We must turn to foreign capital because Canadians are not saving enough to finance public debt, business investment, and consumer borrowing (in the form of mortgages and credit card debt). Investment of Canadian savings abroad, both in plant construction and subsidiary acquisition, as well as in shorter-term investments, exacerbates the situation. Canadian pension funds and mutual funds invest a small but ever-increasing portion of their funds outside of Canada. At the end of 1994, Canadian institutions held $78 billion in foreign securities, principally in the form of American stocks — five times more than a decade before. But these holdings amount to only one-fifth the size of Canadian securities portfolios held by foreigners.

PUBLIC DEBT SKYROCKETS IN 1982
Net debt of the federal, provincial, territorial, and local governments at March 31

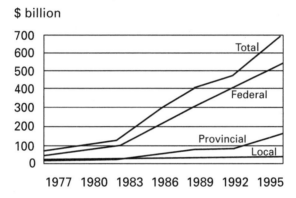

Source: Statistics Canada, Public Sector Finances 1994/1995, n° 68-212

A country held hostage

More than any other OECD member country, Canada depends on foreign capital to finance public debt. This is even more true for Quebec. Trussed and bound, subject to the whims of our creditors, we are at the mercy of every tremor that may shake international markets. Whether Canada or Quebec is the nation dearest to your heart, it is being held hostage.

A threat is less dangerous if we understand it. Why do foreigners purchase Canadian Treasury bills and bonds? When and why do they sell these securities, and what are the criteria they base their decisions on?

What risks do they associate with Canadian public borrowers? What do they even know about Canada? Or the Quebec question, for that matter? What are their perceptions? Are they likely to change their minds overnight?

No less important is understanding why and how Canadians invest abroad, and how they divide their Canadian investment portfolio between the federal and provincial governments.

These are the questions I put to more than 175 financial market insiders in twenty-some cities around the world. While my investigation makes no pretense of being scientific, it has been painstaking and detailed. The questions asked were open-ended and unbiased; no rigid questionnaire was used. Persons interviewed were not selected because of their views (of which I was unaware prior to the interview) but because they represented a significant cross-section of credible players. Deliberately focusing on people close to the action, I spoke to some influential analysts, and a very few top executives — but not a single politician. Whether their answers please or shock is immaterial; the fact is that their opinions carry a disproportionate weight. The power of investors is the power of money: the power to give, and to take away; the power to reward, the power to punish. The people who wield this power are managing not their own assets but the savings of wealthy and less wealthy clients around the world. Many of these clients are counting on their savings for retirement, or for rainy day protection. Just like most Canadians.

Chapters 3, 4, 5, and 7 deal with continental Europe, the United Kingdom, Japan, and the United States respectively. They present the views of our foreign creditors. In the course of our travels, you may well come to concur with Graham Allison, an American political scientist, who notes that, on any complex issue, "where you stand depends on where you sit."[5] Needless to say, the outlook of Canadian fund managers described in chapter 6 is of prime importance. These are the people who finance the lion's share of the public debt. Chapter 8 shows how the influential New York rating agencies make their critical decisions. Finally, borrowers, be they the government of Canada, the provinces, or crown corporations, are discussed in chapter 9.

It's not always easy to understand the key players. They speak a language all their own and juggle complex figures and astronomical sums of money. Don't worry, though. No one is asking you to crack the dictionary, to plow through a doctoral dissertation, or to solve complicated equations. Together, in the first chapter, we will learn how the Bank of Canada operates as we observe it at work on the foreign exchange and money markets; in the second chapter we will observe securities traders in the bond market and peer over the shoulder of the country's largest institutional investor, Quebec's Caisse de dépôt et placement.

Financing the public debt is far more than a simple matter of house-keeping, something to be left to the specialists. It has deep implications for democracy. Understanding the debt issue and suggesting credible solutions is impossible without a solid comprehension of how international capital markets function. I've attempted to follow Albert Einstein's advice: make things as simple as possible, but not too simple. Throughout the book, but primarily in the first two chapters, readers will encounter boxed texts that explain the basic concepts in simple language. Terms are defined in a glossary at the end of the book.

When we reach the end of our guided tour, we should be better able to evaluate possible avenues for nursing our public finances back to health, and we'll have a better understanding of how the market might react should Quebec become independent.

Each player's outlook is determined by his geographical location, by his role in the system, by recent events, and, even more, by anticipated events. Each interview in this book carries a date — not to create a day-to-day account of the world of finance, but to keep events in a specific historical perspective. (Attentive readers will note that some dates do not follow chronological order.) Naturally, certain opinions stand the test of time better than others. In the trading rooms, people change their minds more frequently than they change their shirts. But the things they have to say (most of the interviews were tape recorded) remain highly pertinent: they cast a new light on a way of thinking and acting that evolves slowly.

To underscore how important time and place are, let's start off with a thirty-six-hour plunge into the financial markets. Fasten your seat belts!

Chapter 1

THIRTY-SIX
HOURS ON THE
FINANCIAL
MARKETS

TORONTO, MONDAY, SEPTEMBER 12, 1994

HIROKO MATSUMOTO'S FOOTSTEPS echo as she hurries across the lobby of First Canadian Place toward the reception desk, where I'm pacing back and forth. But the desk is empty and the elevators are locked; most of the people who work in the seventy-two-storey office building, Canada's largest, have already gone home. Matsumoto, a currency trader with the Bank of Montreal, glances impatiently at the small black device clipped to her belt. It looks like a pager, but instead of a telephone number the tiny screen displays the current Canadian dollar exchange rate. Matsumoto is late getting back from her dinner break, and she's afraid she might be keeping her boss waiting. Finally a security guard appears and unlocks the elevator.

Of the one hundred employees who work in the bank's seventeenth-floor trading room during the day, only a dozen are still on duty, eyes focused on computer screens, telephones wedged against their ears. A wall-mounted television set tuned to CBC Newsworld is broadcasting the first results of the Quebec elections.

Normally only one trader is on duty for what bank insiders call "the Tokyo shift," but when a political event like a budget speech or an election

10

is likely to have an impact on markets, Canada's chartered banks set up quick-response teams to handle client orders. Pre-election polls have predicted a comfortable majority for the Parti Québécois, which wants to turn Quebec from a province into an independent country. "If we see a P.Q. majority of at least eighty-five seats or with more than 40 percent of the vote, there may be a sell-off of the Canadian dollar," warns a husky forty-something with a blond moustache. Chief foreign exchange dealer Nick Howell is the man who quotes spot prices for the Canadian dollar for people who want to sell to the Bank of Montreal or buy from it. He's a market maker, always prepared to close a deal at the quoted price. Howell is not alone: an assistant helps him analyze incoming information, and a sales team keeps in constant touch with clients. Meanwhile, Matsumoto is on the phone to Japan, where it's now 10:00 a.m. An institutional investor wants to sell 75 million Canadian dollars at a rate of $1.3643 (CA). According to bank rules, Matsumoto must ask Howell's permission. He gives her a "no" signal. The only offer he's obliged to accept is at his quoted price. For the time being the Japanese offer is too high.

The chief foreign exchange dealer sits between two rows of facing work stations. With a swing of his chair he can call out to a subordinate or flash a hand signal. The atmosphere crackles with tension and nervous energy. Behind the rows of computer screens are the bank's invisible clients and competitors. As close as the building next door, or halfway around the world, they are connected with the trading room by telephone, by computer, or through middlemen. Traders use a special code to joke and trade information with colleagues who may be friends one day, enemies the next, and sometimes both at once. The trading room isn't a war room — not quite. The people who work there are full-time players in an open-ended poker game where the chips stand for millions. Buy low, sell high is the name of the game, and bluffing plays a central role. But professionalism always prevails.

At 8:12 a salesman shouts: "CTV projects a minimum of seventy seats." The information hasn't come from the television, which will remain tuned to Newsworld all evening. He's picked it up over the phone. In fact, television doesn't get watched much this evening: everyone is too busy. Besides, it's almost impossible to hear what the analysts are saying over the surrounding din. The only useful information transmitted by the

11

THE EXCHANGE RATE

The exchange rate is the international price of a given currency. Foreign exchange markets are the imaginary places where currencies are traded. Like any commodity, the price of a currency is determined by supply and demand. Steady buying sends prices upward, sustained sales drive them down, under the influence of factors such as international investment, trade, and tourism. The American dollar is the currency of reference on international capital markets; its price is measured against a variety of other currencies to determine exchange rates. By convention, traders always quote the price of the American dollar in other currencies, including the Canadian dollar, rather than the opposite. When a trader declares that the American dollar is worth $1.3635 Canadian dollars, he means that the Canadian dollar is worth $0.7334 (US). When a trader wants to indicate that the Canadian dollar is losing value, he quotes a greater value for the American dollar. Conversely, for a rising loonie he quotes a diminishing amount for the U.S. dollar. When the Canadian dollar drops, the American dollar rises, and vice versa.

---

television is from the coloured band at the bottom of the screen showing computer projections of the number of seats attributed to each party: won, or simply leading, the band doesn't specify.

"Sixty-five/eighty," squawks a metallic voice from a loudspeaker. "Sixty-five/eighty." Is the voice projecting the final tally of seats? No, it's the voice of a specialized broker, an intermediary who links all the banks and who provides a constant, anonymous update on the best buy and sell prices transmitted to him. If Nick Howell likes one of the offers he pushes a button connecting him to the broker and, in a matter of seconds, buys or sells without ever knowing the identity of the other party. "Sixty-five" refers to the two final decimals of the American exchange rate expressed in Canadian dollars. To be specific, $1.3665 (CA) is the price a buyer is prepared to pay to buy American dollars — the bid price. "Eighty" is the seller's asking price, $1.3680 (CA) — the ask price. The difference between the two is larger than usual, indicating that the market hasn't yet decided which way it wants to head.

Trade in Canadian dollars is usually carried out in multiples of five million dollars, called "five bucks." A five-buck transaction is a small one, 100 million a large one; more than 300 million qualifies as a blockbuster.

12

Daily volumes traded on Canadian foreign exchange markets run into the $30 billion (US) range. Canada-U.S. exchange operations account for 71 percent of the total, the Deutschmark 13 percent, the yen 6 percent, the pound sterling 4 percent, the Swiss franc 3 percent, and all other currencies 3 percent. Studies have shown that 61 percent of all transactions take place between banks; only 39 percent involve clients, mostly institutional investors and commercial firms. "Spot" transactions, Howell's baby, make up 39 percent of the total.[1]

"What do you call that third party?" asks Matsumoto.

"Parti de l'Action démocratique," I reply.

"Spell that please."

I sit down in front of her terminal and type the four words. In a paragraph, Matsumoto brings a client in the Far East up to date on the Quebec situation. Foreign exchange markets handle fabulous sums of money, but the most exciting give and take involves information.

Traders keep up a steady stream of banter with clients and competitors, often with more than one at a time, eyes glued to the constantly updated graphs and charts that fill the three computer screens in front of them. They are bombarded with information. How do they ever find the time to steal a glance at the pictures of their kids pasted next to the computer screen? Even with interruptions, a conversation rarely lasts longer than a minute, but into this brief instant a trader crams several micro-arguments, each complete with subject, verb, and predicate. If there's a degree of complexity involved, he might throw in a dependent clause. A typical exchange can touch on a dozen apparently unrelated subjects. For the casual onlooker, it's a hodgepodge, but for market insiders, each argument is grounded in economic theory, in whatever ideas happen to be in fashion, or in plain old-fashioned prejudice. The trading room of a major bank is hardly the place for a sophisticated, cool-headed evaluation of the causes and possible consequences of a political event. Perhaps more troubling still, traders don't even wait until the dust has settled before rushing to judgment, and into action. Tonight's election results are still fragmentary, and already the phones are ringing. Millions begin to dance across the screens. Stress levels are climbing toward the stratosphere. One trader ducks around a corner for a quick puff. He's committing a misdemeanour: federal law prohibits smoking on bank premises.

Howell quotes bid and ask prices on request and concludes transactions for his clients at those prices. His objective, of course, is to buy cheaper than he sells most of the time. Easier said than done, as prices are in constant flux. But Howell is accustomed to calculated risks. Within clearly established limits, the chief currency dealer speculates on the appreciation or depreciation of a given currency, relying on a mix of incoming information and his own flair and experience. This evening, a little voice is counselling caution. He begins with a small, long position of $10–15 million, next to nothing for a major player like the Bank of Montreal. Generally, professional dealers take market positions that reflect their expectations, either "long" or "short." When a dealer can't tell which way the market is moving, he stays neutral. Or, like Howell, he takes a small position.

By 8:30 CBC predicts a Parti Québécois majority government. I sense no emotion in the trading room, not even a reaction. But on the computer screens the Canadian dollar is appreciating. "Canada is behaving very, very well," says Howell, with a hint of a British accent. In fact, its behaviour seems to bear out the old adage: Buy on rumours, sell on news. Markets are future-obsessed, constantly trying to predict what will happen. Buy and sell decisions are made long before the event, as soon as the outcome

---

THE LONG AND SHORT OF IT

A long position means that an investor possesses a security — bonds, stocks, or foreign exchange — whose price he believes will increase. By selling for more than he paid, he will take a profit. If the same investor anticipates a drop in price he can still profit by taking a short position. This involves selling a security that he does not possess, or selling more of a given security than he possesses. This he accomplishes by borrowing the sold securities from a third party. If prices fall as anticipated, the dealer buys back the same security and returns it to the third party from whom he had "rented" it. He thus obtains a profit, since the selling price is superior to the purchase price, even though the normal transaction sequence has been reversed. However, should prices increase while an investor is short, he will take a loss. For example, a dealer sells a bond short at $100. If the price falls to $98, he buys back the same bond at the lower price for a profit of $2. But if the price climbs to $102, he will pay more for the bond than the purchase price, for a $2 loss.

---

has become predictable. Spring polls pointed to Liberal fatigue and a surge of support for the Parti Québécois. A change of government was in the wind, an eventuality dealers were prompt to put a price on. But this price is almost impossible to pinpoint. The Canadian dollar had been weakening for the previous three years for several reasons, including the deficit and the deterioration in public finances. Throughout the summer it had held steady. Tonight, as political uncertainty dissipated, investors were buying Canadian dollars again.

Every transaction brings together a buyer and a seller, each with distinct opinions and interests. To Howell's right, dealer Darren Kosack is conducting a transaction on his computer screen. On the first line he enters the price: 50-57 ($1.3650 [CA] bid and $1.3657 [CA] ask). After a lapse of a few seconds, a second line appears on the screen. The reply comes from Singapore; a currency trader for a large American investment banker is buying $25 million (US) worth of Canadian dollars. The two trade brief greetings, and the deal is done.

Just after 9:00 p.m., a good half of the bank's traders call it a night. Most clients — corporations, insurance companies, pension funds — have called up to check market reaction to the election; only a few really wanted to carry out transactions. Canada's institutional investors are a conservative lot who don't like doing business outside normal business hours. The sky hasn't fallen on anyone's head. They will still have time to take another look at their positions tomorrow.

On the television, the coloured band shows the P.Q. with eighty seats, the Liberals with forty-four. Howell shrugs his shoulders. "I don't care any more. This is history. Canada will be there tomorrow." His interpretation reflects the feeling in the room: the P.Q. victory has been closer than predicted. The likelihood that the government will be able to win a referendum on Quebec independence next spring seems remote. This is good news for investors, who are leery of the uncertainty surrounding the whole idea of independence. That's one reason why the Canadian dollar has risen by sixteen one-hundredths of a cent U.S. since the polls closed. But Howell is already thinking about the next market turnaround. His game plan is to protect himself against a drop in the dollar; the fear is that a backlash will occur if several investors decide to sell their Canadian dollars. "It's my feeling there will be profit taking." At 8:00 p.m. the Bank of Montreal was in a long position of $10–15 million. One hour and a half later, it is short to the tune of $30–35 million. But it is still a modest position, one that can be quickly altered.

By 10:00 p.m., transactions have climbed past the $250-million mark — slow going for an election night, or for a trading team that claims to be a top player in Canadian foreign exchange. Transactions have been mostly speculative. Buyers are from North America, mostly big Wall Street firms; sellers are from the Far East, primarily the Japanese banks. Canadians are also net sellers. The night's biggest transaction saw a Japanese bank trading $50 million (CA) for U.S. dollars. Nothing new, explains Matsumoto. Since the beginning of the year, the Japanese have been sellers.

Now it's almost 11:00 p.m. Shirttail flapping, Howell leaves the trading room without waiting for Jacques Parizeau's victory speech. He's been hard at it since 6:30 in the morning, and now he's ready to drop. The Bank of Montreal's Singapore branch will take over for the next few hours. It will be up to them to decode the Parti Québécois leader's message. The night is still young.

OTTAWA, TUESDAY, SEPTEMBER 13, 1994

Ten people file into the small beige room. Their faces match the colour of the walls. They're uneasy at having a stranger in their midst. It's never happened before. Authorization at the highest level, along with iron-clad guarantees that participants would not be identified, were needed before I, as a journalist, could set foot in the holy of holies. We take our places around a rectangular table dominated by a bank of microphones that look so retro they could have come straight from the heroic early days of the CBC. But we're here for a serious reason: the morning meeting of the Bank of Canada's securities department. The meeting is chaired by the deputy governor who heads the department. One after another, each participant makes a brief presentation in either English or French. The microphones carry the discussion straight to the bank's Montreal and Toronto offices via a direct telephone line. The purpose of the daily meeting is to discuss the previous night's market developments and to identify events that might influence markets during the day.

"Quebeckers have spoken and the markets, which feared a more decisive P.Q. victory, have reacted positively," states the chairman, in French, in his opening remarks. The analysis is fair and even-handed. The morning papers have confirmed that the Parti Québécois has won seventy-seven seats, the Liberals forty-seven, and the Parti de l'Action démocratique only one. A more telling detail for the upcoming referendum is the P.Q.'s narrow plurality: 44.7 percent against 44.3 percent for the Liberals. No further political remarks will be uttered for the rest of the meeting. The Bank of Canada never strays across the invisible line that marks out its territory. It keeps strictly out of politics and never places the finance minister in an awkward position. In return, it enjoys considerable latitude in setting and acting on a monetary policy whose sole objective — some might even call it an obsession — is price stability.

It is a compromise that has been carefully safeguarded ever since the celebrated dustup between then prime minister John Diefenbaker and bank governor James Coyne, in 1961. The bank's anti-inflationary monetary policy had irritated the Diefenbaker government, whose overriding concern was unemployment and the stability of Canadian bonds on the eve of Victory Bond conversion. Coyne had to go. Since then, in the grand old central bank tradition, the institution speaks with only one voice: that of the bank's governor. As one of the group of ten puts it, "We prefer being boring." When the governor makes a public statement, his comments are more scrupulously scripted than a papal encyclical. In the past, central bank presidents or governors have created market turbulence with remarks that deviated, however subtly, from normal policy. It's hard to imagine anything more prudent, more orthodox, than a speech by a central banker.

Today the bank will maintain its target rate for overnight funds at $5\frac{1}{8}$ percent, continues the deputy governor. The overnight rate — little known to the general public — is the tool most frequently used by the Bank of Canada to influence short-term interest rates. It is a truism that increased rates slow the economy, while reduced rates stimulate it.

The delicate task of fine-tuning the overnight rate falls to the second speaker, a woman who unleashes a mind-numbing cascade of technical data so arcane that even some of the participants have trouble following her. To sighs of relief she finishes quickly. This woman is the chief

---

THE OVERNIGHT RATE

The overnight rate is the price of money charged by the banks for very short-term loans. The rate, which fluctuates within a half percentage point operating band, is a prime target for central bank intervention. As of April 1996, the Bank of Canada rate will be set at the upper end of the range. Banks that temporarily hold excess funds lend them to other banks at the overnight rate. They also lend their overnight funds to investment dealers to finance their holdings of Treasury bills, a key consideration in monetary policy. Lower rates mean dealers are more inclined to hold Treasury bills, and to act more aggressively at the Tuesday T-bill auction. The more hotly Treasury bills are sought, the lower will be the rate paid by the government on these short-term debt securities. The overnight rate tends to be close to the three-month T-bill yield. A lower rate can be read as a sign that the bank wants to promote lower interest rates, or to slow rising rates; the central bank is then said to be following an easing policy. A higher rate generally indicates that the Bank of Canada intends to encourage higher interest rates, or slow a decline; the bank is then said to be pursuing a restrictive policy.

"plumber" at the Bank of Canada. By a complex system of cash transfers she makes sure that the overnight rate remains remarkably close to the bank's target most of the time. In order to do so she manipulates the balances of government accounts held with each of the chartered banks. The main purpose of these accounts is to honour the numerous cheques issued by the government, and to collect tax revenues. The government's cash needs fluctuate wildly from day to day. One of the Bank of Canada's numerous tasks is to manage cash inflows and outflows.

The era of behind-the-scenes string-pulling is coming to an end. The central bank wants the banks to speed up the settlement process and encourage freer circulation of overnight funds. Soon the bank will be adopting a new method for influencing the overnight rate via the clearing system. This system is what makes it possible to calculate and settle net amounts owed to one institution by another, as when a person deposits in the Royal Bank a cheque drawn on a CIBC account. Every night, clearing is carried out via accounts held by the financial institutions at the Bank of Canada. The system currently in use will be maintained for cheques, but beginning in 1997 banks will use an electronic payment system, meaning instant settlement for large transactions. New rules will come into force.

THE MONEY MARKET

The money market is a general term covering lending instruments with maturities of one year or less. These instruments include Treasury bills, bonds with less than a year to maturity, commercial paper (notes issued by private corporations), banker's acceptances (notes issued by private corporations but guaranteed by the banks), and tradable certificates of deposit. Taken together, these securities account for a highly liquid mass of some $300 billion, more than half of which consists of Canadian government Treasury bills. The Bank of Canada intervenes in the money market to influence short-term interest rates, indirectly through overnight rates but also occasionally by direct buying and selling of Treasury bills. The central bank rarely intervenes in the bond market, which consists of lending instruments in maturities ranging from one to thirty years. In Canada, long-term rates are determined entirely by market forces. The money market must not be confused with the foreign exchange market.

Positive balances held by banks in their Bank of Canada accounts will be paid at an interest rate set at the lower end of the overnight operating range. In the event of an overdraft, banks will pay interest set at the higher end of the differential, that is to say, the bank rate. Since the overnight rate falls between the two, banks with excess liquidity will find it more profitable to lend to other banks than to let the money gather dust at the Bank of Canada. Banks looking for funds will find it less expensive to borrow from rivals than from the Bank of Canada.[2] Changes to the overnight rate differential will be made by the most simple of expedients: the public announcement of a new bank rate. But let's not get too far ahead of ourselves. For the moment, the bank rate is still tied to the sale of Treasury bills.

The third speaker is the Montreal bureau chief, one of the group's most experienced members. His review of the foreign exchange market climaxes with a torrent of figures indicating that the Canadian dollar has appreciated substantially during the night: 0.7 cents U.S., or nearly 1 percent. The upswing is in sharp contrast to the stability of the American dollar against the Deutschmark and the yen. The message crackling over the loudspeaker is that Canadians, Japanese, and Europeans have been buying the loonie at increasingly high prices during the night, both in Singapore and London. In Europe it peaked at $1.3527 (CA) (73.93 cents [US]) before Bank of Canada intervention drove the loonie back to $1.3550 (CA) (73.80 cents [US]). The

---

WHEN ISSUED (WI)

When Issueds — WIs — are Treasury bills that will be issued during the next auction. They are traded among financial institutions on an extremely active market. On average, a Treasury bill is bought and sold three times during the week preceding its issue. The weekly market cycle begins immediately after the Tuesday auction. It deals in the next week's T-bills, whose characteristics are already common knowledge. Until 1996, WI rates acted as a barometer of bank rate expectations.

---

morning's briefing from Montreal is based on information gathered earlier through telephone contacts with foreign exchange (forex) dealers. But even before the presentation is over it has been overtaken by events. While the bureau chief is speaking, the Canadian dollar has leapt upward to $1.3500 (CA) (74.07 cents [US]). It has now gained almost a full cent since the polls closed, much too rapidly to suit the Bank of Canada.

The meeting is strictly business: no doughnuts, no coffee, no small talk. The next presentation, from Toronto, focuses on the money market. This morning, the price of Treasury bills is rising (their interest rates are dropping) for the same reasons that drove the dollar upward: foreign investors have bought heavily in the wake of the election results. "The auction should go extremely well," says this third participant. After having sounded out the dealers, the voice from Toronto estimates that "the street is short by about $3.1 billion." "The street" is the expression used to describe the investment community, and takes its name from New York's Wall Street. The street is short because it has already sold half of the $6.8 billion in Treasury bills it will buy at auction early this afternoon. The practice is standard, and it reduces the risk to banks and dealers who will buy the issue. Before the meeting began WI rates on three-month bonds stood at 5.55 percent, suggesting a bank rate of about 5.80 percent, down twelve basis points from the previous week (one hundred basis points = 1 percent). The major part of the drop has taken place over the last few hours.

The American bond market — the next subject — is up slightly this morning following publication of the latest consumer price index figures, which turn out to be less alarming than anticipated. Another rise in short-term rates is always possible, but the Fed (Federal Reserve Board, the

American central bank) is determined to hold the line until mid-term elections, in November. Another participant interjects that on the Canadian bond market there are more information requests from institutional investors than actual transactions. The yield spread between Canadian and American bonds, considered an added risk premium, has narrowed. The same holds true for the spreads between provincial and Government of Canada bonds. Here, too, it's been a quiet night. Investment dealers are now anticipating new provincial bond issues as political uncertainty eases.

Late this afternoon, at 4:15, the same group will meet again. If necessary it will suggest adjustments to chartered bank liquidity and to the following day's overnight rate. Then, at 5:00, its proposals will be submitted for approval to the governor and his closest advisers.

As quickly as it began, the meeting ends. Once outside the cramped, windowless, beige room, I pause to admire the modern, functional elegance of the building itself, designed by architect Arthur Erickson. Is the luxury of the Wellington Street institution — just a stone's throw from Parliament — a vestige of affluence in an era of downsizing and cutbacks, or is it solid proof of the bank's independence?

"A huge intervention in London"

The bank has made a "huge intervention in London," a senior official whispers. The action, to slow the rise of the Canadian dollar, is still underway. The scene is the fifth floor of the east wing of the Bank of Canada, in the international trading room, where foreign exchange transactions and gold sales are conducted. The room is decorated in calming shades of khaki and forest green and illuminated with natural light. With only four people at work, the atmosphere is calm compared to that at the Bank of Montreal.

Last night the bank kept a currency trader on duty as the election results were coming in, but he didn't have to lift a finger: the Canadian dollar was moving up smoothly on its own. "We make no attempt to maintain a particular level, or to set the external value of our currency," one of the traders explains. "Our policy is to dampen short-term movements. We couldn't defend the dollar even if we wanted to." A fixed exchange rate relative to the American dollar is a theoretical possibility, but in that case the bank would have to drop its inflation-fighting stance and import the American inflation rate, no questions asked. No central bank can keep its finger in more than one pie. The Bank of Canada has opted for price stability; it must tolerate fluctuations in the value of the dollar.

Before going home at 10:00 last night, the trader left instructions with an agent in Europe: "Sell Canadian dollars and buy U.S. currency if the greenback hits $1.3650 (CA) (73.26 cents [US])." The trader refuses to divulge the identity of the mystery agent, but it's common knowledge that he's referring to the Bank of England. That's standard operating procedure. Each night the Bank of Canada leaves detailed instructions with its sister bank in London. These instructions are to be acted on if the dollar starts acting up during the night. Shortly after midnight, it did just that. At 1:15 a.m. the Bank of England rang the trader at home, seeking fresh instructions. Suddenly, all bets were off. The market had crossed the technical level of $1.3630 (CA) (73.37 cents [US]), leaping suddenly up to $1.3580 (CA) (73.64 [US]). It was then 7:15 a.m. in Europe, and the first Canadian-dollar purchases joined those pouring in from the Far East, where the work day had not yet ended. To halt the buying spree, the Bank of Canada issued fresh sell orders. When London markets opened an hour later, the volume of Canadian-dollar transactions was still on the rise. At 6:25 a.m. in Ottawa, the Bank of England once again roused our poor trader from his sleep. All allotted funds had been spent and the dollar, now at $1.3540 (CA) (73.85 cents [US]), was still climbing. The Bank of Canada trader quickly released new funds and set new intervention targets. At last the loonie levelled off. Sales of Canadian dollars, exchanged for American dollars, had swollen the country's foreign exchange reserves. In late August, Canada's international reserves totalled $14.8 billion. By the end of September, they had grown by nearly one billion dollars.

Instead of returning to bed after the second call from London, our bleary-eyed trader returned to the Bank of Canada trading room to keep on top of the situation. Now the Bank of England remains in control, since the North American market is not yet open for business. This it will do at 8:00 a.m., when trading gets underway on the Chicago Mercantile Exchange. One of the four Chicago exchanges, the CME specializes in currency trading. The dollar is currently trading at $1.3530 (CA) (73.91 cents

---

INTERNATIONAL RESERVES

Canada's international reserves, or foreign exchange reserves, are used to defend the Canadian dollar on the foreign exchange market. They are made up of foreign currencies (primarily American dollars invested in highly liquid securities), of gold bullion held in a basement vault, and of Special Drawing Rights (SDR), an International Monetary Fund–issued accounting unit that represents a basket of selected currencies. These reserves, which belong to the government and are managed by the Bank of Canada under the general instructions of the finance minister, don't show up in the budget. A country's financial health is generally considered to be more robust when reserves are high; if reserves become exhausted, the government must borrow abroad to replenish them. As a rule, foreign reserves increase when the Canadian dollar gains strength and diminish when it falters.

[US]). After a hectic night in Asia and in Europe, what will the Chicago-based speculators do?

On the CME floor, dealers mill around in the pit, shouting and waving their arms. They're trading futures contracts that allow standard lots of $100,000 (CA) to be bought and sold for delivery at predetermined dates during the coming months. Futures contracts are distinctive in that upcoming transaction prices are determined beforehand, meaning that importers or exporters can immediately lock in the value of the future payments to be received or made in another currency. Futures contracts function as hedging instruments. At the same time they allow traders to speculate on what a currency might do in future. That's what's behind the furious activity in the pit. The Bank of Canada does not intervene in Chicago, but it monitors developments there closely, since the futures market and the spot market play off on one another.

The market is calm until 9:00 a.m. Then suddenly, as the Bank of Canada committee is meeting in Ottawa, it goes haywire, with the dollar surging to $1.3500 (CA) (74.07 cents [US]). The bank sells off tens of millions of Canadian dollars, managing to blunt the thrust. Other sellers move in and by lunchtime the dollar has begun to dip, pausing while most traders step out for a bite. Last winter, at the sight of coatless women smoking cigarettes, an out-of-town visitor wondered aloud why ladies of the night were tolerated so close to the central bank! The shady ladies turned out to be law-abiding Bank of Canada employees who nip outside for a quick smoke and a stroll on Sparks Street, a downtown pedestrian mall.

Back from lunch, the rejuvenated buyers resume their assault on the dollar. At 4:00 p.m., the official closing rings up $1.3486 (CA) (74.15 cents [US]). But the market never sleeps. The dollar will continue to creep upward, then level off during the night.

Except for transactions like those made last night in its name by the Bank of England, the Bank of Canada usually deals with the Canadian chartered banks for its foreign exchange operations. The trader has jotted down on a sheet of paper a list of the day's operations, noting times and amounts. A furtive glance shows about fifteen. The day's transaction volume totals several hundred million dollars, well below the single-day record of nearly one billion dollars. It's both a lot and a little. The average daily foreign exchange transaction volume is around $30 billion (US), including $9 billion on the spot market alone.

Until policy was changed (a few months after my visit to the Bank of Canada), transactions usually took place in lots of $5 to $25 million, at a relatively rapid pace. The Bank of Canada set itself apart from other central banks by the greater frequency and smaller size of its transactions. Market makers privately concede that these transactions made life easier for them, as the central bank acted as buyer or seller of last resort. "Now we intervene less often, but more actively. Our job is dealing with short-term dollar fluctuations, which can turn into disorderly movements, and not trends driven by underlying economic factors," explains Tim Noël, deputy governor in charge of financial markets.[3] Stopping strong speculative pressures will remain a tough task, but a central bank can maximize its impact if it waits until a small correction appears before weighing in with hundreds of millions of dollars.

Joint interventions involving the Fed and the Buba (short for the Bundesbank, the German central bank) are rare, and the record is spotty. Occasionally, the Bank of Canada joins the fray. Contact with the major central banks of the world is a daily affair. The head trader uses a small black-and-brown box with a tiny built-in loudspeaker and a series of buttons identified by country names. This private network is used five times a day to exchange information by conference call. The Bank of Canada usually participates in two or three of the five conferences that fall into its time zone. Since NAFTA has taken effect, the network is also used for weekly phone conferences with the Fed and the Bank of Mexico.

Insiders disagree over the effectiveness of central bank intervention on the foreign exchange market. Like giving a gorilla bananas to make it go away, the policy simply won't work, some say.[4] Certainly, when the Bank of Canada does intervene, it's a small fish in a big pond. But on the money market, the pond is smaller. Here, the bank can increase its impact on the price of the loonie by manipulating short-term interest rates.

The gatekeepers of the money market

Two floors down, in an even larger trading room decorated in the same forest hues, sunlight streaming through the windows falls on three large desks, seating roughly half a dozen people, each desk as peaceful as a landscape painting. Two managers operate out of open corner cubicles, set like summer cottages around a lake. Their desks, made of natural wood, are bare, except for a computer terminal large enough to display several pages of information from a wide range of sources. A few people are talking quietly on the telephone, but not with receivers jammed between their ears and shoulders. Like telephone operators they use lightweight headsets connected to miniature microphones. Although we're in the Securities Trading Room, the atmosphere reminds me of an academic library. Even the name is misleading: nothing is actually traded here. The far work station is reserved for run-of-the-mill clerical tasks; the one close to the window is occupied by two employees who invest Canada's international reserves in high-quality instruments, such as American, Japanese, and German government bonds. The last group — the heart of the operation — is made up of five analysts and a supervisor who scrutinize every aspect of Canadian money and bond markets. They pull in information like a vacuum cleaner, sift through it, and transmit it in condensed form to Bank of Canada decision-makers.

The bank's headquarters in Ottawa has no direct contact with the dealers of Bay Street or Montreal's Rue Saint-Jacques. This job falls to the bank's eyes, ears, and hands in Toronto and Montreal. Working out of these regional offices, traders — who occasionally make transactions —

telephone banks and dealers across Canada several times a day, taking the pulse of the market. Each call lasts several minutes; the central bank trader checks a long list of prices, asks questions about volume, what kind of clients have been active, and which parts of the world are issuing buy and sell orders. The information is confidential and clients' names are usually not revealed. This morning, the Bank of Canada wants to understand how various dealers are reading the market. Most important, it wants to find out whether they will be taking long or short positions for the upcoming Treasury bill issue. In return, the Bank of Canada trader provides cautiously worded information on the market. The conversation, which gives traders a feel for the central bank's intentions, is part of Ottawa's efforts to become more open and explicit. Talking to the Bank of Canada is a little like appearing in court: tell the whole truth and nothing but the truth. But this may be too much to ask of inveterate poker players. Every one "talks his book," or "talks his own position and reflects his own view of the world," says a trading room manager. "It's not always in their interest to tell everything. That's why we would never rely on only one or two sources."

The regional traders report back regularly to Ottawa. The analysts who synthesize the information look for three variables: the overnight rate, the yield on three-month Treasury bills on the spot market, and the yield on three-month WIs to be issued at the next auction. They also keep a close watch on the dollar, even though this job remains the responsibility of the international team, because many foreigners who buy Canadian dollars invest them in Treasury bills and bonds.

"The global market" is not just a hollow slogan: the bank has to know where capital is coming from and where it is going in order to determine which trends are likely to last. In this ongoing international shell game, the ability to read the American market is crucial. Today, the analysts are watching the Canadian money market rally, fuelled by foreign purchases closely linked to the rise of the dollar. At 10:00 the yield on WIs — Treasury bills to be issued — points to a small drop in the bank rate of about ten basis points. This pace suits the central bank. But not long after, rates drop suddenly. T-bills promise to sell like hotcakes.

The auction takes place every Tuesday — electronically. Bankers and dealers fill out a form on their computer screens. They have until 12:30

sharp to present one or more offers for the bills to be sold. This week, the Bank of Canada is selling, in the name of the Finance department, $3.8 billion of three-month bills, $2 billion of six-month bills, and $1 billion of one-year bills. Each offer must list the number, maturity, and the yield the bidder is prepared to pay the government. The interest rate is quoted to three decimal points. The total offer may not exceed one-third of the bills auctioned for each maturity.

At 1:30 p.m., the bank replies to the offers submitted by a form that appears on the same screen. A computer program has sifted through the bills, starting with the bidder whose offer or offers indicate the lowest yield, then the bidder offering the next-lowest yield, and so on until the entire issue has been placed. The system minimizes the government's borrowing costs while creating a level playing field for dealers. Under a special provision for smaller investment dealers, all participants are eligible to purchase at least one $2-million lot at the average auction rate. Twenty-five basis points are added to this average to determine the bank rate, a method that will be modified in 1996. On this day, the rate is set at 5.71 percent, a "fairly large" but not abnormal drop of twenty-one points. The result is immediately disseminated by press release, which also gives maximum and minimum yields on accepted bids. The difference between the average and the highest yield is a dispersion indicator called the "auction tail," which shows market uncertainty levels. The difference is usually one basis point, indicating a high degree of consensus on

---

TREASURY BILLS

Treasury bills are securities for which the government of Canada promises to pay the holder a fixed amount (face value) after a given number of days have elapsed. Periods are normally three months, six months, and one year. These securities are issued in denominations varying between one thousand and one million dollars. They are sold for less than their face value — at discount; for the government, the borrowing cost (yield, for the investor) is the difference between the selling price and the face value. For example, if a Treasury bill that the government will redeem three months later for $100 is sold for $99, the one-dollar difference is equivalent to an annual yield of 4.05 percent. Yield, not face value, drives Treasury bill transactions. T-bills are also issued by provincial governments and some large municipalities.

appropriate bill yields — exactly what is happening today. A difference of seven or eight points would point to market uncertainty. The characteristics of the following week's auction are also released. Using the information, banks and dealers immediately begin trading a new generation of WIs. Negotiable Government of Canada bonds, with maturities of two, three, five, ten, and thirty years, are sold using the same procedure, but with only one maturity being issued per auction, held most Wednesdays.

Nearly forty banks and investment dealers enjoy primary dealer status for Treasury bills, meaning they may purchase the issue in order to resell it. A sub-group of eleven big players (the Canadian chartered banks or their brokerage subsidiaries, as well as the American brokers Merrill Lynch and Goldman Sachs), known as jobbers, are active auction participants, agreeing to purchase the entire issue should the other players drop out. Their responsibility is to maintain an active secondary market following the issue by quoting bid and ask prices. This is called an over-the-counter market, meaning that bills are traded among financial institutions, by telephone, and not on an exchange. Jobbers usually snap up from 90 percent to 95 percent of a Treasury bill issue, and it's not unusual for a single player to rack up a third, the allowable maximum. The Bank of Canada is also a bidder, buying a portion of the week's Treasury bills for its own needs, as well as for other central banks that want to place their Canadian dollar reserves in Canadian dollars in a high-quality, liquid investment.

TORONTO

Later that same morning, Canada's money market traders are chattering away on the telephone. It's time for the curious ritual that precedes every auction. The street is humming with rumours, gossip, false confidences, and insinuations as each dealer tries to guess which way everyone else will go at auction. Collusion of this kind is strictly illegal, of course, but bluffing is so common that no one believes every word. Everyone on the street remembers one serious breach, however. In May 1991, five dealers swept up the entire bond issue with bids each set at the allowed maximum of 20 percent of the total (which is lower than the T-bill limit). Yields were identical to the last decimal point — much too neat for pure happenstance. In the United States, the incident would have touched off a scandal, followed closely by public investigation and legal action. In 1990 and 1991, Salomon Brothers was convicted of violating American regulations that restrict the amount of Treasury bills a single dealer may purchase to 35 percent. The brokerage firm had attempted to create an artificial shortage and fix prices. Salomon management was forced to resign and was subject to heavy fines. Canadians prefer to wash their dirty linen in private. The Bank of Canada carried out a low-key investigation, but no wrong-doing could be proved. The institutions involved were given a sharp reprimand and rules tightened, and the affair was swept under the carpet.

The dance of the seven veils that precedes the auction gives experienced dealers an opportunity to detect key signals. Today, Steve Scrimshaw, chief money market dealer for the Royal Bank, intuits that institutional investors have scooped up Treasury bills on the WI market. Over the last few days Scrimshaw has received overseas orders, including one from a Hong Kong–based speculative account that has acquired several hundred million dollars in one-year bills. A sizable portion of these deals involved operations of great complexity.

As a jobber, the Royal Bank must participate in the weekly auction, but Scrimshaw is torn between taking an aggressive position and holding back. This morning, several of his clients have sold WIs to take a profit, but he doesn't know how many others might have done the same thing, and that bothers him. Prior to the auction, the Royal Bank was short by more than $100 million in one-year bills, so Scrimshaw bids for a quarter of the paper to be sold, not far from the bank's usual market share. At 2:00 he learns that he's only got $700 million, or 10.3 percent of the paper offered. When the Royal Bank buys bills on the secondary market in order to deliver bills sold short, it must pay more than the sale price, and has to swallow a loss of $200,000.

Another player had too much of what he wanted. Bob Telley, vice president and money market manager at the Toronto office of Lévesque, Beaubien, Geoffrion, is astonished to find out that he's corralled 12 percent of bills offered, four times more than usual. "I didn't like the market," he says. "It was clearly short." But twenty minutes before the auction Telley

> **HEDGING**
>
> Hedging protects short or long positions that would otherwise be considered too risky. Dealers protect themselves by taking a second position contrary to the first: losses from the first are compensated by gains from the second. For example: to cover a Treasury bill purchase (a long position), a dealer will short-sell BAX, futures contracts made up of a standard quantity of three-month banker's acceptances. Banker's acceptance and Treasury bill prices fluctuate concurrently, meaning that losses due to a drop in Treasury bills held by the dealer will be compensated by an equivalent profit on BAX. Brokers settle their BAX contracts as they sell Treasury bills.

received a fat order from an American "hedge fund," a speculative investment fund that wanted $200 million in six-month bills. Lévesque's order book already listed two orders from Canadian insurance companies, plus a third from a pension fund, for a total of $375 million in orders for six-month and one-year bills. For three-month maturities, nothing. Telley must act quickly. Based on his orders, he places a high bid. Too high. He gets $890 million in bills, $250 million of it in three-month bills. To cut risks, Telley hedges his position by selling future contracts on the Montreal Stock Exchange. The Lévesque sales staff will have to work hard in the coming week to place these bills, an operation that will cost the brokerage firm $25,000. Meanwhile, in Montreal, the treasury of the National Bank — Lévesque, Beaubien, Geoffrion's parent firm — has brought in $270 million in bills, but not even a scrap of one-year paper, an area where it had been a bit short. "Someone squeezed them," says trader Jérôme Bernier, who has no idea of Telley's position. Strangely enough, even though they work for the same bank, the two men are competitors. (This bizarre situation ended in 1996, when bank and broker merged their trading rooms, driven by the Canada-wide move toward consolidation of all fixed income instruments [bonds and bills].)

After-auction dealing in T-bills is hectic. In the week to come, volume will hit $110 billion, twenty-three times the volume of all transactions on the Montreal and Toronto stock exchanges. Trade between primary dealers accounts for fully two-thirds of the total, the rest going to financial institutions like insurance companies, mutual funds, and trust companies;

only one transaction in ten involves a foreign investor. Canadian financial institutions do more than trade in Treasury bills; they buy enormous quantities as investments. In 1992, they held more than 44 percent of all Treasury bills outstanding, while 22 percent were held by individuals, 7 percent by corporations, 9 percent by the Bank of Canada, 4 percent by other levels of government and public administration, and 13 percent by foreigners.

High media visibility for the bank rate gives the banks a convenient pretext for changing their rates. This afternoon, one minute after the bank rate has been announced, the Royal Bank drops its prime rate by a modest twenty-five basis points, to 7 percent. The other financial institutions rapidly follow suit.

The money market has not been the only strong performer of the day. Rates on the longer-term bond market have plummeted even more rapidly than in the United States, shrinking yield spreads between Canadian and American securities by ten to twenty-one points. Spreads between Canada and Quebec bonds have also narrowed by seven points. Meanwhile, CBRS, a Montreal-based bond rating service, has confirmed the province's A-plus rating. Just after 6:00 p.m. the Bank of Montreal, picking up on the upbeat mood, announces a 25-percent basis point reduction in its one- to ten-year mortgage rates. The Royal Bank quickly ups the ante, trimming rates by thirty-five basis points. The chartered banks normally set mortgage rates at about 2 percent above Canada bond yields for the same maturity. That same evening the Canadian stock exchange registers a small upswing, following an American trend.

THE BANK RATE

The bank rate is the interest rate that the Bank of Canada charges for overdrafts or for the cash advances it provides to the chartered banks. Formerly set automatically by adding twenty-five basis points to the average Tuesday auction rate for three-month Treasury bills, as of April 1996 the bank rate is set at the high end of the Bank of Canada overnight rate operating range. The bank rate will no longer keep pace with Treasury bill prices. Changes in the bank rate announced by the central bank will be clear indicators of whether credit is being relaxed or tightened.

THE PRIME RATE

The prime rate is frequently described as the rate offered to a bank's best commercial customers. As a matter of fact, these customers often pay a much lower rate. The prime rate is a point of reference for setting all banks' short-term rates, from personal lines of credit to open one-year mortgages. Banks rely on banker's acceptances and commercial paper in setting their prime rate. This rate must remain competitive at all times; corporations can borrow short-term capital from the banks, or they can issue commercial paper or banker's acceptances.

OTTAWA, SEPTEMBER 14, 1994

"Euphoria on Financial Markets" blares the headline in this morning's *La Presse*. "$ Soars Free From Politics" cries *The Financial Post*. But the specialists in the Bank of Canada trading room are wondering if it isn't a case of too much, too soon. We're looking at a market overreaction, explains a veteran analyst: "Markets have a herd instinct, and fashions can create problems. All participants fear they will miss something if they don't jump in. So they all jump on the same end of the boat and it tips." The central bank's job is to keep the boat from tipping.

Early this morning, the Royal Bank is having trouble interpreting the presence of excess cash in the government's account. Is the central bank

---

OPEN MARKET OPERATIONS

Direct interventions by the central banks in the money market are known as Open Market Operations. The decision to intervene is made in Ottawa but carried out by traders in the Toronto and Montreal offices. Though the Bank of Canada resorts to it infrequently, the classic operation consists of buying or selling three-month Treasury bills on the secondary market. Purchases increase the demand for Treasury bills, which pushes up prices and reduces yield. Sales have the opposite effect. Remember, Treasury bill yield is equal to the difference between the face value at redemption and the purchase price. The higher the price, and the smaller the difference between it and face value, the weaker the yield. Thus, bond buying drives yield down, while bond selling has the opposite effect. The central bank prefers other methods, but if they do not have the desired effect, it can still revert to this classic technique to stabilize the money market.

---

angling for another drop in rates? To put its mind at ease, the Royal Bank decides to test how far the Bank of Canada is prepared to go, and it authorizes two loans of overnight funds at $4\frac{7}{8}$ percent, well below the current floor price. Fifteen minutes later, at 10:45, the central bank steps in to clear up any misunderstanding. "We told the market: for a short while, even if the dollar has recovered, enough is enough," says a manager. For the time being, overnight funds are not to fall below 5 percent.

This morning the central bank has offered the big banks a special kind of loan transaction called repurchase agreements, or repos, at 5 percent, the threshold level it hopes to maintain for overnight funds. There is only one taker, but everyone gets the message. A typical transaction with a single bank usually ranges from $100–$300 million, while the total of all

REPURCHASE AGREEMENTS (REPOS)

Repurchase agreements enable financial institutions to borrow or lend cash for very short periods of time at an interest rate that is the overnight rate. These agreements are much like a loan whose repayment is insured by securities given as collateral. Daily volumes for repurchase agreements in Canada currently stand at around $50 billion. In a more formal sense, a repurchase agreement can be described as a sale of bonds or Treasury bills that will be bought back at a later date. The dealer who sells securities under a repurchase agreement gets cash in return, paying out interest until he repurchases the securities. In a reverse repurchase agreement the dealer buys securities from another dealer — lending his cash, in other words — and receives interest until the securities are resold. Sale and repurchase are made at the same price. When the Bank of Canada enters into repurchase agreements, it offers an interest rate that dealers acknowledge as the overnight rate desired by the financial authorities. Announcements of a new operating range for the overnight rate (or announcements of a new bank rate, for that matter) dictated by underlying economic factors or to fine-tune monetary conditions (the mix of foreign exchange rates and short-term interest rates) are usually made at 9:00 a.m. But interventions to calm the market may take place at any time. They may take the form of Special Purchase and Resale Agreements (SPRA) or Sale and Repurchase Agreements (SRA), transactions that are settled the following day. In an SPRA, the bank buys Treasury bills and sometimes three-year bonds and undertakes to sell them the next day. In an SRA, the bank sells bills and undertakes to purchase them the next day.[5]

transactions may go as high as $1 billion. Occasionally the bank's offer gets no response. Economics textbooks tell us that the Bank of Canada will indulge in moral suasion to encourage banks to modify their behaviour, but the tactic hasn't been used for years, insists Ottawa. The tool of persuasion has grown rusty from lack of use. Nowadays, when the bank wants to push interest rates and the dollar up or down, it relies on financial market levers.

What's at stake?

The world capital market isn't just on the horizon, it's a reality. A Hong Kong investor who has never set foot in Canada, who may not even know that French is spoken in Quebec, can buy up hundreds of millions of dollars worth of Treasury bills before a provincial election and sell them at a loss or a profit a few days later. All an investor has to do is pick up his telephone; the capital will do his bidding. Perhaps we'd prefer not to admit it, but Canadians are doing precisely the same thing for a few hundredths of a percentage point. The quest for profit is relentless, and it's information-driven. Every rumour is seized, interpreted, and judged in a matter of seconds. There is no going back.

Nothing pumps up the markets like the hot breath of inflation. On budget day, in February 1991, Bank of Canada governor John Crow and Finance minister Michael Wilson formally undertook to "bring inflation down to 2 percent between now and 1995 and to move thereafter toward price stability." The policy succeeded beyond their wildest dreams: from 6 percent in 1991, inflation plummeted to nearly zero in 1994. But the price to be paid was a longer, harder recession than that in other industrialized countries. As a side effect, government deficits ballooned. In its all-out war on inflation the Bank of Canada adopted a tight money strategy, promising lower rates when rising prices had been wrestled to the ground. The bank finally managed to lower interest rates when the Fed began to move in that direction. But in February 1994, when the U.S. central bank reversed itself to dampen a possible inflationary flare-up, the Bank of Canada backed off, its fingertips singed. Foreigners had stopped buying Treasury bills and Canada bonds the moment those investments stopped yielding higher rates of return than American securities. Although inflation in Canada stayed well below U.S. levels, although the prospect of inflation was next to nil, although real interest rates in Canada remained among the most generous of all the OECD member-countries, the Bank of Canada was forced to rein in credit. To keep from smothering the nascent economic recovery, it let the dollar slide.

The mix of foreign exchange and interest rates ultimately determines what the Bank of Canada calls monetary conditions. A decline in the value of the Canadian dollar, which activates the export locomotive, can partially offset higher rates and keep monetary conditions neutral.[6] The Bank of Canada is not able to set the interest rates it desires, nor can it dictate the exchange rate. If it could, it would opt for low rates and a strong dollar. The bank can affect these variables by dampening or stimulating trends driven by market forces, but over the long haul it cannot reverse such trends. Despite its vast expertise and access to privileged information, the Bank of Canada cannot even forecast dollar levels or interest rates; as recently as last year, no one in the venerable Wellington Street institution believed that interest rates would be as high as they are today. Right or wrong, the bank's economic forecasts are for the finance minister's eyes only: they will never be made public.

Perhaps foreign investors demand higher nominal yields in Canada than they do in the United States because the Bank of Canada has not been able to convince them it can keep prices stable over the long term. Because the simplest solution to overindebtedness is to print more money, to "monetize" the debt. All central banks have this power, providing the debt is expressed in the national currency, as it is for the government of Canada.[7] The Bank of Canada could simply purchase more bonds and Treasury bills, paying for them with new bank notes, which Ottawa would then use to pay for goods and services, or fund old age pensions and business subsidies. The new money would begin to circulate in the economy, bloating the money supply. But when the amount of money increases more rapidly than goods and services available, prices skyrocket. History has repeatedly shown that when a central bank abuses its power to print money, inflation is bound to follow.

Inflation brings with it a broad spectrum of problems. But it has a seductive appeal for heavily indebted governments and individuals. Debt load lessens over time. Paying back $100 in ten years will cost less if an annual inflation rate of 5 percent reduces purchasing power to $60, particularly if government revenues keep pace with inflation, as often happens when wages driven upwards by rising prices are taxed at higher marginal rates. Individuals discover that their buying power has been transferred to the state. Unplanned inflation is a disaster for lenders, who will be repaid in devalued capital. Throughout the 1970s, when double-digit inflation was the order of the day in the West, interest earned by lenders of capital fell below the inflation rate. If investors fear that the debt may be monetized, it's unlikely they will wait for a second bout of inflation before taking action. Foreign investors in Canada will demand even higher interest rates to offset the risk. These foreigners do not make Canada their home; they will certainly not suffer if prices climb. But they do know that a country that tolerates rates of inflation higher than its neighbours' risks seeing its national currency depreciate in relation to other currencies. Foreign exchange fluctuations have come to play a crucial role in a foreigner's decision to invest in Canadian securities. One of the things investors fear most is being repaid in Canadian dollars that will be worth less when reconverted into their national currency. Bank of Canada governor Gordon Thiessen admits that "large deficits, and the accumulation of debt which results, can cause nervousness in financial markets because, in the past, countries have frequently tried to reduce the burden of their debts by inflating the problem away. So to protect themselves against this risk, investors require higher interest rates." The Bank of Canada, he adds, will carry on with its policy of price stability irrespective of the government's fiscal situation.[8]

On Tuesday, September 13, 1994, the Bank of Canada issued $6.8 billion of Treasury bills, of which $5.9 billion were used to redeem expired bills. Acting as agent for the Finance department, the central bank on that day refinanced one one-thousandth of 1 percent of the federal debt. The following week it issued securities for $8 billion. Over the next five years, the government is expected to sell $400 billion in Treasury bills and bonds, the equivalent of existing federal debt. New deficits not included.

Chapter 2

THE CANADIAN BOND MARKET

WEDNESDAY, SEPTEMBER 21, 1994

AS JIM BREEZES into the trading room at 7:30 a.m., Frank hurries over.

"The Japanese were really selling last night!"

"Is that so?"

"Were you hedged?"

"Sure was."

Jim is a market maker in provincial securities; Frank sells these securities to institutional investors. The two men are chatting excitedly about the latest from the rumour mill: Japanese investors have sold off $4 billion (CA) of Saskatchewan, Newfoundland, Quebec, British Columbia, and Prince Edward Island bonds.

There's no such thing as privacy for the people who work cheek by jowl in the trading room. Still, a few traders manage to personalize their work space. Jim has posted sayings on his computer terminal, the kind of thing you might associate with a teenage romantic: "Better a live dog than a dead lion." "Patience and discipline." "Think wrongly if you please, but in all cases think for yourself." "Uncertainty breeds opportunity."

BONDS

A bond is a debt security issued by a government, a public agency, or a corporation to those who lend it capital for a period of between two and thirty years. Bonds are made up of two parts: the principal, or face value, which is equivalent to the amount borrowed and repaid at maturity; and the interest coupon, an amount that is generally paid to the holder twice yearly. Bonds, sold in denominations of $1,000 to $1,000,000, are purchased by institutional investors such as pension funds, insurance companies, banks, mutual funds, etc. Government bonds are not redeemable prior to maturity, but paper issued by corporations may be redeemed earlier, under certain conditions. Once issued by the borrower, bonds may be bought and sold at any time on the secondary market. Bonds should not be confused with savings bonds, which are purchased by small investors and sold in small denominations of $100 to $1,000. Savings bonds are redeemable at any time, at the holder's discretion, but cannot be traded on the secondary market.

I'm here as a trainee, to learn the basics of the Canadian bond market from a respected but highly secretive bond dealer. The firm insists on anonymity; discretion is their watchword. For the first and only time in this book, both the names of individuals and the amounts (not the prices) of bond transactions have been changed. Everything else is described exactly as I saw and heard it.

The Canadian bond market weighs in at more than $500 billion, fully $100 billion more than the capitalization of the Canadian stock market, which is defined as the total share value of all corporations listed. Federal government borrowing accounts for 64 percent of the total, provincial securities for 24 percent, corporate paper for 10 percent, and municipal bonds for 1 percent. When governments borrow, dealers place bonds with investors: this is known as the primary market. When an original investor no longer wants to hold a bond acquired earlier, he resells it through a dealer to other investors on the secondary market. In this way, the same security can change hands several times. Daily volume on the secondary bond market hovers around the $70-billion mark, more than three times the volume of Canada's stock exchanges combined. Dealers are more than intermediaries between institutional investors; they also buy bonds for their own accounts.

The rumour mill

The rumour mill says the province of Quebec might be about to proceed with a bond issue. Jim is bearish about the market; he doesn't want to be overloaded with Quebecs when the government moves. Tongues are wagging this morning in the trading room. Is a bond issue likely before the new government has been sworn in? What and where is demand, if any? A Quebec issue on the Canadian market normally runs between $300 and $400 million (CA). As a member of the province's financial syndicate, my anonymous investment dealer will have to place several million dollars' worth of bonds.

Jim decides to jettison a chunk of his Quebecs. (Quebecs, Ontarios, and Canadas are trading room shorthand for Government of Quebec, Ontario, or Canada bonds.) At 9:00 a.m. he sells a medium-sized pension fund $6.5 million (CA) of Quebec bonds maturing in 2000. Jim picked up the bonds six weeks ago, prior to the election, from a London-based Japanese investment banker, paying $104.06 per $100 of face value. At resale he got $104.73, a gross profit of 67 cents.

BOND PRICES

Bond prices are always expressed in terms of $100 face value. Face value is the amount to be paid at maturity. When a trader says that five-year Quebecs have gained 67 cents, he means that Quebec bonds redeemable in five years have appreciated by 0.67 percent (67 cents per $100 = 0.67 percent). If he announces that ten-year Canadas have lost one dollar, he means that Canada bonds maturing in ten years have depreciated by 1 percent ($1 per $100 = 1 percent). The five-year bonds Jim is selling offer a coupon rate of 10 percent, the market rate at the time of issue, in October 1989. Today's interest rate is 9 percent. Because the bond's coupon rate brings more than the market rate, today's price is higher. A bond is sold at a price higher than its face value when the interest paid by the coupon is higher than the market rate; a bond is then said to be trading at a premium. On the other hand, a bond sells for less than its face value when coupon interest is lower than the market rate; it is then said to be trading at discount. When coupon interest is equivalent to the market rate, a bond is termed at par. Thus the following rule: *When interest rates increase, bond values decline; when interest rates decline, bond values increase.*

When he buys bonds, Jim jots down the price and transaction size on pink slips; blue slips are for sales transactions. Price is an important factor, but Jim's primary consideration is bond yield. Yield, which incorporates both price (which is constantly changing) and coupon interest (which never changes), provides a much more useful measuring stick. Simply defined, yield at maturity represents the annual revenue derived from a security that will be held until maturity, taking into account the purchase price. These revenue flows are discounted to reflect the fact that a dollar received in the future is worth less than a dollar received today. Jim quotes prices to his clients while keeping an eye on yields; his primary focus is on the yield spread between Quebec and Canada bonds. On the bond market, everything is measured as a spread. In Canada, the benchmark used to measure all other debt securities is the federal government bond. Canada bonds are themselves measured in terms of spreads vis-à-vis American government bonds, known as U.S. Treasuries.

When Jim bought the five-year Quebecs, they offered a yield fifty-six basis points higher than Canadas for the same maturity. He resold them at a forty-three-point spread. The market has concluded that Quebec bonds are a better risk, meaning they are worth more, now that pre-election jitters have been dispelled.

Determining net profit will be a slightly more complicated task. Jim will also have to factor in the cost of hedging. When he bought the Quebecs, he sold short an identical quantity of Canadas of the same maturity. His short position in the Canadas cancelled out his long position in the Quebecs as far as the risks inherent in interest rate changes were concerned. Whatever had been lost on the long position after a rise in rates would be compensated for by an identical gain on the short position. Conversely, any gain in the long position on the heels of a drop in interest rates would be offset by a corresponding loss in the short position.

It was ideal protection as long the spread between Quebecs and Canadas remained stable, but Jim wagered that the spread would shrink after the elections, as it had after previous ballots. He took care to protect himself against interest rate volatility, but he speculated on a drop in the perceived risk of Quebec bonds. On that transaction he took a profit of $43,717 on the Quebecs but a loss of $21,007 when he repurchased the Canadas he'd sold short earlier. Including interest earned for the time he

SPREADS

A spread is the difference between the yields of two bonds of the same maturity but issued by different borrowers. Traders track secondary market spreads closely, as they provide a tool for evaluating the risk that distinguishes one borrower from another, an important variable. The wider the spread, the riskier the bond being compared to a "benchmark" bond. If a borrower's credit deteriorates, the relative value of his bonds will decrease, and vice versa. The borrower's financial situation, the state of the economy, and the political climate are the principal risk factors that distinguish government bonds from one another. A bond whose spread is narrowing is performing better than the benchmark bond. A bond whose spread is widening is performing worse. Spreads fluctuate within a bracket: investors consider a bond whose spread is large in relation to the historical average to be relatively inexpensive; when the spread is narrow, a bond is considered expensive. Generally, investors purchase bonds when the spread is wide (when they are cheap) if they believe the spread will narrow and the bond will increase in value. But they sell bonds trading at historically narrow spreads (when they are expensive) if they believe the spread will widen and the bond's relative value will decline. The spread for bond A will narrow if its yield increases more slowly than that of bond B, the benchmark. As all increases in yield lower a bond's price, A will have lost less value than B; the spread also narrows if A's yield decreases faster than B's. In this case, A will have delivered a greater capital gain than B. Portfolio managers can minimize losses in a bear bond market, and earn more in a bull market, by the careful monitoring of spreads.

held the Quebecs, his net profit is $34,485.

"The market is like a hungry animal," says Frank, his fellow salesman. "You've got to respect it. If you're not careful, it can eat you alive in five minutes." In most transactions, he explains, the seller wants to sell his bonds at a high price, the buyer wants to buy at a low price. Since the two parties rarely meet, the broker buys the bond, enters it in his books, and attempts to resell it within the following hours or days. Buying a commodity one party considers expensive or of poor quality for resale to a buyer who will consider it cheap or of high quality is risky work at the best of times. Like any broker, a trader is looking to make a dollar by selling his merchandise for more than he paid for it. When prices are in constant flux, it's no tea party. "You're happy if you make a buck two times out of three," says Frank.

A Canada bond issue

Rumours of a Quebec bond issue are impossible to pin down; the provinces always announce their borrowing plans at the very last minute. As it happens, Quebec will not be making a public issue on the Canadian market this year. What is certain, however, is that $2.3 billion of five-year Canada bonds will be auctioned this afternoon. This is where Tom comes in. While the provinces try to select the optimum moment for borrowing, Ottawa follows a rigid quarterly schedule, irrespective of the mood of the market. Today the market is unfavourable: all indices, except for the Canadian dollar and gold, are reflecting sharp declines. Prices for Canadas are following the bearish movement of U.S. Treasuries (U.S. government bonds). But, rain or shine, Canadian dealers must take part in all auctions.

Tom points to a number blinking on and off on a computer screen. "Look, a $120-million deal; five-year Canadas," he says. The dedicated screen displays transactions handled by special brokers — middlemen between the dealers — called Freedom Bond Brokers. Any bank or dealer can notify Freedom (or its competitor, Shorcan International Brokers) of its buy or sell price for a given size of the Canada bonds issued. For each bond, Freedom posts the best price offered, the best price asked, and the corresponding amounts — keeping individual dealers' identities secret, of course. Traders anywhere in the world can ring up the broker to confirm that they wish to make one of the transactions available. The deal, part of the more than 40 percent of trading volume on the secondary market that flows through these special brokers, blinks on the screen, then disappears, all under conditions of strictest confidentiality. Tom notes that "the market is bouncing on the floor." Bond prices have been low in recent days; there is a nagging concern that the market might fall right on through.

Tom has some tough choices to make. Should he be daring or cautious on the five-year bond issue? Should he take a long position at auction, or a short one? At 9:30 he chats with a trader for an American dealer who has detected no interest in the securities. At 9:45 Tom puts himself in a short position to the tune of some $120 million; before the auction actually begins, he'll be selling the lion's share of the roughly $128 million of bonds he contemplates picking up. "I don't like the Canadian market," he says. "The Canadas are too expensive."

At 10:45 Tom calls a Bank of Canada rep and during the course of the conversation lets him know that I'll be sitting at the bond desk. Then he unveils his position on the five-year paper. After asking him for a long list of prices, the Bank of Canada dealer wants to know if he's picked up any interest in the upcoming bond issue. "Not yet," Tom answers. A New York–based analyst has been predicting another interest rate hike by the Fed, the sixth since the beginning of the year — what does Tom think? Then the central bank trader passes on the story behind last night's sell-off of Canadian paper: the Japanese simply wanted to balance their books prior to publication of that semester's results. The conversation is about to wind up when he lets drop that the Bank of Canada has just made a special Treasury bill repurchase at 4.75 percent; the overnight rate has dropped by twenty-five basis points.

The conversation has left Tom feeling a bit perkier: he's pleased to learn that the cost of financing his securities has dropped. But the overnight rate still hasn't dropped enough for the street to go for five-years, Tom hears from an American dealer. The better part of the next hour he spends talking with Canadian and American traders, including one, he tells me, with a reputation as a liar. The idea is to figure out which way the four or five major players are likely to go. Each dealer attempts to extract the maximum amount of information while revealing nothing about his own tender. To pass on information would be worse than breaking a taboo: it would be collusion. But to survive, a trader must have the most accurate possible picture of capital flows: who is buying and selling, in what quantities, and why. Traders need the information to figure out which direction the market is heading in the days — or minutes — to come. But no single market participant, not even the Bank of Canada, can possibly have a complete overview of everything that goes on in the market. Information circulates rapidly, but distortions are frequent. Often, traders find themselves groping in the fog, never knowing when the ground will fall away from beneath their feet.

Later in the morning Tom buys $120 million of five-year Canada bonds and sells short $90 million of ten-years, a classic operation known as an arbitrage on the yield curve, a simultaneous buy-sell transaction designed to profit from short-term market anomalies. The yield curve is a graph that

THE YIELD CURVE IS STEEP IN THE SHORT AND MEDIUM TERM, FLAT IN THE LONG TERM

Yield curve on Canada bonds, September 21, 1994

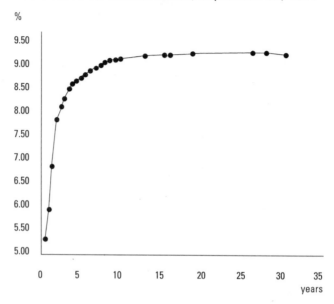

indicates the yield at maturity of Treasury bills and Canada bonds for all maturities, from short to long term. The idea is to purchase that portion of the curve that is temporarily cheap because it is under pressure for whatever reason, while simultaneously selling a stable section to contain risk. When the curve returns to its normal shape the operation is reversed. Today, five-years are feeling the heat as the market gears up for the extra offer on the afternoon's auction. The arbitrage has been structured to bring a profit of 1 cent per $100 of face value. "You're always looking for the steak," laughs Tom. "But when there isn't any, you go for the chicken bones and suck the marrow." When times are tough, no profit is too small.

The Bank of Canada calls Tom back at 12:20 looking for the latest prices; everything is looking good for the issue, they add. At 12:25 Tom prepares his tender: "I need $118 million, but I'm going for $210 million." Tom might have been pessimistic this morning, but now he's feeling positively bullish. He dictates his tender to a trader, who types it into the on-screen form with a direct Bank of Canada link. Size: $210 million. When he comes to the interest rate, Tom specifies 8.6 percent, then adds the last two decimal places: 8.630 percent. He hesitates for an instant,

44

then orders a change: 8.629 percent. "Send!" he orders. On the Freedom and Shorcan screens, five-years are trading at 8.64 percent. Tom's offer is a hefty one, designed to pull in the $210 million of bonds he wants. $120 million of them have already been sold short, so he's looking at a $90-million long position. In an hour the auction results will be in. "If the market flops, you're toast," he says, rushing off to wolf down a sandwich in a nearby café. But it's not long before Tom comes rushing back upstairs; he's changed his mind again. At 1:08 he gives the order to sell $69 million more of five-years.

At 1:30 sharp the auction results flash across the screen. Five-year bonds come in at 8.640 percent. Tom gets his $210 million plus the $2 million shared out automatically to participants — 9 percent of the total issue. By subtracting what he has already sold short, Tom ends up with a long position of $29 million. "Bad auction," he mutters, as he analyses the outcome. The "auction tail," the spread between the average and the strongest bid, is abnormally long, at two basis points. The coverage ratio — total bids against the number of bonds available — has never been weaker, at 1.8:1.

By 1:55 the bonds have already lost 25 cents, meaning that the overall value of the bonds sold has dropped by $5.7 million in twenty-five minutes. Tom is fit to be tied, and his colleagues are on his case. He hedged his $29-million position by selling short an equivalent size of U.S. Treasuries. But other brokers appear to have had the same idea: the American five-year market has dropped. His hedge turns out to be less than perfect. On paper, Tom has lost $90,000 because the Canadian market has slipped faster than the American market. Canada-U.S. spreads have widened.

Other traders are beating the bushes for five-year buyers. Frank is on the phone, trying to interest a crown corporation pension fund manager. Canadas? No thanks, says the man; he would rather buy American. Institutional buyers are waiting until the market has bottomed out before buying. Now the street is keeping the issue afloat on its own. By 2:15 Tom's theoretical loss has soared to $180,000, but he's confident he'll be able to sell off his position at a profit during the week. By 4:10 the loss is back to $42,000, as Canada-U.S. spreads have tightened.

Now it's 4:50 and Tom impatiently attempts to solicit bids from other dealers. "I don't like the market," he says. Unfortunately for Tom, most traders feel exactly the same way he does; the offers that trickle in are insignificant. Tom will just have to wait. The day began with slippage on the American market; Canada followed suit with a downturn in the medium and long term. Lower overnight rates have kept T-bills alive, but that's done nothing for the five-year bonds.

Tom is one of the top traders on the Canadian bond market, a man with sophisticated technical training who commands banks of computers displaying a constant stream of up-to-the-minute information, accurate to the last decimal place. And yet his attitude can be summed up in two short sentences: "I like the market" and "I don't like the market."

A day at the Caisse de dépôt

MONTREAL, THURSDAY, OCTOBER 13, 1994

Every morning, the money and bond market traders at Quebec's Caisse de dépôt et placement meet to review the events of the previous night and to preview the economic developments expected that day. Today's main event will be the United States wholesale price index. At 8:30 sharp the number flashes on the screens: a drop of 0.5 percent. "Bull!" exclaims a dealer, picking up the positive aspect of the number. Economists had been predicting a 1 percent increase. "It's volatile," says another, noting the immediate rise in American bonds. The traders listen as a small loud-speaker broadcasts a conference call organized by New York–based investment banker Goldman Sachs. "The report is not as good as it looks on the surface," says the American analyst.

The blue of the Quebec flag highlights the light blue of the trading room walls. The office has glass-walled corridors on one side, and the other side overlooks Montreal's swish McGill College Avenue. Two large desks, each with eight work stations, occupy the middle of the room: one is for bond traders, the second for money market and foreign exchange traders. Stocks are traded in another room.

In front of every trader stands a keyboard and a large-screen computer displaying a constant flow of graphic information, price lists, and the latest-breaking financial news. A huge bank of financial data is available on a small orange side-screen from the Bloomberg Agency. To call a dealer, a trader simply touches his name on a sensitive screen linked to a telephone, which records all conversations — standard industry practice. For Canadian securities, the Caisse does business with any brokerage house, large or small, providing it has a Montreal office. But for bonds denominated in foreign currencies, the Caisse deals with traders in the world's financial capitals. Here, where daily transaction volumes hover around the $200-million mark, the atmosphere is noisier than at the Bank of Canada but less hectic than at investment dealers or in the banks' trading rooms.

Ranked 123rd worldwide, the Caisse de dépôt et placement du Québec is Canada's largest fund manager, administering funds for eighteen government agencies, including the Quebec Pension Plan (the equivalent of the Canada Pension Plan) and the government employees' pension fund. At first glance it looks like a curious hybrid, but the Caisse does nothing that isn't already being done across North America: the Quebec fund manager simply puts these activities together in a different way. Some critics accuse the Caisse of behaving like a bull in a china shop — of attempting to influence individual corporations in which it owns large blocks of shares — but several American institutions take an even heavier-handed approach. The critics also tend to forget that bonds account for half of its $47-billion assets, and they ignore the substantial portfolio management expertise the Caisse has built up over the years.

Like all major institutional investors, "we are evaluated in relation to a benchmark and our mandate is to outperform it," explains Ernest

WHAT IS A PORTFOLIO?

Portfolio is the term used to designate all securities held by an investor. Portfolios can be specialized or diversified. When selecting securities for a portfolio, a manager searches for an optimum combination of risk and yield. Major institutional investors are happy when they marginally outperform the market; they know widely diversified portfolios rarely generate much higher returns for several years running. Such portfolios are too much like the market itself. Less diversified portfolios, while generating more striking results, can also lead to disaster: precisely the kind of high-risk situation large fund managers prefer to avoid.

Bastien, the Ph.D. in economics who heads the Caisse's strategic bond portfolios division. The ScotiaMcLeod Universe Bond Index provides the benchmark used by the Caisse to compare its performance with the yield rate for the Canadian bond market as a whole. "This year, bond yields are negative. If the index drops 5 percent and we only sink by 4.5 percent, we're doing a good job. If the index hits 22 percent and we only manage 20 percent, then we're doing a bad job," adds André Duchesne, a Caisse vice president. But Jean-Claude Scraire, the Caisse's new president, is insisting on both profits and protection of capital year in, year out.

A portfolio profile

The Caisse manages a portfolio of portfolios: traditional portfolios in each asset class — shares, bonds, real estate, etc. — but also portfolios containing the same asset classes differentiated by management style. For example, a "tactical" portfolio employs derivative instruments to change short-term weighting of asset classes without sale or purchase of a single share or bond. For risk management, the Caisse has developed a complex, quantitative model updated daily by four technicians applying between eighty and ninety parameters.

The house heavyweight is a $22-billion, two-part bond portfolio structured to meet the Caisse's long-term objectives for yield. The first section, which represents 85 percent of portfolio assets, is made up of less liquid securities and holds all provincial bonds, including those issued by Hydro-Québec and the municipalities. This reflects prevailing wisdom that the Caisse, as a significant player, should not deal actively in these securities, meaning that most are held for the long term, or traded for other kinds of Quebec securities with different characteristics. Liquid securities, such as Canada, U.S., and European government bonds, make up the remaining 15 percent, and here the dealing is significantly more active.

Since January 1993, a tactical bond portfolio has been piggybacked onto the Caisse's strategic bond portfolio. Its more active style lets managers take positions that fit their own market outlook. Portfolio director Yvon Gaudreau matches his own economic perspective against the market

---

DERIVATIVES

Derivatives are complex products whose value is derived from one or more simpler financial instruments, such as shares, bonds, currencies, or indices. The principal derivatives are options, futures, and swaps. An option is the right (but not the obligation) to buy or sell a standard financial product at an agreed-upon date and price. A future contract is an obligation to buy or to sell a financial product at an agreed-upon date and price. Some standard derivatives are traded on stock exchanges. Others, because of their complexity or one-of-a-kind nature, are traded over the counter. Derivatives have become controversial because most are used to create leverage, accentuating the speculative character of certain positions. But derivatives can also be used to reduce risk in certain types of investments. A solid understanding of how they work, combined with hands-on management of their cumulative effects on a portfolio, is essential.

---

consensus. When the two are on converging paths he does nothing, but when the paths diverge, there's an opportunity to exploit the difference. "We are trying to evaluate the accuracy of market expectations," says Gaudreau. He then takes a more daring, shorter-term position in derivatives, backed up by the resources of the strategic portfolio. At the beginning of each year, the Caisse hands Gaudreau a chunk of capital and a mandate to earn a rate of return of 20 percent. Losses may not exceed the total amount, which is a well-kept secret. Thus far, he's delivered the goods.

A recent tactical operation focused on the long-running wager on the short-term impact of political uncertainty on Canada-U.S. interest rate spreads. In June 1994, investors began to realize that the Parti Québécois would probably be elected. The value of Canadian bonds declined relative to those of the United States, pushing up the yield spread to 215 basis points. The Caisse promptly stepped in to purchase $650 million of Canada bonds, viewed as cheap, and sold an equivalent amount of American bonds, seen as expensive. While trader Denis Sénécal sold U.S. Treasuries short, his colleague Jean-Pierre Desloges took a long position on Canada bonds by purchasing a derivative, a future contract on ten-year Canada bonds called a CGB, which is traded on the Montreal Stock Exchange. After the elections, Sénécal and Desloges reversed the transaction; the profit was $20 million.

Negotiating with Quebec

Today, Finance department officials have come to discuss placement plans for the upcoming Quebec bond issue with its chief fund provider. The two parties — Caisse and government — decide on an overall amount for the year; this amount is then broken down into equal quarterly portions, each of which is then divided into one to five private placements. In a private placement, an issuer places his securities with a single investor. Where a small number of investors are involved, the placement is described as semi-private. Provincial and Hydro-Québec borrowings tend to alternate.

After determining its depositors' investment needs, the Caisse purchases the required bonds. In the short term, its managers enjoy a 5 percent leeway. In 1994, the Caisse purchased $1.4 billion (CA) in Quebec government bonds, for 60 percent of the province's borrowing in Canadian dollars and 20 percent of its total borrowing. No private Hydro-Québec investment was made; borrowing needs that year were soft.

The framework for negotiations between the Caisse and the government is well established, with bond maturities heading the agenda. The government might wish to borrow for seven years, while the Caisse needs a ten-year investment. "There have been king-size arguments over maturities," claims Bastien. The price-setting process, which follows, is more mechanical, thus less controversial. If a bond is traded on the market, a cross section of dealers is canvassed for price, and the average is chosen. If the bond does not exist, its price is derived from the price of a Canada bond of the same maturity.

The Caisse may occasionally subscribe to a public offering, but doing so might stimulate dealer curiosity. Should it purchase a significant portion of the issue, some people will claim that it is compensating for a weak demand for Quebec paper; if it does not take part in the issue, the same people will argue that the price is wrong. Things can get sticky. But neither the government nor Hydro-Québec pays dealers a commission for bonds sold to the Caisse.

Of the Caisse's bond portfolio, 45 percent consists of Quebec government paper and 27 percent of government-guaranteed securities, primarily

Hydro-Québec borrowings. Fully 30 percent of all Canadian dollar issues by the Quebec government and its electric utility are controlled by the institution — a powerful argument for caution in its operations on the secondary market for Quebec securities.

How the Caisse influences Quebec bonds

Earlier in the summer, a twenty-nine-year-old chartered financial analyst (CFA) and Quebec bond market maker gave the market an important message. Normally, Sylvain Choquette's job is to quote bid and ask prices on Quebec bonds and to conclude transactions initiated by dealers. But in June, the spread between Quebec and Canada bonds became "far too wide," says the man who buys and sells as many as sixty different Quebec government and Hydro-Québec securities. On the 27th, when the spread on ten-year bonds hit 108 basis points, he purchased $10 million (CA) on his own initiative, followed by another $5 million, hinting that he might be prepared to go even further. Dealers, who had been speculating on a drop in the value of Quebec bonds, were short, and the solid, stolid Caisse had just done something rash — and scary. If prices rose after Choquette's move, they could be big losers. These same dealers moved into heavy buying of Quebec bonds to cover their positions, ratcheting down the spread by about ten points.

In the tradition of the central banks, the Caisse's well-timed intervention turned the tide. But it was the exception to the rule. "There's nothing we can do about the way the spreads are moving," maintains Choquette. "But we can have an impact on the size of the spreads." Adds Bastien: "We don't have the capacity to set prices" — any more than the Bank of Canada can control the price of federal government bonds.

Choquette's real task is ensuring that Quebec securities remain liquid. "I always show a price" in order to avoid "panic reactions" among dealers stuck with large blocks, or encountering difficulties in processing a large order. "I want to facilitate transactions, not give them away. With my prices, I try not to give dealers a chance to make excessive profits." His policy for maintaining the equilibrium of the strategic portfolio vis-à-vis interest rate fluctuations: sell Canada when he buys Quebec, and buy Canada when he sells Quebec.

A feverish market will see Choquette change prices frequently. If dealers rush together to sell or buy Quebec, he slows the rush by posting less and less attractive prices. "We don't want to get caught in front of an oncoming train," he says. Besides, explains Bastien, the Caisse cannot possibly absorb the full volume. "We can't take the place of the dealers. After all, Quebec is paying them to distribute Quebec bonds." Being a market maker, he explains, means "swimming against the current." This year, at the first sign of political nervousness, the Caisse turned sell offers to its advantage, buying Quebec at low prices. Prices rose after the election; now the Caisse is attempting to reduce its position to rebuild its liquidity. "Whenever people let their emotions run away with them, it's profitable for us," says Bastien. A market maker's job is far from neutral. Still, the Caisse does not speculate on Quebec bonds; in fact, they are not even a component of its tactical portfolio.

It's been a quiet day. Choquette has purchased Quebecs maturing in 1999 for $20 million from a large dealer and sold $16 million maturing in 2000. From a boutique (the expression for a small broker) he has also bought $1.5 million in securities maturing in 1998, and sold $1.2 million maturing one year later. The spreads haven't budged. It was the same approach that saw the Caisse last year trade a volume of $27 billion in Quebec and Hydro-Québec bonds. Even though the activity does not generate either significant profits or losses, it enhances the liquidity of Quebec securities. Active management makes them a more attractive item for investors — including the Caisse itself — and smooths the process of government borrowing. But some people believe that this amounts to manipulating the market, making Quebec securities less attractive.

The Caisse, the institutional investor handling the largest foreign exchange volume in Canada, at $154.2 billion per year, has been known to make waves. Its investments in foreign bonds and shares, accounting for some 95 percent of its foreign exchange volume, are entirely hedged for currency risks. But through its tactical portfolio the Caisse speculates on currency fluctuations. When it has a firm opinion on the direction prices are moving, it takes a position equivalent to up to 10 percent of the value of its international portfolio, explains Laurent Desbois, manager of foreign exchange and money markets. In other words, the Caisse never drops its hedge below 90 percent, an extremely conservative management practice. It's all done through derivatives. "We operate without cash," explains Desbois, a CFA whose taste in clothing runs to heavy wool socks in traditional wing-tips. Right now, adds his assistant Marc Tremblay, "we're being very cautious. We can't tell which direction the market is headed."

By late afternoon the pace has slackened. As in most trading rooms, the bulk of transactions take place in the morning. Tensions have relaxed, traders are joking on the phones: "You got a country house? A gun? I'm recruiting for a traders' sect." A copy of *La Presse* is lying on the floor, with a banner headline about the Solar Temple affair.

Lining up the next coup

At 4:30, ten people meet in a closed room to plan investment tactics. A bowl of Marks & Spencer toffees lies at the centre of the table, a treat for the end of the afternoon. A soft-spoken Bastien chairs the meeting. The morning's encounter with the Finance department people elicits one laconic sentence: "We don't quite see eye to eye about maturities with our friends in Quebec City; we won't be buying."

The group analyzes the latest inflation figures and goes over the events of the day before getting down to the nuts and bolts of an arbitrage project. The idea is to sell Ontario and buy British Columbia bonds. The buzz is that the Ontarios are too high-priced; they are expected to drop in value as soon as investors realize the size of the provincial deficit. On the other hand, the B.C.s could well climb if the NDP government were to be turfed out. The transaction would be worth from $20 to $50 million, but might expand to $200 or $300 million. Plan B would be to sell Quebecs and purchase B.C.s, but in smaller sizes. If the Caisse sells Ontarios, it would be selling short; but if it decides to sell Quebecs, the securities would be pulled from the strategic portfolio, which is currently saturated, thanks to its market-making activity over the last few months,

The participants pass around graphs and pore over lists, looking for the bonds that best fit the operation. Not an easy matter. B.C.s are scarce on the market; the province has been cutting its deficit. After a brisk discussion, Bastien decides to start out with a block of $50 million, then winds up the meeting with a word of caution to the troops: "Don't let them see you coming; call people one at a time."

Putting our savings in the blender

Large or small, middleman or major investor, every player on the market has one goal: to make money in an uncertain environment. But as the traders and market makers wheel, deal, and churn the paper, they are also managing the savings of Mr. and Mrs. John Q. Public under a double mandate. When depositors entrust their savings to a bank, an insurance company, or a mutual fund, when they forego a portion of their wages in the form of pension plan contributions, they are hoping the people managing their capital will both preserve it and make it grow.

Savings are part of the equation that governs capital supply and demand, and that equation can be tested by a price: the interest rate. Capital supply originates in household savings and corporate profits. Demand includes consumer credit, mortgages, corporate capital investments, and government deficits. But the equation becomes more complicated as, with the growth of globalization, an ever-increasing portion of savings jumps from one country to another, toward the supplier who offers a better price.

Why should a person who has built up savings over time forego possession of his capital if he has no prospect of increasing it? When an investor rents capital, he hopes that his tenants will prove quiet and accommodating. Without his knowing it, a significant portion of his savings are channelled through negotiable instruments called Treasury bills and bonds. The fund managers who purchase these securities in his name face a double risk: interest rate fluctuation and the quality of the borrower's credit.

The inflation rate expected by investors is the main factor in determining the general interest rate level. An investor who fears that inflation will cause the value of the capital to be repaid him in ten years to depreciate will insist on a higher interest rate than if he were persuaded that the dollars he has lent will maintain their purchasing power. But, as inflation forecasts fluctuate along with the business cycle, interest rates also rise and fall. Rate volatility carries with it a capital liquidity risk that is directly related to a bond's maturity. The longer the maturity, the greater the sensitivity of the bond's price to interest rate fluctuations. Money lent out through long-term securities will not be paid back before the maturity date. If interest rates rise in the meantime, the money cannot be transferred to a new security offering a more generous rate. To release himself from the contract, the holder must sell the bond at a reduced price and take a loss. Thirty-year bonds are far more risky than two-year paper, no matter who the issuer is. A lot can happen in twenty or thirty years, particularly deterioration of the borrower's credit.

The insolvency or default risk depends on the quality of the borrower's signature. It would be an error to assume that the default risk for securities issued by public bodies is nil simply because the governments of the industrial countries never declare bankruptcy. The method investors use to evaluate default risk is much more subtle than that. An overindebted government, for instance, can always print money to finance its debt, driving up inflation. But between the extremes of debt repudiation and the solidity of the government of a wealthy country with sound public finances there exists an entire range of gradations, each with its corresponding risk premium. The evaluation process is never purely objective, as some might think. The size of the debt is a precise figure, but the capacity to raise additional taxes to finance the debt, or the strength of the economy that must support it, can be evaluated in a variety of ways. How can we measure such factors as political stability or the capacity of governments to bring in and enforce unpopular corrective policies?

The savings equation in Canada points to an imbalance that must be compensated for by foreign capital. Without it, the price of Canadian savings would be far too high. That is why our governments must borrow abroad.

But what motivates a foreign investor to purchase our securities? As our investigation unfolds, we will be piecing together what looks like a jigsaw puzzle. Be patient, dear reader, because the puzzle takes shape slowly. You might get the feeling that the only pieces in hand are sky-blue, but beneath that sky lies a fascinating landscape which is ours to discover.

Chapter 3

MONEY FROM EUROPE

PARIS, OCTOBER 18, 1994

IS THIS REALLY Paris? Maybe it's just jet lag. The newspapers are full of talk about political uncertainty, nervous capital markets, and widening bond spreads. *Le Monde* headlines "the rise of political 'risk' in France" following the resignation of the country's minister of Industry, Post and Telecommunications and Foreign Trade. Gérard Longuet, leader of the Parti républicain, is the latest in a long line of French politicians forced to resign in a rash of corruption-related scandals. The re-election of Chancellor Helmut Kohl has also intensified political risk, says the prestigious Parisian daily. Under Kohl, Germany is expected to adopt restrictive fiscal policies just as France's presidential campaign is getting underway, driving a wedge between French and German government bond yields.[1]

"Bickering within the current government majority is beginning to undermine the confidence of international investors. A weakening of political power inevitably has an effect on currency parities. There is no reason why France should be an exception," laments *La Tribune*, one of Paris's two financial dailies.[2]

Seen from a distance, Canada's problems suddenly loom less large. Still, both dailies run a press agency report on Finance minister Paul Martin's promise to wrestle the deficit down to $25 billion by 1997. "We're up to our eyeballs in debt," they quote the minister as saying. Meanwhile, the mainstream press is agog over the latest British royal family melo-drama. In an authorized biography, Prince Charles has just revealed that he never loved Princess Diana.

The historic Château de la Muette, on the outskirts of Paris, in the chic Sixteenth arrondissement, is where the Organization for Economic Co-operation and Development makes its headquarters. The thirty-five-year-old organization brings together the twenty-five richest industrial nations, but it has no decision-making power, and its public statements often sound more like diplomatic communiqués than international economic reports. Still, the OECD remains an unparalleled source of information on the economic situations and policies of its member-states.[3] OECD statistics confirm that Canada is the fourth most indebted country in relation to the size of its economy, after Belgium, Italy, and Greece, and just before Sweden, on the informal watch-list of five countries whose deficits are seen as unsustainable. In the OECD's eyes, these countries are vulnerable to rising interest rates, and are in danger of becoming caught up in a "rising spiral of debt."[4] The five delinquents should take advantage of the current economic recovery to reduce their deficits even more ener-getically, it argues.

For Deborah Roseveare, the OECD's principal fiscal policy analyst, analyzing the debt dilemma is a full-time job. "When is debt too high? That's one of those very, very difficult questions to answer. It's like asking, what is the optimal amount of government spending? You can't find any-where in the literature something that would say the ideal is 32.4 percent. It is not that straightforward; it depends on the preferences of the country." But, I ask, can you identify a breaking point, a line that a country cannot cross without touching off a crisis? "The simple answer is no. If anybody had been asked what Belgium's breaking point was ten years ago, we would all have been proved wrong, because there is a country which, by virtually everybody's standard, should have reached the point of no return, the breaking point, already. And yet, by the criterion of interest rate differential with Germany, they are not there yet. The country's not broke yet." In fact, Belgium borrows at interest rates that are only slightly higher than those of its neighbours with healthier public finances.

What do you think of Canada? "At nearly 100 percent of GDP, the Canadian debt, by anybody's standard, should raise considerable concerns.

CANADA: ONE OF THE MOST INDEBTED COUNTRIES

Gross financial liabilities of public administrations as a percentage of GDP

	1985	1995*
United States	48.9	63.1
Japan	67.0	83.1**
Germany	42.5	60.0
France	38.6	57.5
Italy	82.3	124.4
United Kingdom	58.9	56.8
Canada	64.7	97.3
Total of countries shown	*54.6*	*71.6*
Australia	—	38.1
Belgium	122.6	134.6
Greece	48.3	117.5
Sweden	66.7	80.8
Total of 25 OECD countries	*55.2*	*72.1*

* Estimates and forecasts
** Japan has large gross financial liabilities but also large financial assets, and a smaller net public debt.

Source: OECD, Economic Outlook, December, 1995

If I were a Canadian, it is a situation that I would be quite concerned about." Particularly, she adds, since deterioration was so rapid during the 1980s. How does Belgium, where indebtedness stands at 142 percent of GDP, manage where Canada seemingly cannot? Is it because Belgium's record as an inflation-fighter has convinced investors that the chances of it monetizing its debt are slim? Canadian inflation rates are just as low as Belgium's, but the trend is only a recent one. Investors are not sure whether it can last. Despite the differences between countries, Roseveare believes that a breaking point does exist, a point where debt can spiral out of control, driven by the high interest rates it creates. No one can foretell the critical moment, so "the safest course is to act as if it's just around the corner."

Anything like New Zealand in 1984? I ask. Ms. Roseveare seems embarrassed by the question. It's not that she doesn't know the answer. In fact, she is a native Kiwi, and was an employee of the New Zealand Treasury when Finance minister Roger Douglas declared that the country had "hit the debt wall." Foreign investors were refusing to finance recurring deficits, Douglas asserted. The only solution was to slice government spending to the bone. Ms. Roseveare feels unable to speak freely on the subject, but I come away with the impression that, in her opinion, New Zealand could have chosen the deeper debt route. Other countries — such as Sweden, in 1994 — have survived greater financial crises without prescribing such bitter medicine, she notes. Sweden's social democratic government leaned toward preservation of a generous welfare state, while attempting to control the deficit with a combination of new taxes and spending restrictions.

The Swedish response showed that there are other ways of dealing with a foreign exchange crisis, the crisis of confidence that erupts when speculators become convinced that the exchange rate that governments attempt to maintain has, for whatever reason, become indefensible. In New Zealand, publication of a Labour Party document forecasting a 20 percent devaluation after elections triggered a wave of speculation. Canada is far less vulnerable to such an outbreak, since the Bank of Canada has no specific exchange rate to protect. The potential payoff is greater, and the risk higher, for speculators who attack a national currency defended by a country's central bank rather than a free-floating currency protected only against sudden swings by punctual interventions.

Still, Ms. Roseveare believes that Canada must act without further ado. "The message we would be sending is: the more you can get your debt under control, the sooner the better. It would give you more room to manoeuvre; the fiscal boat takes a long time to turn around." If Canadians wait until capital markets give them the push, they will be forced into taking "brutal, painful" measures which are unlikely to encourage optimal distribution of economic resources.

••••••••••••••••••••••••

The City of Light has probably generated as many clichés as fond memories, but neither are likely to involve its great financial centre. The tourists who troop through the Eighth arrondissement don't think of it as the Business District; instead their gazes turn to the Louvre, the Place de l'Opéra, and the great department stores. In a nondescript building just

---

THE EUROCURRENCY MARKET

A Eurocurrency is a currency deposited in a bank located outside the country where that currency has been minted. The Eurocurrency market is also known as the Eurodollar market, a name originating in the 1960s and '70s, when European banks accumulated a pool of American dollars. Over time, this capital was invested in negotiable securities called Eurobonds. The principal Eurocurrencies, in order of importance, are the American dollar, the Deutschmark, the yen, the pound sterling, the French franc, the ECU (European Currency Unit, which will become the Euro, the European Union's single currency, at the turn of the century), the Canadian dollar, and the Australian dollar. These currencies also constitute the principal segments of the Eurobond market. London is the nerve centre of the Euromarket.[5]

---

across the street from Les Galeries Lafayette lurks the Société Générale's office for relations with issuers. The offices are run-down, and the staff is restive, hoping to be transferred soon to La Défense, the newly built business district springing up around a node of office towers just outside the city walls. Pascal Bay picks up the phone, and in two minutes a waiter from a nearby café hurries across the street, balancing two bottles of Perrier on a tray.

"Our job is to obtain mandates from Canadian issuers," Bay explains as we sip the fizzy spring water. The Société Générale is one of France's largest banks (twice as big as Canada's Royal Bank), and, in keeping with continental tradition, it handles a wide variety of financial specialty services, including the task of piloting bond issues as lead bank, or joining sales efforts as part of a distribution syndicate. Bay's department scours the market for financing opportunities for issuers and formulates proposals from which its clients can pick and choose. Similar departments exist in all the major American, European, and Asian banks. The Société Générale's strength is the Eurofranc, one of the many niches on the huge, complex Eurocurrency market.

From its vantage point close to the "*zinzins*" — French banking slang for institutional investors (from *zinvestisseurs zinstitutionnels*) — the Société Générale can easily canvass interest in a new bond carrying a Canadian signature, and pin down interest rate, volume, and maturity. It must, of course, advise its Canadian client of the swap, the vital contract

---

SWAPS

A swap is an exchange of future payments flows between two parties. The practice, which makes it possible to alter radically the characteristics of a borrowing, is common in international finance. In an interest rate swap, two entities can exchange borrowings of different rates and maturities. Specifically, borrower A is able to obtain good conditions for a variable interest loan; he finds it to his advantage to trade this loan for a fixed-rate loan that borrower B can obtain at better conditions than A. In currency swaps, a borrowing in one currency can be exchanged for a borrowing in another. Both types of swaps are occasionally joined to create a hybrid form. Banks at one time played the role of intermediary between the two parties. But given the difficulty of meeting the needs of both borrowers at the appropriate time, the bank (or dealer) actually acts as the other party to the swap (i.e., becomes the counterparty). A bank manages a swap portfolio made up of opposing commitments to minimize its counterparty risk. Managing counterparty risks has become a critical aspect of this high-volume market. Swap protection is effective only as long as the banker can respect his commitments during the life of the borrowing.

---

that will convert French francs, useless to the Canadian issuer, into Canadian dollars. Even more critical is the fact that the swap locks in at its current level the exchange rate that will be used to calculate interest payments and repayment of capital at maturity. It comes as no surprise that most governments in Canada prefer not to borrow in a currency if they are not certain beforehand what exchange rate will determine the service of a particular debt. Nova Scotia, which ventured into this hornets' nest several years ago, is still extracting the stingers; the Deutschmarks that the province was forced to reimburse had a much higher Canadian dollar cost than those that it had borrowed.

The most recent financial operation to be led by the Société Générale for a Canadian borrower was a "jumbo" issue of 20 billion French francs (FF) for the Province of Quebec, in March 1994. "We solicited French investors who were looking for yield," Bay explains. The ten-year bond offered sixty-five basis points (one hundred basis points = 1 percent) more than an OAT (French government bond, or Obligation assimilable au Trésor) of the same maturity. Merrill Lynch acted as the Société Générale's co-lead bank in the deal, with the two firms placing 65 percent of the issue between them. Both have also been members of the Quebec government and Hydro-Québec international syndicate for several years. Nine other banks and investment dealers also participated in the distribution.

European institutional investors are paying increased attention to credit ratings set by the New York bond rating agencies. When Quebec was downgraded in the spring of 1993, they sat up and took notice. But, says Bay, "the franc is an open currency when it comes to rating." Most of the investors who participated in the 1994 deal were French, he continues; they knew Quebec well and were not worried by the situation in the province. Insurance companies also have no difficulty purchasing Quebec bonds. But they tend to look much more closely at the intrinsic risks of a name. The sheer size of the borrowing in this deal was enough to ensure good liquidity, considered an essential quality. The operation went smoothly, even though it took a while to complete the sale, Bay concludes.

The industry's judgment is harsher. The financing was hard to place; it was simply too large for the market, a competitor later told me. Conversion of the borrowing into French francs took place in two phases. First phase: five swaps negotiated with three dealers produced a floating rate borrowing in U.S. dollars, distributed among maturities of one, four, and five years. Second phase: the borrowings denominated in U.S. dollars were converted into a total of $1.2 billion (CA) at maturities of between three and ten years, with certain tranches (blocks) at fixed rates, others at a floating rate. The cost to Quebec was theoretically equivalent to borrowing on the Canadian market — theoretically, because the Canadian market could not possibly have absorbed such a large financing at current rates.

•••••••••••••••••••••

Five minutes away, at the Banque nationale de Paris (BNP) on boulevard des Italiens, François-Xavier Chevalier's department handles, on a discretionary or consulting basis, funds worth 400 billion francs, twice what Quebec's Caisse de dépôt et placement deals with. Chevalier, an MBA from the University of Chicago, wears several hats at once: those of a portfolio manager, strategist, and quantitative management specialist. A frequent visitor to Quebec, he likes "our American cousins. They've kept a freshness you no longer find in France."

His rumpled shirt and receding hairline give the fiftyish fund manager the look of a friendly version of the eccentric Dr. Tournesol from a Tintin comic book. With a professorial air, he explains the link between the economy and portfolio management. "We begin with an economic argument. There is a relationship between the business cycle and the yield rate curve. Think of the economic cycle as four seasons: expansion is like summer, and during the summer the yield curve stays normal, with short-term rates lower than long-term rates. When the economy begins to heat up, the central bank raises short-term rates to counteract inflation. When short-term rates go higher than long-term ones, we enter the autumn solstice. When interest rates peak, the period of overheating ends and recession begins. Long- and short-term rates meet and begin to fall. At the spring solstice, short-term rates go lower than long-term rates and recovery is underway."

Geographic diversification of investments, explains Chevalier, now makes it possible to profit from the time-lag between the cycles of different countries. International portfolio distribution is guided by world benchmarks, particularly the indices compiled by J. P. Morgan and Salomon Brothers. These indices are weighted according to the volume of existing issues in each national bond market. Hoping to improve his position, a

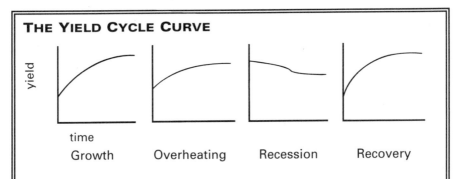

THE YIELD CYCLE CURVE

yield

time

Growth Overheating Recession Recovery

The curve illustrates the yield of Treasury bills and bonds from a benchmark issuer such as the Government of Canada for several maturities, from short to long term. Portfolio managers track each segment of the yield curve, and shift their capital back and forth in response to fluctuations. The rise in interest rates that precedes a recession has a sharp negative impact on the price of long-term securities. Conversely, falling rates prior to recovery are more propitious to long-term securities. Confident investors lengthen the average maturity of their portfolio; worried investors shorten it.

manager will over-weight or under-weight a given country's index share, depending on his analysis of the cycle. Index-driven management has become the rule in France over the last four or five years. In this context, and considering the close relationship between the Canadian and American cycles, "Canadian securities are viewed as a supplement to American ones, a more profitable, but also a riskier supplement," he says. Foremost among the risks is a drop in the Canadian dollar, which has been uncoupled from raw material prices. Next comes the Quebec question. "If Canada breaks up, confidence in the Canadian dollar will erode." But "over-indebtedness is common to all industrialized countries," says Chevalier.

Les Échos, Paris's other financial daily, profiles a BNP mutual fund specializing in international bonds. The story quotes fund manager Alain Jegou as saying that "three quarters of the performance of products in our category can be attributed to currency fluctuations, and only one quarter to changes in interest rates."[6] Jegou and I meet in the small trading room where he supervises some twenty other bank employees. Jegou manages a retirement fund bond portfolio, but his pride and joy is a *sicav* worth 500 billion francs ($500 million [CA]) called Natio-Inter. A *sicav* — a French abbreviation for *société d'investissement de capital variable* — is a mutual fund that enjoys autonomous legal status and boasts its own board of directors. Shares are sold in bank branches to small players on the French market who have a distinct preference for investment vehicles of this kind. Jegou's goal is to beat the J. P. Morgan World Government Bond Index, which assigns Canada a weight of 2.93 percent, compared with 41.81 percent for the United States. Jegou's *sicav* boasts a separate dollar compartment which includes the currencies of the United States, Canada, Australia, and New Zealand. All four have been lumped together "because of the stable, proven correlation" among them. Their relative weight is adjusted according to interest rate spreads. At the present time, says Jegou with a glance at his computer screen, "the 135-point spread isn't bad." He's alluding to the yield spread that separates Canadian and American ten-year bonds. If the spread drops to 80 points, he will sell Canadas and buy U.S. Treasuries. European money is more patient than North American, he says. But even his two-year investment horizon doesn't stop him from regularly reviewing his positions.

When he picks securities, Jegou always looks for the Standard & Poor's and Moody's rating, never going below AA. When it comes to Canadian dollar investments he prefers the federal debt "because it has a better rating and because we like to have plenty of liquidity." In Jegou's trade, currency fluctuations represent the principal income as well as danger to investors, which explains why he occasionally hedges his foreign exchange risk on the Chicago futures market. Among the other risks is provincial indebtedness, but it is not so extreme that it could result in default on payment. A downgrading, on the other hand, can hurt, since it reduces the market value of the bonds, which "wipes out the yield pick-up on provincial bonds." The federal debt is also a matter of concern. Jegou is critical of the decision to "postpone cuts in government spending" until 1995. Quebec independence won't happen, he believes, but should it appear probable "we would sell Canadas before the referendum. I think all traders would do the same thing. There would be a danger of a sell-off. The markets are terrified of uncertainty. That's clear." Jegou won't be selling any Quebecs, for the simple reason that there are none in his portfolio.

So where does Jegou get his information on Canada? He pulls a recent study by the American brokerage firm Goldman Sachs from the wastebasket. A paragraph is marked with yellow highlighter: "We are nervous about the Canadian capital markets because the recent rally has been based mainly on a downward revision to investors' assessment about the likelihood of Quebec separation. The budgetary problems remain and could be adversely affected by developments in the United States,"[7] particularly with regard to interest rates. Jegou also studies the research papers published by J. P. Morgan, TD Securities, and Lehman Brothers, not to mention press clippings faxed from Montreal. And, like every dealer on earth, he keeps a constant eye on the news from Reuters and Telerate (a Dow Jones subsidiary).

Philippe Rakotovao, born of Malagasy parents, is in charge of domestic and international bond markets at the BNP. His decisions are completely independent of Jegou's and Chevalier's. The trading room where we meet, which is shaped like a triangle with rounded ends, shares a global mission with its London sister office. Paris covers the franc and the ECU; London covers all other currencies; the Hong Kong branch handles the night shift. Rakotovao and his colleagues describe themselves as market makers.

"We like to talk about the fundamentals, but our job is to make prices, to try to come up with a margin, even if it's weak, on large volumes." The bank is not in the habit of taking daring positions, but it will "scratch for basis points" by playing the spreads, or by selling an expensive-looking security and buying a cheaper one.

How do French market insiders view Canadian issuers? "An entity, before it can call itself Quebec or Ontario, is Canadian first of all. For all issuers, the political risk is quite important. But we have trouble figuring out what's going on in Canada. The rate spreads between Canada and the United States seem absurd to us. We don't have much information on political developments in Canada. It's hard to understand what Quebec independence means. We buy Quebec on feeling," even though the collapse of Toronto-based Confederation Life made more than a few investors think twice. "Look, a bond is a product which has to be sold. The French public debt was a pile of shit! But they did road shows, had a marketing plan, and now there are these accounts you can't even imagine, way out in deepest Colorado, holding French Treasury paper. Canada ought to stage its own road shows to sell its debt," advises Rakotovao. But while we're talking about Quebec and Canada, political uncertainty, the bugbear that keeps European dealers awake nights, hovers over France. OATs have dropped relative to Bunds (German government borrowings), with the spread between ten-year securities widening two basis points, to seventy. It stood at fifty points in September; some observers are predicting one hundred before year's end.

As the TGV slows down before pulling into the Geneva station, I leaf through the current issue of *L'Express*, a major French newsweekly: "Quebec: the independence trap" reads the headline, setting the tone for the article beneath it. The lead quotes "distinguished Université du Québec à Montréal economist Pierre Fortin: 'Sovereignty will swell the Quebec deficit to 3.5 billion dollars . . . Jurisdictional transfers involving Ottawa and Quebec would cost $1.7 billion; sovereignty would touch off an economic slowdown. In the short term at least.'"[8] Reading further, I note that a public opinion poll taken after the election of the Parti Québécois showed that 32.8 percent of Quebeckers would answer "Yes" to a question on sovereignty, while 54 percent would vote "No." I am sure the French bankers will be reading that article.

GENEVA, OCTOBER 19, 1994

Geneva's artificial geyser, the city's trademark, has been shut down for repairs. A lakeshore shuttle chugs across the harbour, past the sailboats moored in impeccable order in the marina. Huge signboards perched atop the roofs of the luxurious buildings overlooking Lac Léman provide a visitor with a crash course in the Swiss economy. There's tourism, with the Hôtel Les Bergues, the Grand Casino, and Kuwait Airways; then comes watchmaking, with Rolex and Patek Philippe; there's insurance, with Genève Assurances, Zurich Assurances, and Union Suisse Assurances; and, of course, banking. Down at the lakefront, the foreign banks are the most visible: the Bank of New York, the British Bank of the Middle East, Citibank, ABN Amro Bank.

Hard statistics are unavailable, but it is estimated in the industry that Switzerland's banks manage funds valued between 1,500 and 2,000 billion Swiss francs (SF), roughly $2,000 billion (CA), or two and a half times Canada's GDP. Which is another way of saying that the Swiss bankers move around enough capital to finance Canada's public debt two and a half times over, even though Switzerland's economy is only half the size of Canada's. Three huge institutions — Credit Suisse, Union Bank of Switzerland, and the Swiss Bank Corp. — hold the bulk of this hoard, which represents between one-fifth and one-quarter of the world wealth management market. But Geneva's specialty is its private banks, those little-known institutions that manage funds as large as Canada's largest institutional investors.

If virtues had nationalities, discretion would wear a "Made in Switzerland" label. A few blocks away from the lakefront, no sign on the roof identifies the venerable greystone, five-storey building at 11, rue de la Corraterie. Beside the main entrance a small bronze plaque reads: "L. O. & Cie." In little more time than it takes to scan the plaque, the massive wrought-iron gate swings open as if by magic, and I step into the premises of Messrs Lombard Odier & Cie, bankers in Geneva since 1798. This is the bank that financed the fictitious lunar cannon in Jules Verne's novel *From the Earth to the Moon*.

Geneva's eight private banks are peculiar institutions. They make no loans and accept no deposits. No numbered accounts here. Their specialty is wealth management. Industry insiders estimate that L. O. & Cie manages assets of between 40 and 50 billion SF (about $45 billion [CA]), two-thirds of which is drawn from the fortunes of individuals, and a third from institutions, including central banks. Fully three-quarters of its funds originate outside of Switzerland — from around the world, in fact. Four men in well-tailored uniforms welcome me politely and relieve me of my trenchcoat. Don't ask me how, but they know my name: the scene is straight out of an American Express commercial. One of them leads me up a flight of stairs to Room 42, a small office furnished with a desk, five chairs, and a computer. Seated behind the desk is Dr. Patrizio Merciai, the bank's chief economist and investment strategy planner. Also present are Guy Barbey, deputy vice president in charge of international fixed-income revenues, and Hervé Siegrist, who manages some client portfolios.

"There are still people who think of us as the gentleman in his library who dazzles the lady with his knowledge, but it's an overworked image," laughs Merciai. The bank performs extensive research; its institutional clients would settle for nothing less. Perhaps one hundred of its eight hundred employees keep constant track of the markets, while another hundred managers supervise client accounts, and then there are the traders who carry out the orders. A strategic committee plans every move and formulates investment grids that serve as asset distribution models. Grids are determined by the client's currency of reference and his propensity for risk, from conservative to daring; the wealth manager can then adapt the appropriate grid to the client's specific needs. Six months is the normal planning period, but strategies are reviewed at least monthly.

Currently, the balanced strategy is solidly defensive. A typical portfolio holds 44 percent in Swiss francs, 40 percent in shares (including 2 percent Canadian), and a mere 16 percent in bonds. "We have been extremely prudent on the bond markets since the first of the year. We may have left the market slightly too soon, but it was the better decision to have made. And it paid off," says Merciai. The bank's withdrawal was particularly noticeable in the United States, where Lombard Odier cut its holdings to 5 percent. The percentage of assets assigned to Canadian bonds was sliced from 4 percent to 2 percent, still twice the country's relative weight on international bond-market indices. Few people use benchmarks here, except on behalf of institutional clients. "We can pick up 150 to 200 additional basis points on the Canadian market," Siegrist explains.

Security and capital protection are the first two commandments of Swiss bank clients, making risk analysis essential. "Currency risk is a strategic risk," explains Merciai. "Of course, this risk can be hedged, but that can be costly. I think the issue is more important than that. The currency's fragility, or lack of it, is what determines the interest rate structure. It's not enough to say that because a given currency is weak the risk must be hedged. We have to ask ourselves whether the weakness of the currency will lead to a shift in Canadian monetary policy, and to even higher interest rates. After a strategic overview, we can adopt more suitable tactics in the options or futures markets to hedge the risk." Siegrist admits that for clients who think in terms of Swiss francs "almost all currencies are risky. But the Canadian dollar, which is more volatile than the American dollar, is even more so."

"We've pulled out of all the heavily indebted countries," Merciai says in response to my question about public indebtedness. Lombard Odier sold Sweden four months ago. "Unfortunately, it's something you see a lot of. Half the world's bond markets find themselves in the same situation. The spreads illustrate the differences in public debt levels. We try to determine whether they are sufficient, or whether they are likely to widen further. One of the reasons why we've been so cautious on securities markets is because of the explosion of public debt around the world. An accident in Canada, in Sweden, or in New Zealand drives up yields and risk premiums. Still, we hold a small portion of Canadian dollars. If the spread is enough, and if the Canadian economy takes off, we might see a rise in tax revenues and avoid the worst. Canada was in a better position than Sweden, which was still in recession [when the institution cut back its bond portfolio]."

Political risk appears not to disturb the Geneva bankers. The firm's Montreal office gives them a listening post at ground zero. "We are quite content with the quality of the debtor. Volatility is normal, considering political uncertainty; we are certainly ready to play," says the chief economist. Prior to the Quebec elections, Barbey adds, taking a cigarette from an elegant box on the desk, "Quebec and Hydro-Québec bonds climbed to more than 9 percent in three- and four-year maturities; with inflation at 1.5 percent, those are fabulous real rates. During the summer we bought quite a few Canadian securities. It was an excellent bargain, and it had nothing to do with the American market."

How do you choose your securities? "Most of the time," Barbey tells me, "we require a minimum rating of AA. But even then, depending on client orders, we will buy debt on emerging markets such as South America, like the paper of Argentina or Brazil. The Canadian provinces don't have much of a following, but some clients like their yields, and that's fine, as long as they accept the risk with full knowledge. We try to avoid these risks in our discretionary mandates. If we buy a province, it will be a British Columbia." For Barbey, what really counts is Canada's AAA rating.

....

A burgundy red Piccard-Pictet stands poised and gleaming in the middle of the bank lobby. The antique luxury sedan, built in Geneva in 1914, is one of nine known to exist. A man in servant's livery unlocks the elevator, then accompanies me to the fifth floor and a waiting bevy of hostesses. They guide me to Room 9, an elegantly appointed, spacious office overlooking a park; antique engravings adorn the walls. Philippe Treyvaud, deputy director, is the first to arrive, followed by Jean-Marc Bongard, Japan and dollar-block bond market specialist. His business card reads "*Fondé de pouvoir de Messieurs Pictet & Cie, banquiers,*" the old-fashioned title used by fund managers who deal directly with the clientele. In this institution, financial analysts also manage funds. "If things go badly, the analyst shares the blame. That obliges us to stay closer to the market," Treyvaud says.

Pictet & Cie is Switzerland's second-largest private bank, after Lombard Odier, and like its sister institution, it prides itself on its long-running, intimate ties with clients Treyvaud describes as "well-to-do, wealthy, or extremely wealthy." The kind of clients who once drove Piccard-Pictets. Each client deals directly with his or her personal manager, or with the manager's substitute, a younger employee learning the trade. Often, when a client bequeaths his fortune to his son, the son will continue with the substitute, who has by then become an experienced manager in his own right. A typical client "does not necessarily want extraordinary performance; what he wants is stable performance; his aim is to preserve his capital," Treyvaud adds.

The investment process begins with an examination of the leading economic indicators by the bank's strategy committee. Its first decision will be how to divide the funds among asset classes: cash, bonds, equity, and precious metals. The second decision will divide the equity by country, and the bonds by currency. Analysts bring highly specialized recommendations to bear in setting up a portfolio, creating eighteen investment grids that managers can tailor to suit their clients.

The primary bond selection criterion is quality of credit, followed by liquidity, and, finally, by specific market conditions. The institution tracks trends but will take no risk to boost yields by a mere twenty-five basis points. Its first choices, as a matter of policy, are AAA ratings, "because there's nothing better." Pictet will also consider AA, but simple A will be purchased only "reluctantly, and only if we think the issuer's rating is likely to improve," Bongard explains. The bank no longer purchases provincial bonds, only Canadas.

Pictet maintains a profile in several key markets: the United States, Germany, Switzerland, the United Kingdom, Japan, the Netherlands, and France. If circumstances are propitious, it will make what it calls "forays" into peripheral markets like Canada, Australia, Spain, Italy, and Denmark. But it won't go near Sweden or Belgium, two countries with high debt loads. Why would you invest in Italy, then? I ask. True, Treyvaud responds, Italy is almost as deeply in debt as Belgium, but the bank made an extremely profitable foray onto the Italian market when spreads with the Bunds became excessive. In Belgium, spreads are far less attractive.

And finally, the inevitable question: what do you think of the situation in Canada? "Investors are extremely sensitive to the deficit. Canada must do something. If not, it runs an enormous risk of an investment hemorrhage," says Bongard. The bankers at Pictet warn against the "portfolio effect," the term they use to describe large flows of capital moving rapidly in and out of a given country. "Portfolio effects can be brutal and massive, and no one can predict either their extent or their timing," adds Treyvaud. But they are a major factor on the Canadian bond market, as they are on "every market where foreigners have a significant presence. We observed the phenomenon at work in Sweden, where the effects were devastating." It doesn't take much. For example, volunteers Bongard, the Japanese repatriated a good portion of their capital from the United States during the tense trade negotiations between the two countries. A statement from a high-profile financier like George Soros could be enough to touch off the process. My hosts say not a word about Quebec, but in a recent study, Pictet's analysts noted that "the fact that the PQ received less than 50 percent of the popular vote indicates that this party has not obtained the mandate to declare independence" and went on to predict that the "No" would likely prevail in the referendum. A good thing, for "the very thought of a division of the federal debt is cause for alarm." They concluded with a recommendation on Canadian bonds: "The only prudent course is to select short maturities."[9]

At a newsstand just down the street from Pictet headquarters, I pick up a copy of *Bilan*. The current issue of the Swiss economic magazine features an interview with James Tobin, the American winner of the Nobel Prize for Economics in 1981 for his analysis of the relationship between capital markets and employment, production, and price movements. A remark on financiers gave me food for thought: "Seated around the clock in front of computer screens, they can simply press a button to unleash huge transactions around the world," he is quoted as saying. "The result of speculation is that we end up investing in the wrong industries, and in the wrong countries. Keynes once compared these distortions to a beauty contest where the judges use newspaper photographs to pick the winner." For all that, the American economist was not predicting a "financial meltdown."[10] *AGEFI*, the Geneva financial daily, takes quite the opposite tack: "The Emmental cartel should be melted down into fondue," it insists.[11]

ZURICH, OCTOBER 21, 1994

Back in 1967, Expo year, some kids collected postage stamps. I collected foreign coins. The Canadian dollar was worth four Swiss francs back then; today, I can't even get one franc for a dollar. Zurich is a wonderful city, its old neighbourhoods are enchanting, but it's a chillingly expensive place: $6.00 (CA) for a bottom-of-the-line Big Mac, no fries; between $400 and $700 for a sport jacket; $27 for Sinead O'Connor's latest chart-topping CD; $7 for a fifteen-minute streetcar journey, and don't even think about a taxi. The Swiss are rich, and I'm poor. As I stroll along the shore of Lake Zurich, swans paddle over begging for a crust of bread; is that a loon I see toward the back of the flock?

Dusty-rose carpets, potted plants, and the playful beeping of electronic devices give a festive atmosphere to the huge trading room of the UBS

(Union Bank of Switzerland). So, this is the lair of the "gnomes of Zurich," as British Labour prime minister Harold Wilson branded the speculators who unleashed the attack on the pound sterling in the mid 1960s. Armin Bischofberger leads me over to his trading desk. On the way, I'm surprised to see a close-up of a basketball player finishing off a slam-dunk on one of the room's outsize computer screens. A fraction of a second later, the CNN-International logo flashes onto the screen; the gnomes have joined the global village.

Bischofberger is a market maker for bonds denominated in Swiss francs, a cartel-dominated business that was able to stave off attempts to establish a Euromarket in Swiss francs. If there is anything the Swiss don't like, it is the lack of regulation on the Euromarkets. But at the same time, the local bond market boasts an extensive foreign sector, where Bischofberger quotes bid and asked prices for a wide range of names, including Canadian ones.

"Liquidity is a big problem in the Swiss market," he explains. "As long as we are in the primary phase, after launching the bonds, there is quite good liquidity. But after a while, people tend to hold these bonds and not trade them actively." Does this apply to Canadian names? Bischofberger isn't listening. I repeat the question. He's still not listening. As I look over my shoulder, I notice that his eyes, like those of everyone else in the place, are fixed on a gorgeous woman who's just stepped into the trading room. Finally I get my answer: "Unfortunately, with Canadian names in particular, people got burned. I remember when I began trading in 1988, the province of Manitoba was regarded as an AAA name. Best-quality name. But with all the downgrading over the last two years, it is now extremely difficult to trade Canadian names. People want to reduce their large Canadian holdings, but there are no buyers." Still, they aren't ready to sell their paper at a loss. Just then the man at the next workstation barks out something in German; I can hardly hear Bischofberger's reply.

Bischofberger brandishes a sheet listing the Canadian provinces from his black book. The list is a long one. He's not interested in further buying because reselling will be tough, so he quotes prohibitive purchase prices. "Canadians used to come to market here a lot. If I were to show you the portfolios of some of our clients, you would see between 10 percent and 15 percent Canadian names." For the time being, the situation looks like a standoff: institutional investors are not selling, but they are not buying either.

Fredy Flury is a recycling specialist. He gives me a twenty-minute crash course in the inner workings of the high-flying financial gymnastics known as asset swaps. Flury buys cast-off securities at a low price, changes their characteristics to make them more attractive, and sells them at a profit. The technique consists of breaking up bonds into tiny parcels, scrambling them vigorously, and pasting them together in a new shape.

A little farther on Nef Jürg manages a portion of the bank's proprietary trading portfolio. "We have been net sellers of Canadas and U.S. Treasuries for the last nine months," says Jürg, who has a highly negative view of the North American market, primarily because he expects the Fed to rein in credit further. UBS portfolio management is decentralized, and the New York, London, and Tokyo trading rooms can make decisions that contradict his own. "I don't have to follow the bank view every day. I may have a six-hour view that is completely different." It's a tough trade. Like every other bank and brokerage house in the world, UBS lost heavily on the dismal bond market of 1994.

••••••••••••••••••••••••

Two toddlers stick their hands through the fence to feed the lambs, but the animals don't bat an eye: they just keep on nibbling the grass, bells tinkling. Just like Swiss bankers, I thought. The pastoral scene is only a few steps away from the main entrance to the Schweizerische Kreditanstalt (SKA), better known as Credit Suisse, the landlocked country's most powerful banking institution. Its main offices in the Zurich suburbs, ringed by a woodland path, remind me of a university campus. Some of the bank's buildings appear to have been carved out of the rock; panoramic windows look out over the valley below. It's hard to believe that more than three thousand people work here. In the cafeteria, the subject of discussion is an article in this morning's *Neue Zürcher Zeitung*, Switzerland's leading daily. "*Kanadas Haushalt bedarf dringender Sanierung*" proclaims the headline. "Canada's budget needs an urgent overhaul," translates Peter Luetscher, who handles Swiss issues for foreign borrowers. The previous day, Canada's *Finanzminister* Paul Martin had promised spending cuts and a deficit reduction.

"This information is not news to me," says Dr. Theresia Tolxdorff, a senior economist. "For a long time, I am not optimistic about reducing the budget deficit." Canadians may think they can reduce the deficit strictly through economic growth, but there is likely to be a slowdown starting next year, and a recession before the end of century, she says, reeling off enough statistics from memory to convince me that she knows all the intricacies of the subject. "Canada has a huge problem. The price of reducing the deficit will be low growth rate, maybe even a recession. You have to act now. It is important to have a plan the market believes can be successful."

"Well, it remains to be seen whether Mr. Martin's proposals will be a part of next year's budget," adds Mr. Luetscher. "People aren't ready to believe what the politicians tell them. What is positive, however, is that certain provinces have succeeded in cutting their budget deficits dramatically, particularly British Columbia and Alberta."

Andreas Aemisegger, a bond credit analyst, displays a graph showing how interest rate spreads widened when Government of Canada bonds denominated in foreign currencies were downgraded in 1992. "Investors choose the countries with the best situations; it would appear that Canada does not, at this moment, have the best of situations." In the 1980s, explains Luetscher, the provinces were treated as though they had AAA names. "Manitoba, for example, had performed thirty-five transactions in Swiss francs, the last early in 1993." Ever since, Swiss investors have been turning up their noses, refusing to lend to Canadians at the same rates they can get on other markets. "People ask me to quote prices for Hydro-Québec, for the province of Quebec, for Ontario, Ontario Hydro, the Export Development Corporation, and so on. But it is extremely difficult to make them a competitive offer for an issue, even though many of them would like to get back on our market." This is because "the market has become more selective. This year, it's been nothing but AAA." The bear market might explain part of the swing to quality, but Herr Luetscher does not rule out a deeper, structural shift.

Canada's constitutional debate is another factor. If the country were to break up in acrimony, the Swiss would not buy Canadian securities during the transition. "But after twelve months, maximum, the situation would level off. The two countries would work things out. After two years, there would be no impact at all," says Tolxdorff. Bond rating agency assessments of the Quebec debt would be crucial for potential investors, suggests

Luetscher. Says a Credit Suisse report, "the province is unlikely to opt for independence. But if it does, there will be ructions in the financial markets. The Canadian dollar would come under intense pressure, forcing the Bank of Canada to push up interest rates, and capital market yields would probably go through the roof. Even higher borrowing costs would seriously erode economic momentum, and a reduction of the public sector deficit would become a distant prospect."[12] In another publication, however, Credit Suisse concedes that "it is not difficult to recognize that separation involves many short-term difficulties, as much from the reaction of businessmen and investors as from the difficulty of splitting assets and liabilities, including even the territory of Quebec. Commentators may, however, be overly pessimistic about the long-term viability of Quebec (i.e., after a few years), an entity larger and more populous than Switzerland."[13]

As we part, Luetscher attempts to fine-tune the Credit Suisse position: "Let's be quite clear about that. Nobody here believes that Canada is a basket case. Canada is still an immensely rich country. But what we are saying is that, the consequence of inaction would be dramatic, especially at a societal level, for the Canadian people." As I leave Zurich I recall Voltaire's advice: "If a Swiss banker leaps from a window, follow him; there is surely some profit to be gained." Today, our Swiss banker is seriously considering pulling out of Canada.

FRANKFURT, OCTOBER 25, 1994

Frankfurt, with its pell-mell mixture of the beautiful and the ugly, claims to be Germany's most Americanized city. Junkies huddle on downtown sidewalks littered with discarded syringes, while in a small park across the street from the opera house, two reclining figures by Henry Moore bathe in a fountain. Further on, a bronze plaque pays tribute to George C. Marshall, the U.S. secretary of state who gave his name to the plan that financed the reconstruction of war-torn Europe, vanquished Germany included. The result is hard to miss: in front of me, on the Mainzer Landstrasse, the two trapezoidal, mirror-clad towers of the Deutsche Bank, Europe's most powerful, soar skyward.

When my appointment with Dr. Tran, the bank's director of research, was confirmed I fully expected a tall blond; instead, I encountered a short, slender Vietnamese with all the Teutonic virtues of clarity and hard-nosed precision. Dr. Hung Q. Tran left his country in 1968 for the United States, took his Ph.D. in economics at New York University, gravitated to Wall Street, where he worked for Salomon Brothers, then moved on to Merrill Lynch. In 1987 Tran joined the Deutsche Bank in Frankfurt, where today he administers a department of two hundred employees.

Ask Dr. Tran a question and his answer inevitably begins with "two things," even though he may add on a third or a fourth as he goes. I begin by asking what determines capital allocation among countries. "Two things," he replies, right on cue. "Currency movements and interest rate movements. At the end of the day, it's the total rate of return in the local currency of the investor that is the driving force. Investors in Japan or in the United States or Europe will look at Canada and ask themselves: are the interest rates generous compared with rates that can be obtained at home? Will interest rates in the future move in the upward or downward direction? If they move in the upward direction, then it means a decline in the price of the instrument and capital losses. Vice versa. Will the Canadian dollar appreciate or depreciate against the yen, DM, pound sterling, or U.S. dollar?" What will an investment in Canada be worth when it is converted into the local currency of the investor? These are the kinds of questions being asked in the investment community as the move toward international investment diversification intensifies, he explains. The major pension funds, mutual funds, and other institutions believe it is to their advantage to have a presence in countries whose economic cycles are not all moving at the same pace as their own. Canadian borrowers have benefited from this bedrock trend, Tran adds. But Canada can offer all the high interest rates it wants; this is one basket in which no foreign investor is willing to put all his eggs.

Canada accounts for only a fraction of the world securities market, and risk diversification is crucial. "Investors who don't have their mind made up about Canada one way or another tend to purchase roughly its share in the indices, meaning around 3 or 4 percent. If they are bullish about the country, they may go as high as 5 or 6 percent; but if they're bearish, they will reduce it, of course, down to zero." On the other hand, such investors will never withdraw from the pivotal markets such as

Germany, the United States, or Japan. Too risky. All the major European institutions manage their portfolios against such benchmarks. Still, individuals or small funds who don't have the resources to manage a truly international portfolio can be more selective in their decision-making. Practically speaking, says Tran, management by the indices can be boiled down to management by currency block — dollars, Deutschmarks, or yen — where shifts in the American dollar and in interest rates are the key factors. Canada is in the game as long as its yields are marginally higher than American ones.

"There are two reasons" why Canadian real rates are as high as they are, Tran continues. "One is what we see as real interest rates may not be real interest rates. The real interest rate is a theoretical concept, not something we can observe in real life. For a ten-year bond yielding 9 percent, it is not the 1 percent inflation at the moment that we should use to subtract from 9 percent to get 8 percent and call it real yield. It is the expected inflation over the course of the next ten years that will give you the expected real yield. The real yield will only be known at the end of that period. Market participants do not expect the 1 to 2 percent inflation rate we have today to be obtained every year over the next ten years. Second, you have to look at Canada in the context of what happens everywhere else. All around the globe, we observe this simple real yield to be historically high in Europe, in Japan, in the United States. It might simply reflect the fact that, overall around the globe, there is very strong demand for credit, for reconstruction in Central Europe, for building up infrastructures in Asia, for investment spending in OECD countries that are undergoing economic recovery. High real interest rates are necessary to stimulate high real savings and satisfy the stronger demand for credit."

Moreover, nominal interest rates have a built-in risk premium, he adds. "The risk premium for government bonds is not so much the credit risk of default, which is minimal for Canada, but the risk that the current policies are not sufficient to reduce the debt and the deficit problem in a credible time frame." For Tran, Finance minister Paul Martin's objective of hauling the deficit down to 3 percent of GDP is "not radical enough." To stabilize Canada's debt at 100 percent of GDP, a primary surplus (before payment of interest) of 2.6 percent is needed, and "they are nowhere near that in the planning horizon of Mr. Paul Martin." But the trend has to be reversed. "It may take five or ten years to reduce debt levels to 60 percent. But that is not the question. The question is: is there a clear and credible program with the active support of the provinces? So far we don't have that in place." Failing such a program, investors are concerned that the government might be tempted to finance its debt by printing more money, thus fuelling inflation and undermining the value of their bonds.

Dr. Tran is not the only one who's caught a whiff of inflation. Today's editorial in the prestigious *Financial Times*, the newspaper of record for the European business community, expresses the same doubts about Mr. Martin's determination to reduce government spending, and echoes market fears about possible monetization of Canada's debt, which it labels "a form of internal default through inflation."[14]

Political risk, for Dr. Tran, boils down to knowing whether the government will adopt the right policies. The question of Quebec independence, however, is a little more complicated. "It's very difficult to assess; international investors do not have historical benchmarks to help in the analysis. The fears are twofold: one is that no one knows how long the issue will simmer without a clear resolution. If it goes on in the way it has in the past two decades, then it might interfere with the federal government's efforts to reduce the deficit, which involve a lot of belt-tightening by the provinces. The second issue is, if Quebec finally decides to opt for separation — and here nobody knows if they will — then it will affect the strength of the economy of the remainder of Canada, which will back the value of Canadian government bonds. Canada with Quebec and Canada without Quebec are two different countries. There is therefore uncertainty, and markets tend to price uncertainty into risk premium. Here, the key question is really not of right or wrong. I don't think international investors are in the business of making moral judgments; they are in the business of trying to come up with the best guess in terms of what will produce the highest return for their funds or for their clients. And one of the things they feel unable to cope with is uncertainty."

Canada could hit the debt wall, some observers say. And if that happens, foreign investors would simply stop buying Canadian paper. But "hitting the wall" is a simpleminded way of looking at the investment process, argues Dr. Tran. "Sure, there will always be people willing to lend, to buy the debt of federal or provincial governments. The question is, what kind of investors, and at what price? Canada, in the universe of government debt, is still a high investment grade." Nevertheless, Tran isn't convinced that the foreigners who have already built up substantial quantities of Canadian paper will be adding to their stocks at the same pace as they did in the past. The saturation point might not be far off.

And what about a sovereign Quebec? "It is one of those difficult questions. Because we don't know what would be its share of assets and liabilities of the federal government. If you look at the spread of interest rates between Quebec debt and federal debt, that can give some indication of how the risk premium of an independent Quebec is already put into the price."

DÜSSELDORF, OCTOBER 26, 1994

From the outside, the pure functional elegance of the WestLB bank building is a perfect fit for Düsseldorf, Germany's second-ranking financial centre. But the bank's labyrinth of seemingly endless corridors remind me of a children's tale set in the Black Forest. Luckily, like a forest spirit, a secretary escorts me to Dr. Peter Kuhlmann's office. Cautionary reminders that governments have repudiated their debts before — ancient bonds in sterling issued by the Imperial Chinese Government, the Russian Railways, and the City of Moscow — decorate the walls. I had been scheduled to meet the man in charge of bond issues, but he has departed unexpectedly for South Africa. Still, Kuhlmann, who will be sitting in for him, has ten years' experience in the field. At his side is Dr. Hans-Peter Rathjens, who heads the bank's bond research group.

WestLB is Germany's number three; it is also the state bank of the country's wealthiest Land (the German equivalent of Canada's provinces), North Rhine-Westphalia. Germany boasts three distinct kinds of banking institutions: the private banks, such as the Deutsche Bank; cooperatives, like the Raifheisenbanken or the Volksbanken; and credit unions, called Sparkassen, which belong to the municipalities. In each Land, the Sparkassen delegate certain functions to a central banking agency such as WestLB, which numbers the Sparkassen and the Land among its shareholders.

Canadian borrowers are generally very well received in Germany,

Dr. Kuhlmann assures me. Canada has what Germany does not: space, nature, and natural resources. And on an emotional level, Germans feel closer to Canada than to the United States. WestLB has already organized several issues for Quebec, Nova Scotia, British Columbia, and Manitoba. In the early 1980s, when they offered high rates and the dollar was appreciating in relation to the Deutschmark, Canadian dollar bonds were extremely popular with German investors.

Investors in Germany, says Rathjens, might purchase securities directly from the Sparkassen, sometimes after reading an article in the Sunday paper. But more often they will pick from a list of bonds on hand bearing the bank's recommendation (the country has no stockbrokers). Retail clients are not very conscious of the risks associated with higher yields, he says, and "People make a broad judgment on the dollar." Adds Kuhlmann: "I believe that people treat currency like shares, they go up and down. You make losses, you make gains. The movement of currency is very important, but it does not mean that someone who has lost on it is never buying again. On the contrary, now is maybe the time to buy again. The dollar can only go up." WestCapital, the bank's portfolio management subsidiary, certainly hopes that's true. In February 1994, it bet its entire dollar block on the beleaguered loonie. Its foreign exchange losses have been substantial.

German investors do not pay as much attention to credit ratings as their Swiss counterparts. The country's banks possess their own, internal rating systems for establishing credit limits. WestLB has lowered Canada's rating, and will not hesitate to lower it further if public debt increases, says Kuhlmann.

Competition between bankers for issuers' mandates is stiff. "A Canadian name or province will always find an issuing house, especially the ones that have traditionally regarded themselves as their issuing house. They will try very hard, and maybe sacrifice some profits in order to keep the client. But there are limits. We consider ourselves as Quebec's house bank [in Germany, along with Commerzbank], and would be very cross if it came to the market with Deutsche Bank, for instance."

The German market remains receptive, Dr. Kuhlmann says. "Canadian provinces, even the province of Quebec, are still of a good quality; the ratings are still acceptable. It's still Canada. They may have to pay a little more than they did before in terms of spreads." What would happen if Quebec were to become independent? "It would be very difficult for them to raise funds in the international markets during that transition period. After it, they might be able to do it again, but at a totally different cost."

LUXEMBOURG, OCTOBER 27, 1994

The "Coupon Express" glides to a stop at the Luxembourg station; the passengers detrain and rush off down the platform. A Banque Internationale au Luxembourg billboard trumpets the miniature country's natural resources: term deposits, discounted coupons, investment counselling, *sicavs*, financial management, holding companies. I've just arrived in the tax haven of the European Union, the place where Europeans come to collect interest on their bonds. In fact, Luxembourg is an investors' paradise for outsiders only; the taxes paid by the Grand Duchy's 380,000 subjects are just as high as in neighbouring countries.

Luxembourg's capital market — the world's seventh-largest — took off in 1961 when the Belgian government slapped a withholding tax on revenues generated by foreign securities. Belgian dentists were the first to cross the border to redeem their bond coupons. The trip was short, the bank was the same, and the currency was almost identical (the Luxembourg franc is set at par with the Belgian franc). Germany followed Belgium's lead, and German citizens rapidly developed a taste for travel. The legendary Belgian dentist, the stereotype of the tax-dodging European professional who came to symbolize the typical Eurobond retail market client, had touched off a chain reaction. Today more than two hundred banks, from Europe and beyond, have opened their doors in Luxembourg.

Kredietbank is Belgium's third-ranking bank. Its lobby is straight out of any major Canadian bank branch, except for the leather-upholstered armchairs and the inscriptions in four languages: English, French, Flemish, and German. But the real action is upstairs. On the street side of the building, first-time clients with less than 20 million BF ($875,000 [CA]) to invest meet a financial adviser in one of twenty alcoves. Wealthier investors will be steered into a private salon on the other side of the building, where the carpets are thicker and the walls are upholstered with velvet fabric. Director Michel Hubert has been a private banker for thirty years, providing wealthy clients with financial advice, portfolio management, mutual funds, term deposits, and precious metals, all in the currency of the client's choice. A client need not come to Luxembourg to get those services, but Monsieur Hubert can also offer bank secrecy, which, he claims, enjoys greater protection here than in Switzerland. Numbered accounts do not exist; all accounts are confidential. But clients must reveal their full identity, identify their ultimate economic beneficiary, and specify the origin of funds deposited. Money-laundering is illegal, but secrecy can be lifted by a judge only if the alleged infraction constitutes a criminal offence. Tax evasion is not considered a criminal offence in the Grand Duchy. Foreigners are totally ignored and pay no taxes or at-source deductions.

Luxembourg cannot boast the long tradition that has given Swiss banks their enviable reputation, in spite of the fact that Swiss institutions collect a 35 percent withholding tax which is handed over to the government. Most of Luxembourg's clients are drawn from neighbouring countries. Unlike Geneva, Kredietbank demands no minimum for portfolio management services. "Switzerland draws the 1,000 richest people; here in Luxembourg, we want to attract the next 100,000," says Hubert. "Switzerland is for billionaires; we are for millionaires," adds Vim Van Mulder, director of institutional operations. Belgian franc millionaires, that is. A typical client invests between 1 and 3 million BF ($44,000 and $130,000 [CA]). Some people walk in with a suitcase full of bills; others simply deposit a cheque. The people who open an account in Luxembourg want to protect themselves from taxes and protect their capital, explains Van Mulder. Speculation and complex financial instruments don't interest them. "The product such clients are looking for is discretion and good advice," adds Hubert. "Belgians are money conscious." They follow the newspapers and financial newsletters, and are often attracted by fashionable ideas. But deep down, Belgians are prudent people deeply attached to bonds.

Today, the list of newly issued Eurobonds features securities denominated in American dollars, Deutschmarks, ECUs, Dutch guilders, French and Luxembourg francs, and pounds sterling. The sole Canadian dollar paper is issued by the Kredietbank itself. On the secondary market list I spot several Canadian names: Ville de Montréal, Vancouver City Saving, Caisse Centrale Desjardins, Ford Credit Canada, Quebec Province, the City of Toronto, and the Société Québécoise d'assainissement des eaux, virtually all of them custom-tailored for the retail clientele. For reasons of confidentiality, all are bearer securities, contrary to Canadian practice, where securities are registered in the name of the buyer.

Clients tend to rely on familiar names when they buy a security, paying less attention to credit ratings and more to coupon interest, which should be substantial. As a rule they purchase securities at issue and hold onto them until maturity: the Belgian dentist is not interested in buying when markets are low and selling when markets are high. Investors of this kind are said to have the kind of "strong hands" that issuers look for. Belgians, more accustomed than most Europeans to investing abroad, are drawn to high-yield currencies, a role that the Canadian dollar played for many years. Currently, our dentist is looking to bonds denominated in Luxembourg francs, with a coupon above 8 percent; he will probably reinvest them in the same currency at maturity.

"Canada is the kind of investment destination our clients are looking for. Investors here have never had a problem with Canadian issuers," Hubert says. Renewing an investment in the same currency is simpler. Our dentist is not really concerned about Canadian indebtedness; the solid image of the country's natural resources provides him with all the security he needs. How do you evaluate Quebec-related political risks? I ask. "People really aren't all that aware of the situation, but they become more sensitive to it at election time. It isn't the first time they've heard about it, and nothing has happened," Hubert replies. Belgians may also be immunized by all the deficit talk and constitutional squabbling they are surrounded with at home.

An intensive week of interviews later, a few basic ideas have begun to take shape: Europeans are concerned about the value of the Canadian dollar, about high debt levels, and about political uncertainty. But before jumping to conclusions, let's complete our whirlwind tour with a stopover in the City, financial capital of Europe.

Chapter 4

THE
CITY

LONDON, WEEK OF OCTOBER 31, 1994

A LONG, BLACK Bentley whispers by me as I stroll down the narrow street. On the front fender a fluttering white flag, emblazoned with a St. George's Cross and sword, identifies its illustrious occupant. Inside, I catch a glimpse of the Lord Mayor of London, elected representative of the five thousand permanent residents and fifteen thousand businessmen and women who live and work in the City of London, the man who symbolizes its commercial liberty. The curious government he heads derives its power from the eighty-four Guilds that have ruled the City since 1319. Under his authority, the Corporation of the City of London administers a compact area known as the Square Mile, which corresponds approximately to the ancient Roman settlement on the banks of the Thames. It might be small, but its influence reaches to every nook and cranny of the international capital market.

Lacking New York's or Tokyo's vast domestic markets, London has turned to the world at large, and the world has come running. London's markets — though they are generally well policed and honest — tend to be freer and less restrictive than its rivals'. Its financial techniques might not match those of New York in sophistication, and the City's institutions might not equal the Japanese behemoths for sheer size, but London uses its tradition of openness to compensate for its handicaps. The City is the heart of the international securities trade; the world's financial giants, whatever their nationality, run their own trading houses, many of which chalk up higher business volumes than their English counterparts.

Competition is the name of the game, and inevitably there are both fantastic wins and devastating losses.

The modern building that houses Hambros overlooks the Tower of London, its square profile in keeping with the squat bulk of the historic structure. Like most of Britain's merchant banks, Hambros was founded by an immigrant from the continent, a Dane named Carl Joachim Hambro, who set up shop in London in 1839. Hambro and the other merchant bankers not only financed international trade but lent money to the rulers of the day. Hambros underwrote Denmark's war against Prussia and provided capital to Greece and Italy. Today, its activities have become perhaps more prosaic. Hambros has withdrawn from the stock exchange, but the bank's remaining operations correspond to those of a Canadian investment dealer.

It's 7:45 — time for the morning meeting of the bond group. The room is packed. A number of people are standing around a table while others are crowding in the doorway as the review of last night's market activity begins. I jot down some notes: "U.S. dollar weak, Fed intervenes. Eurocan extremely quiet. Australian domestic market slow; active in Europe." Each participant is handed two sheets of paper. The first lists, in table form, the day's anticipated economic news and its estimated release time. On the second I read: "The purpose of this page is to emphasize the positions that can make us — or lose us — a lot of money." Under the Canadian dollars heading, the objective is to buy Canadas at $7\frac{1}{4}$ percent, maturity 2008. The firm has sold them short to assist a client. In the pounds sterling section, it suggests inexpensive Ontario 2000, at only 48 below the gilts (United Kingdom government bonds). Clients have reacted well to inquiries about a possible ten-year Australian dollar issue by Quebec or Hydro-Québec, says a trader. "We'll wait to see when they might want to make a deal." Transactions of this kind usually have only a one in four chance of actually taking place. The brief meeting ends, and the troops disperse to their battle stations in front of computer screens, telephones at the ready.

Hambros's thirty-four-year-old director and Head of Origination is a Canadian. The telltale clue is a tattered copy of the *Globe and Mail* lying on a corner of Mark Warren's desk, overlooking the trading room, where a good hundred employees are hard at work. The next floor up houses a trading room specializing in money and foreign exchange markets. After graduating from the University of Toronto and the London School of Economics, Warren joined Hambros in 1986. Since then his career has spanned seven years in London, two years in Tokyo, and one in his home town of Toronto. Warren's firm might not be as large as the leading European banks or the biggest American investment houses, but it has carved out a reputation as a powerhouse in narrow segments of the Euromarket — Canadian and Australian dollars, pounds sterling, and ECUs.

Right this minute, no one is buying Canada on the institutional scene, Warren tells me. Since the start of the week, Hambros has sold only $1.3 million. It's dead. Canada can find retail takers, he adds, but the bank deals only with institutions. Australia is more popular, offering 11 percent for ten years, against 9.75 percent for Canadian paper. But even the "down under" market is anemic because "the level of confidence on the dollar bloc is so low." Warren calls Australia five or six times daily; Canada only once.

I take a turn around the room. Mat Davis is in charge of that part of the secondary market in Canadian dollar bonds nicknamed "Eurocan," where three market makers handle the work according to name and maturity, trading with counterparts in London and Europe. One calls for the price of "Quebec $10\frac{1}{2}$ percent, 1998," indicating the bond's coupon rate and maturation date. The request comes from a bank that wants the securities for a private client. Davis offers $104.28 (CA) and nails down a tiny deal worth $50,000.

In another section of the trading room, reserved for institutional sales, Jeremy Cox handles Switzerland, which generates fully one-quarter of the bank's sales. "I sell to banks who sell to clients," he says. The Swiss demand at least AA quality, and prefer European names. "I think I could sell Quebec, even if they were only rated A, but it would be a tough sell." Right now, Hambros is suggesting selling Quebecs in Canadian dollars and buying them in Australian dollars. The credit risk is identical, but investors would gain from a higher yield. This arbitrage is the rationale for the Quebec-Aussie dollar bond that was discussed at the morning's meeting. Marc Jaskowiak and his sidekick Phil Cassen cover the Benelux countries, where "all the provinces sell well, even Newfoundland! People

are looking for yield," says Jaskowiak. On the down side, the collapse of
Confederation Life hurt Canada's image among fund managers, adds
Cassen. Anke Grève handles the bank's German accounts. People are
abandoning the Canadian dollar for the Spanish peseta, the Italian lira,
and the South African Rand. "Germans have been patient with the
Canadian names, but their hopes have never been fulfilled," he says. Still,
it remains relatively easy to sell Vancouver, British Columbia, or Alberta.
Placing Ontario and Quebec is harder.

Suddenly Warren's voice echoes over the loudspeakers. Hambros has
been invited to participate in the sale of a 100 million ECU borrowing
issued by a German bank. While the trading room is still buzzing, I chat
with Denise Petrozzi, an expectant mother who is also the in-house Italy
and Monaco specialist. "Italians are the highest per capita savers in
Europe, which helps finance their enormous public debt," she says. The
Italian bond market is not a terribly sophisticated one. People buy retail
through their banks, and names are more important than credit ratings.
Only recently have they begun investing in foreign currencies. "Huge
quantities of Canadian dollars went to Italy last year," as savers were
attracted by the long-term yields offered by Ontario and Quebec.
"Unfortunately, they got the shock of their life," when heavy losses hit in
1994. They didn't realize that long-term bonds were riskier than short-
term paper. Like all Hambros salespeople, Petrozzi deals with her clients
in their native language. "You've got to be Italian to sell to Italians," she
says. "Personal contacts are important." She interrupts our conversation
to nail down a small sale: $15,000 (CA) of Quebec, $9\frac{3}{8}$ percent, 2003, trans-
ferred to a bank in the Piedmont. She points to a headline in the Milan
financial journal *Il Sole–24 Ore* listing the bond as a good buy: "I just
don't know how they make their recommendations — some bonds are
terribly non-liquid."

North American accounts are Peter Ryan's job. A substantial portion
of the Eurobonds signed by Canadian issuers find their way back to
Canada via the secondary market. Canadian investors consider Eurocan
yields too low, and rarely buy them on issue, he explains. For some, the
preferred tactic is to monitor the secondary market for imperfections and
snatch up the bargains on the fly. Pension funds do subscribe on issue,
however, when a Canadian issuer's borrowing is denominated in a

currency other than the loonie, since these securities are not included in the maximum 20 percent of the portfolio that can legally be invested abroad. These foreign currency Canadian securities follow bond market fluctuations associated with that currency and give the Canadian portfolio added market risk diversification. A Canadian manager who purchases an Ontario Hydro bond denominated in Deutschmarks faces all the ups and downs of the German bond market and runs a foreign exchange risk. The credit risk, which is linked to Ontario Hydro's capacity to repay its borrowings, is identical to a Canadian-dollar-denominated Ontario Hydro bond. Few Canadian names issued on the Euromarket are traded in the United States, for regulatory reasons, but in tax havens like Barbados, the Bahamas, and Bermuda, fund managers buy them freely. One such manager, Ryan tells me, holds $750-million worth.

One floor up, research economist Khim Murphy is expecting me. I want to know why investors insist on lumping Canada and Australia together. Should I blame it on the Queen? Probably, she explains, because both countries are rich in natural resources, share similar growth outlooks, and run both current accounts and budget deficits. Compared with the United States, neither country has a very deep bond market; furthermore, the two markets have historically had a tendency to move in parallel. Until last September, that is, when they came to a parting of the ways: Canadian rates went down, while Australian rates went up. "Why should Canada have lower interest rates?" she asks with a certain irritation. After all, Australia's debt is proportionally only half as large as Canada's. "My worry is that the Bank of Canada won't raise interest rates to the same extent as the United States, hoping that the narrowing of the spreads with U.S. rates will lower the value of the Canadian dollar." Murphy is convinced that the central bank is behaving as it does because "you need a weak currency to help reduce the current accounts deficit and alleviate the debt service." But considering the rarity of available capital, Canadian rates will have to rise. "It will be increasingly difficult for marginal countries with big deficits to attract capital without a bigger premium."

At lunchtime, Warren invites me to join him and colleague James Kowalishin. If the two Canadians working for Hambros had nicknames, those names would be "Fear" and "Greed," the two forces that make the market run. Warren is as fretful as his face is long, and his look fits perfectly with his message: World markets are no longer prepared to finance Canada's debt. "Why are international investors who were buying lots of Canada not buying any more this year? America is the only source of capital that keeps the country afloat. I fear that U.S. money will also go elsewhere, like Latin America. We have a free ride right now. I wonder how long it will continue. The rest of the world is not responsible for running Canada's social programs. Ontario is up against the wall. When overnight money goes to 300 percent, as in Sweden [in 1992], this is hitting the wall."

Taxes are too high back in Toronto, the home town Warren says he's happy to have left. Before leaving the province he fired off a parting shot to Premier Bob Rae detailing his grievances. "Look, I'm as nationalist as they come, but I'm not so blind that I can't see our biggest problem. If I'm pessimistic, I've got my reasons. And it scares me to see that our politicians aren't pessimistic enough." But according to Warren, we would be wrong to blame capital markets. "We are like a thin person discovering chocolate, eating lots of it, and then suing the chocolate manufacturers for being fat as a beast."

At thirty, Kowalishin, born and raised in Saskatoon, handles the swaps market for Hambros, and he has already carved out a reputation as a wheeler-dealer in derivatives. He puts in fourteen to fifteen hours a day and boasts of not having taken a single day off in the last ten months. At home he spends his evening on the phone with the New York traders, running up a monthly telephone bill of £800 ($1,700 [CA]). "If I don't, I will be pushed off," he admits, adding: "I hope to retire at thirty-five, with enough money. A friend of mine quit at forty." Now, with a glass of claret under our belts, the atmosphere has mellowed. Retire at thirty-five? And then what? I ask. "Buy a bookstore in the Caribbean," he says with a broad smile. "I'm a Saskatoon kid who wanted to make it big in the world — and here I am."

....

A 1993 survey by *Euromoney*, the publication of record in the international financial community, named the Deutsche Bank "Top Eurobond Trader."[1] But to win the honour, the German bank had to turn its back on its home town of Frankfurt and set up shop in the City, nerve centre of the international capital market. True, the Deutsche Bank's German client base gives it an immense placing capacity, but its really important business is done in London, a move confirmed by the recent merger with Morgan Grenfell, a prestigious British merchant bank acquired in 1990.

Roger Bates, an Englishman in charge of underwriting for Deutsche Bank, leads all new issues. When I join him in a large meeting room, he's accompanied by Stuart Young, a Toronto-based vice president in charge of liaison with Canadian issuers, and a third person who barely opens his mouth during our three-hour meeting. Into my hands Bates thrusts a blue binder stuffed with statistical printouts compiled the night before. Outstanding debt on the Eurobond market has reached the sum of $1,700 billion (US), three times the size of the Canadian bond market; 5 percent of this paper carries Canadian names. U.S. dollar borrowings stand astride the Eurobond market like a colossus, explains Bates, accounting for nearly 40 percent of the total, followed by three key currencies: the Deutschmark, the pound sterling, and the yen. The Canadian dollar is part of a group of secondary currencies, with each one accounting for from 5 to 8 percent of total borrowing, a kind of flavour-of-the-month arrangement.

Forty-six percent of Canadian financing has been in Canadian dollars, Bates adds as he ticks off the list of the top Canadian dollar borrowers since the beginning of the decade. Ontario Hydro tops the charts, with forty-eight issues totalling $10.6 billion, a full 10 percent of Eurocan volume,[2] followed by the Government of Ontario, Hydro-Québec, General Electric, British Columbia, the European Investment Bank, Quebec, Crédit local de France, KFW (the German government's export bank), and the Deutsche Bank itself. Further down the list I spot familiar names like the Canada Mortgage and Housing Corporation, the Caisse Centrale Desjardins, New Brunswick, the City of Toronto, the City of Montreal and the Montreal Urban Community, the Federal Business Development Bank, and Saskatchewan. Of course, European Canadian dollar borrowers have moved rapidly to swap their newly acquired loonies for other currencies.

Canadians, it turns out, are major-league players in U.S. Eurodollars, which alone account for 35 percent of their Euro borrowings. Since 1990, the Government of Ontario and Ontario Hydro have launched seventy-eight issues for a total of $33.3 billion, with Hydro-Québec and the Quebec government weighing in with thirty-five issues worth $13.7 billion.

Canadians also occasionally borrow in yen, in Deutschmarks, pounds sterling, French francs, ECUs, Australian dollars, Luxembourg francs, Dutch guilders, lira, Finnish marks, and New Zealand dollars.

Bates's list is not complete; a substantial number of recent Canadian borrowings are missing from the statistics. Following the sharp downturn in the bond market earlier in the year, institutional investors have become cautious and selective, turning to complex, shorter-term instruments called medium-term notes (MTN). Many such deals are private, and thus do not appear in the blue binder. Young picks up the phone and asks for an estimate, then jots down a figure. The private market for medium-term notes is worth a good $100 billion (US), he says.

"If you have a hot market, it goes just like that," Bates says with a snap of his fingers. "You can sell an issue in half an hour. In a difficult market like this one, it will take longer." The better-known names always get grabbed up first, he adds. "You try to distribute the bonds as quickly as possible." Among institutional investors, the world's central banks — which can easily subscribe up to 20 percent of the total — are the prime market for placing an issue. But the banks apply strict criteria, nothing lower than AA. Since they are investing their reserves, banks prefer paper with high liquidity, generally denominated in American dollars or Deutschmarks; other sovereign OECD member states are also highly rated, and quasi-sovereign issuers like British Columbia, Alberta, and crown corporations might also pass muster. The central banks of smaller countries might find higher-yield bonds more attractive when their own borrowing costs are high.

"By far the largest buyers are the regular banks themselves, for investment management purposes or for their own accounts," says Bates. "On the low side they will buy 30 percent, and on the high side about 60 percent." These are flexible buyers, who will purchase bonds for resale on the retail market in the weeks to come. If the borrower is a household name, from 60 to 70 percent can be placed directly in individual portfolios, with the banks acting as a buffer between the borrower and the end-investor. In a bull market the banks resell a portion of their paper to lock in profits. If the market is bearish, they are prepared to wait.

We adjourn for lunch to an Italian restaurant crammed with financiers. We can dally over the meal longer than usual today, explains Bates,

---

MEDIUM-TERM NOTES

The expression medium-term notes (MTN) is used, and often misused, to describe a wide variety of transactions. A medium-term note program usually indicates a credit facility (credit arrangement) negotiated between a borrower and one or more lenders, shaped to respond to their specific needs. The borrowing is drawn by tranches, with each possessing its own specific characteristics in terms of maturity, interest rate, or currency. Some highly complex securities are true derivatives and incorporate financial leverage. When several lenders are involved, programs are public; when only a few participate, they are private. Liquidity of these instruments on the secondary market is limited due to their non-standard characteristics and the relatively small size of the issue. As the name suggests, they are primarily medium-term borrowings, although thirty-year notes are not unheard of. Securities are distributed outside conventional placement syndicates. Once the legal documents are prepared, issuing fees are low and flexibility is greater than for normal issues, as tranches are issued in response to borrowing needs. Borrowing programs in the Euromarket are also termed Euro medium-term notes (EMTN).

---

because half of Europe is enjoying a civic holiday. What kind of risks will an investor be facing when he buys a security bearing a Canadian signature? I ask between the pasta and the veal. "There are three main risks: the first, which is an intermittent risk, is the heightened political tension; the second is the size of Canadian government borrowing requirements, what the debt servicing cost looks like relative to domestic revenue; and the third, overlapping these, is the perception that credit is deteriorating," Bates explains, and Stuart chimes in, adding to the list the state of the Canadian dollar and the direction in which interest rates are moving. "These days, many investors tend to look at the currency considerations before they look at anything else in the market," Bates continues. On the risk of Quebec independence he adds: "Some see it as an opportunity, others run away from it." Nowadays, most are running away. The bond market has been flat since the beginning of 1994; people are adopting defensive positions. "Now it is more difficult to do size in the current market for all issuers," and larger numbers of borrowers, particularly in the United States, are trying their luck on the Euro market. Still, Bates has "no sentiment the market is getting saturated with Canadian names."

••••••••••••••••••••••••

Just around the corner from the venerable Old Lady of Threadneedle Street, as the Bank of England is affectionately known, lurks the London office of BMO Nesbitt Burns. The three initials — pronounced "bimo" — are the stock market abbreviation and trading room nickname for the Bank of Montreal, which owns the firm. Managing director Michael Chapman is a market veteran who moved to the City five years ago to sell Europeans Canadian shares and bonds after a twenty-year career in charge of Wood Gundy's New York operations.

Chapman doubles as president of the Association of Canadian Investment Dealers, an august London institution which once wielded regulatory powers but today promotes Canada to European investors in close cooperation with the Canadian High Commission.[3] Canadian brokers are betting they can provide their clients with a propaganda-free, Canadian perspective on events. "It's easier for a Canadian or an American to explain why what Clinton or Mulroney did was stupid than it is for a European," he laughs. When newly elected federal and provincial politicians come to the City to meet the financiers, the Association looks after all the details.

Information flow is a two-way street. "We're not simply dealers, people who buy and sell securities; we're also here to make sure that clients' concerns get looked after, and that if there's a message to be passed on, that it gets where it's supposed to go," he says. Clients are concerned about Canada's currency, the political situation, and its credit rating, but in no particular order. In spite of everything, "the comfort level with Canada is pretty good at this time." In fact, Chapman believes that Europeans are far less concerned about the Quebec situation than people in Canada.

Are the markets likely to turn their backs on Canada because of the debt? I ask. "It's too easy to say: 'Oh! What happens if everybody turns off the tap on Canada?' I think it's very unlikely." In what he terms a "long career," Chapman cannot recall any significant "strike" by investors. When a major California investor dumped Quebec paper after the first election of the PQ, in 1976, the shock waves could be felt throughout the market. But American investors trooped back as soon as New York–based Equitable Life took on provincial paper in a private placement. When the government of Saskatchewan nationalized potash that same year, it had to cancel an issue on the American market, but succeeded the year after.

"The market has a very short memory and sometimes reacts for funny and stupid reasons," he says.

Government bonds issued in Canada, and Eurobonds in Canadian dollars — the kind of investments popular with those notorious Belgian dentists twenty-five years ago — are the bread and butter of the City's Canadian investment community. "Toward the end of the '80s the Canadian dollar market grew fairly dramatically. At that time, European and Asian investors wished to place their money in Canadian dollars, a currency they saw as attractive, and at the same time, European borrowers started to borrow in Canadian dollars and swap into the currency of their choice," Chapman says. Borrowers liked Eurocans because they could get better rates and at the same time diversify their sources of capital. The market ballooned in 1991 with the arrival of global issues from Ontario, and then Quebec. These borrowings, which exceeded one billion Canadian dollars, were placed simultaneously in Canada, Europe, the United States, and Japan.

ISSUING SYNDICATES

An issuing syndicate is a group of banks and dealers that has been set up to assume the financial risks of an issue and to place the securities with investors. A syndicate is usually made up of three sub-groups. One sub-group, known as the managing syndicate, consists of a lead, and one or more co-leads. In Europe, the lead keeps track of the sales book and is also known as a "book runner." This group coordinates, and participates in, each stage of the operation: it negotiates the conditions of the offer with the borrower, organizes the syndicate, and monitors the placement process. Another sub-group, the underwriting syndicate, purchases all bonds issued and assumes resale risks. The members of the managing syndicate are always leading members of the underwriting syndicate, and they assume the bulk of the risks. They are then joined by junior partners, who will distribute the issue to the investors, forming what is called the selling group. The structure is shaped like a pyramid, with the leads enjoying a healthier commission than the underwriters, who are better paid than the rank-and-file members of the selling group. Total commissions paid by the borrower are generally less than 2 percent of the total amount of the issue. Once the issue is complete, the names of all subscribers are listed in order of importance in an advertisement, known, in the specialized press, as a "tombstone."

The City's Canadian dealers are in constant competition with powerful New York firms, with the well-connected European banks, and with the heavily capitalized Japanese houses for lead or co-lead positions in Euro or global financing of Canadian public bodies. The outcome is often determined by the currency of the issue, the part of the world in which sales are concentrated, and particularly by the long-term relationship that exists between key issuers and their banks and dealers. But when a firm has received a mandate, it invites competitors with complementary strengths to share the risk and help place securities with investors. The organizations set up to perform this kind of operation are called issuing syndicates.

The big European banks play a key role in the majority of syndicates, purchasing bonds for themselves, to invest the funds they manage for third parties, and also for resale to their clients via their huge retail networks. "The trick is to get that issue on the buy list of the retail group of banks," says Chapman. "We would only invite people because they have the ability to place bonds. If I give Michael at the Deutsche Bank a million bonds, I don't want to have to buy those bonds back again through somebody else because he can't sell. I will put him there because I know he will use his network to put the bonds in strong hands."

The lead manager takes the lion's share of the issue and must "stabilize" it by keeping the market liquid and orderly once the operation gets underway, a job Chapman is familiar with: "Your job is to maintain the integrity of the issue, to be there to take the bonds back if Michael can't sell them. He won't come to me and tell me 'I can't sell them,' because it's an admission of defeat, but he might sell them through a broker who sells them back to me, and I might end up buying back 10 to 15 percent of the issue on day one. Then I'm sitting there and my job is to replace those bonds. If we are lead manager, we will make a market on the issue until it matures."

For some Canadian names, the Euromarket can provide substantial advantages. As a rule the federal government does not borrow abroad, except when it needs to replenish its foreign currency reserves, when it will issue bonds on the New York or European markets. (Foreigners buy Government of Canada bonds on the Canadian market.) But government agencies like the Export Development Corporation, the Federal Business

Development Bank, and the Canada Mortgage and Housing Corporation regularly turn to foreign markets. And, Chapman explains, they are usually quite well received in Europe. They are able to borrow at a rate close to what the federal government can command, below what they would pay in Canada. Rates lower than those available at home also attract municipal agencies, such as the British Columbia Municipal Financial Authority (BCMFA) and Metro Toronto, which recently borrowed at rates normally restricted to AAA-rated names, even though they fall under the authority of provinces rated AA. According to Chapman, it's because "the perception in Canada is that they cannot get a better rate than the host government, whereas the Europeans are very happy with the AAA. They have had a good experience with those credits in the past; those agencies can borrow at cheaper rates than Ontario or B.C. can. They cannot in Canada."

....

Across the Thames, just outside the storied precincts of the City, stands a Canadian firm that has maintained a high London profile since it was founded at the turn of the century. Wood Gundy, now a subsidiary of the CIBC, employs some one hundred dealers who earn their livelihood trading in Canadian paper, or in foreign paper denominated in Canadian dollars. Wood Gundy and ScotiaMcLeod are the leaders of the Eurocan market.

"Nearly all Euros are sold outside of North America, mostly in Europe, but there's no area of the world where they don't sell," explains Robert J. Edge, the firm's director and vice president. People everywhere are continuing to buy and sell Canadian bonds, he adds. Contrary to what some claim, not a single region has pulled out of Canada. The Japanese have definitely sold their Canadian dollar bonds, but they came right back to the market with Canadian borrowings denominated in yens. Investors act as they do for a nearly infinite variety of reasons. Some dealers make money on the smallest fluctuations of the market, Edge says, moving in and out with high speed and high volume, sometimes moving as much as a billion dollars in a single transaction. Some investors will move to take a profit at sixty basis points, or even fifteen.

There is no such thing as an average deal, Edge continues. Each Euro financing is tailored for a specific market. Characteristics are shaped to fit the issuer's profile, his credit rating, the size of the issue, the currency, the maturity, the yield, and the state of the market at the time of issue. Conditions, meanwhile, are in a constant state of flux. "The market here can turn on a dime. Over time, people have different appetites for different kinds of credit, for different uses, for different reasons," he says. "Today, the Canadian dollar market is fundamentally an attractive one, but not many people are buying. They've lost too much on the currency. In fact, Europeans aren't in a hurry to buy the dollar bloc. And if they don't think highly of the American dollar, it's no easy matter to sell them a favourable view of the Canadian dollar either."

Provincial governments and crown corporations often have little choice; they must borrow in European currencies, and more frequently in yen. But the retail market is still putting out the welcome mat for Canadian dollars, as demonstrated by a recent $150 million (CA) financing for Quebec's Société d'assainissement des eaux, targeted to the Benelux and Switzerland. The operation took place one week before the Quebec election and did "very well." This year, Edge adds, three-quarters of Wood Gundy's sales were directed to its retail clients, and only one-quarter to institutions. The proportions were exactly the opposite during the three preceding years.

Today, borrowers who want to lure big investors have to do more than flutter their eyelashes. Six months ago Wood Gundy set up a complex issue for Quebec composed of medium-term notes denominated in Deutschmarks, which classified it as a derivative. The securities involved in this private placement were designed to please a single institution, a bank in Austria with a strong opinion on the German bond market and an inclination to use financial leverage on a specific fall in interest rates. Quebec was able to provide the paper necessary for the bet. It was the sort of transaction in which the buyer looks for a high yield but accepts a proportional risk; the issuer runs no risk as long as the middlemen who have structured the deal stay solvent. Says Edge: "If some of the Canadian governments had not gone to MTN programs, where they could offer people a better quality of 'soap,' they wouldn't have gotten the money. The Canadian product at the moment is an inferior product." Inferior, he continues "because of the credit. We've been in a one-way direction on Canadian credit for the last few years and the Canadian currency has been on a one-way trend as well. So you're not going to lure investors to buy that 'soap' if it is not refined."

Foreign investor requirements have had an impact on the ability of Canadian governments to borrow, and on the cost of money, Edge adds. "For the last number of years, the pricing, the credit allocation for Canadians, is taking place outside of Toronto. The international clearing price of the securities is being set outside of Toronto."

Clearly a problem exists. In the latest issue of *Euromoney*, a headline blurts out the question: "What's Wrong With Canadian Issuers?" The article leads off: "Canada is coming out of recession, the currency has gained strength [only briefly, following the Quebec election], and a breakup of the country seems unlikely. So why aren't investors buying Canadian bonds?" A few lines down comes the answer: "They continue to be concerned with the magnitude of the federal and provincial budget deficits."[4]

What's under the kilt?

EDINBURGH, FRIDAY, NOVEMBER 4, 1994

The pub walls festooned with pennants flogging Labatt's new Ice Beer remind me of Mordecai Richler's remark that "there is only so much bad wine that one is willing to drink for one's country." Especially when you're soaked to the bone by an unrelenting, cold drizzle. The hell with Canada's trade balance, I grumble as I order a single malt whisky. But Edinburgh is more than a nice place for a stiff drink on a cold, rainy afternoon. The thrifty Scots have built it into the United Kingdom's second-ranking financial centre, as famous for its redoubtable insurance companies, such as Standard Life, as for its banks and fund managers.

Dunedin Fund Managers, a subsidiary of the Bank of Scotland, manages assets of more than $10 billion (CA) for pension funds, mutual funds, and insurance companies from Europe, Asia, and North America, including the Bank of Montreal and the Province of Nova Scotia. Thirty-six-year-old Mark Wauton administers fixed-income securities, using quantitative models to design a portfolio whose performance should outshine the J. P. Morgan World Government Bond Index. "The currency is the driving force" in international bond fund management, he says. "If we think the currency is going to be stable or appreciate, then we will actually invest money there." Currency has emerged as more important than yield. Over the last three years, low interest rate markets have produced the best results, when capital gains and losses and currency fluctuation are factored in. "In the high-yielding markets, investors haven't actually been rewarded for the risks they have taken. Canada is a very good example. For a non-dollar investor, it has been the worst-performing market, yet it used to have the highest yield in the world."

You can hedge the exchange risk associated with the Canadian dollar, adds Wauton, but then you have to give up on the currency lever. In the long run, 60 percent of a portfolio's total yield can be attributed to currency fluctuations, and only 40 percent to the bond market proper. When a currency slips, central banks tend to raise interest rates to slow its drop, but raising rates causes bond values to plummet. Worse, higher rates usually can't stop the currency from slipping in any case. It's a lose-lose game. "You are in a double whammy: if you're in a bond market and believe that the currency is going to weaken, then very often the bond market is actually going to go with it. So it is probably better to avoid it altogether. Currency nowadays tends to drive events rather than lagging behind them."

So goes the theory. In practice, Dunedin brought home its marbles from Canada two years ago. Nowadays, the firm plays only with the United States. Wauton couldn't generate much enthusiasm about the mixture of budget deficits and political developments he had difficulty understanding. When he saw the market post a risk premium, he decided to get out. "When you're aware that the market is pricing risk, the best thing is just not to be involved in it." Early in 1994, half his capital was parked in the United States, but he's brought 30 percent back to Europe. While it might have been an easy matter to cut Canadian holdings from 4 percent to zero, Wauton didn't dare abandon the United States entirely. "If you accept the fact that North American markets constitute just shy of 50 percent of the world index, you've got to be a very brave man not to have any assets in North America."

For this manager, Canada comes rather far down the list. "When I'm thinking about a major shift between the U.S. dollar and the yen, for example, I'm less likely to bother about the fine points of U.S.-Canada spreads. For a global fund, what is most important is to call the

U.S. dollar, the yen, and the Deutschmark correctly." But before he decides to get back into the Canadian market, Wauton would like to see the loonie gain ground against the greenback, and then see the U.S. dollar start to gain value against the European currencies and the yen.

LONDON, TUESDAY, NOVEMBER 1, 1994

H. J. Everitt's twenty-first-floor office commands a nice view of the dome of Saint Paul's Cathedral. Two years ago, every window in the building was shattered by the blast of an IRA bomb. Ever since, security has been tightened in the City, making driving difficult and parking next to impossible. The grey-templed Everitt, as associate director of Commercial Union, one of the U.K.'s five largest insurance companies, and a member of the select club of the world's top twenty, handles fixed-income investments for the firm as well as funds entrusted to it by other institutions, for a total of some £33 billion ($71 billion [CA]) under management.

Everitt's primary objective is to invest insurance premiums prudently over the long term so that the firm is able to respect its commitments when clients die or become incapacitated. Most benefits must be paid out in pounds sterling, making U.K. government bonds the investment of choice. But to improve on local market performance, he invests between a quarter and a third of capital offshore, making sure to hedge the foreign exchange risk. J. P. Morgan or Morgan Stanley weightings play a relatively minor role in his decisions; the company's principal fund has held no North American investments for some time. But one of its specialized smaller funds, a bond Unit Trust (the United Kingdom term for mutual fund), is managed according to international index parameters. The North American segment of these funds has been underweighted for more than two years. Until recently, he explains, he preferred Canadian over American bonds because of their higher yield. But when the spread narrowed seriously, he converted the firm's Canadian position into U.S. Treasuries.

Emotion and decision-making don't mix, ventures Everitt, an actuary by training, after several moments of reflection. "One always tries to avoid the emotional approach, because that does lead to irrational decisions. Having said that, you cannot be a total recluse and ignore what is going on around you. You may believe the market is going in a direction for the wrong reason. But you cannot ignore a tide."

Everitt is as phlegmatic about political risk as he is about feelings. "Political factors are usually unpredictable, and their effects are very sharp but short lived." Markets return to their long trends; political uncertainty is "seldom a sell opportunity, because the market usually falls on such risk." But until now, Canada's recurring political controversies have had minimal effect. "If Quebec were to opt out, I don't think that at the end of the day it would actually be harmful for the market. In fact, I tend to take the opposite view. All the political uncertainties that crop up every year or so would not be there. The problem would be solved once and for all. It could be good for the market." But would a firm like Commercial Union be prepared to hold Canadian bonds throughout the transition period? Everitt weighs his words carefully before replying: "Probably not, because our natural position is not to be there, and we don't think it is appropriate to get involved in a situation where there will be considerable uncertainty." Still, he refuses to rule out the possibility of buying Canadian bonds in such circumstances if their price were to drop.

....

"We are most bullish on the Canadian dollar at the moment," bubbles Charles Thompson, a youthful manager at Barclays de Zoete Wedd Investment Management, a subsidiary of British banking behemoth Barclays that manages more than $100 billion (CA) for pension funds, insurance companies, and Unit Trusts. Perhaps 10 percent of the firm's total funds are held in non-sterling bonds.

Canada's relative weight on the international bond indices, about 3 percent, is Thompson's point of departure. He keeps close track of the interest rate spread between ten-year U.S. and Canada bonds. "It's always good to buy Canada before some event like a general election, and that's what we have done in the last three years." In the spring of 1994, while Bloc Québécois leader Lucien Bouchard was irritating Toronto markets with his trips abroad, and the election of the PQ became almost certain, the spread soared to more than 200 basis points. For Thompson, it was the right time to purchase a fat fistful of seven-year Canada bonds from Goldman Sachs, bringing Canada's weighting in his portfolio up to 5 percent, approximately

$400 million (CA). The way he sees it, 200 basis points are an excellent value, bearing in mind that the spread usually runs between 100 and 150 basis points. Since then, it has fallen back to 124. "Today or tomorrow we are going to take some profits and go back to the index." A narrowing of the spreads would mean that Canadian rates are dropping faster than in the United States, or that they are rising more slowly. In either case, the Canadian bond market's performance would be better than that of the United States.

Thompson would be ready to wager on the impact of political uncertainty on the spreads — up to a point. But if opinion polls indicated that the Parti Québécois could win its referendum, "there is absolutely no doubt that we would underweight to zero. As fixed-income investors, we would run away from that," he says in reply to my question, adding that Barclays de Zoete Wedd doesn't touch provincial bonds, preferring highly liquid securities. "The risk of a country breaking up is an acute worry," he adds. How would they administer the debt? he asks rhetorically. In the same breath, Thompson claims not to be worried by Canada's debt, assuring me that he "can sleep with Canada's rating." Here is a man who says he's bullish on Canada while he's prepared to sell hundreds of millions in Canadian bonds. Sell Canada, by all means, but never short. Such tactics are expressly forbidden by the firm. "The computers show a horrible orange colour and the boss comes to ask what's happening. I know it, it's happened to me!"

....

The young woman insists: this interview will be strictly off the record. I can only reveal that she manages the North American section of one of the United Kingdom's largest bond portfolios for conservative clients like central banks at one of the country's most prestigious, best connected firms. "We have very high rating standards; we primarily invest in AAA names, and strong AA. We don't want to worry."

Ms. Anonymous does not beat around the bush: "We've been mostly underweight in Canada since the beginning of the year, primarily because of the level of debt. And also, obviously, the concerns about the Quebec election." Officials from Canada's Finance department always seem to have excellent arguments when they compare their debt levels with other countries', she explains, but they end up admitting that they are subject to the whims of the capital market. "If you have a country with so much debt, if you are so reliant on foreign investments, you are held hostage. It's just the way things work. Any small bond market like Canada can be influenced by a few sizable accounts." Sizable accounts like the one she manages.

The risk of investing in Canada lies in finding yourself in a bond market whose performance lags behind its rivals. But "the ultimate risk is to end up holding up a debt that defaults, and you don't get all your money back." This is the worst-case scenario. Debt spiralling out of control leads to a downgrading of bond ratings, and that can "cause you pain," since it undercuts the value of the investment. She prides herself on being a bond vigilante, part of a hard-core hit squad of defenders of fiscal orthodoxy, modern-day Crusaders of the bond markets. "Bond vigilantes are people who are strict about their investments and who are punishing countries that fail to take their public finances seriously enough. We do not want to buy their bonds any more. We are a very conservative house." Her hands-off list also includes Sweden, Belgium, and Italy. "Unfortunately, the number of countries we can invest in is shrinking," she says with a sigh.

....

No one is forcing foreigners to invest in Canadian securities. They will take the plunge only if they are convinced that it is in their best interests, which are determined by the institution making the investment, and by the requirements of its clients. Investors who are outwardly cautious and diplomatic in their evaluation of Canada might well be concealing harsher judgments, but investors don't speak with one voice. There are, after all, several European markets, and when they deal with European-based institutions, Canadian borrowers draw on capital from around the world, as well as from their own country. Still, from these complex, shifting perspectives we can draw several general conclusions:

1. The values of the American and Canadian dollars, and their future prospects, play a key role in an investor's decision-making process. For better or for worse, Canada is a tributary of the American bond market, a dollar bloc offshoot.

2. The reputation of the issuer and the generosity of the coupon determine individual choice on the retail market. Name is more important than credit rating, but people purchase familiar names only when they pay high interest.

3. Institutional managers are guided by global indices when they distribute a portfolio geographically. If a manager has no specific opinion about Canada, he will invest 3 percent of his funds; if he is optimistic, he will stake between 5 percent and 10 percent; if he is feeling pessimistic, he will invest nothing at all.

4. European investors see Canadian bonds as a substitute for American paper, a riskier version that pays better. It is inconceivable to them that Canadian bond yields could be equal to or lower than American rates.

5. Canada's image reflects positively on all the country's public borrowers. Generally, professional managers are well versed in Canada's economic and political situation. But more often than not, Canada is little more than a line entry on a statistical chart, a paragraph on a screen, or a newspaper sidebar. If Canada accounts for only 3 percent of a portfolio, why devote more than 3 percent of one's time to studying it — why not even less, if one believes that a good knowledge of the American market is all that's needed to understand the situation in Canada? Fortunately, at several of the largest institutions one person devotes his entire attention to North America, which might leave more time for its northernmost component.

6. The growing risk inherent in public debt constitutes Canada's major image problem. This risk is shared by Italy, Sweden, and Belgium. No one is comparing Canada with a Third World country, but downgrading has restricted the pool of investors who purchase its bonds. Quebec, as a large borrower with a mediocre rating, is particularly vulnerable.

7. Recurring risk linked to political uncertainty is the second factor that penalizes not only Quebec bonds but Canadian borrowing as a whole. But Europeans are accustomed to political complexity, and from a European perspective the prospect of uncertainty looks less dramatic. One European financier put it this way: "Here,

the whole notion of political risk is different. In a two-hour flight from here you have Bosnia-Herzegovina, where people throw grenades at each other. In a three-hour flight, the Russian monolith can blow up at any time. The risk of war in North America looks minuscule."

8. The risks associated with high debt levels and political uncertainty are not always uppermost in investors' minds — but to the extent that they explain the fall of the Canadian dollar against the greenback, they contribute to investor estrangement. In the bear market conditions of 1994, these are the kinds of handicaps that send investors scurrying for safer investments.

9. Fortunately, sharp competition between banks and brokerage houses to nail down lead mandates works to the advantage of Canadian borrowers. The large European banks wield substantial influence over their retail clients' investment decisions. But they cannot sell what clients do not wish to buy. Unattractive merchandise can only be sold at low prices, which, on bond markets, translates into higher interest rates.

10. The prevailing investment perspective in Europe is an international one. Investors will "go where the honey is sweetest," as one investor put it. Well-informed investors will never stake everything on a single country, no matter how attractive it looks — but they will easily abandon a marginal country like Canada.

Chapter 5

SHAKE-UP IN JAPAN

TOKYO, MONDAY, FEBRUARY 6, 1995

METROPOLITAN TOKYO, WITH its population of 12 million, is a crazy-quilt of overlapping neighbourhoods and satellite suburbs stretching as far as the eye can see. Harmony, the quality the Japanese prize above all others, lingers only in the handful of ancient Buddhist temples and Shinto shrines that have escaped the ravages of war, earthquake, and explosive economic growth. In the downtown core, where land prices are among the world's highest, absurdly narrow modern buildings tower over near-hovels. Trees are few and far between; public parks a rarity. But the streets are clean and orderly. Japan's blend of respectful distance and discreet attention seems best exemplified in the innate elegance and politeness of the Japanese themselves. Paris might be a more beautiful city, New York might be more exciting, but Tokyo's inhabitants make it a pleasant place to visit.

The Japanese are still reeling from the shock of the earthquake that devastated the Kobe region three weeks earlier. The disaster is still front-page news, but pain has been quickly masked with stoicism. On the economic front, analysts cannot predict whether the huge investments needed for reconstruction can offset the temporary loss of production and export revenue. The Japanese government is debating a special bond issue of ¥1 trillion (¥1 trillion=¥1,000 billion=$14.6 billion [CA]) to finance rebuilding of the damaged infrastructure and assist Kobe's 200,000 homeless.

Estimated damage stands at more than ¥10 trillion, but the impact of the quake on international bond markets was less than feared. Japanese

107

insurance companies have long considered massive acquisitions of foreign bonds as the best protection against the kind of giant tremor that could destroy Tokyo. Only foreign securities can be sold rapidly in order to pay out claims. Despite its final death toll of 5,200, the Kobe catastrophe remained a manageable one for insurers: large numbers of victims were uninsured older people, and the government moved quickly to compensate material losses over and above a threshold level. Japanese insurers did sell off huge quantities of Canadian and American bonds, but their reasons for doing so turned out to have nothing to do with the quake.

•••••••••••••••••••••••

Bowing slightly from the waist, I offer my calling card with both hands. My host reciprocates, picking it up like a precious object before presenting me with his card. The strict rules of Japanese etiquette have transformed the lowly business card into a badge of social status that must be scrutinized with the greatest attention. I have had mine translated; Japanese in regular contact with Westerners use cards printed vertically on one side in Japanese, and horizontally on the other side in English. My host's card reads: "Takashi Itoda, Manager, International Fixed Investment Division, The Dai-ichi Mutual Life Insurance Company." We lay the cards carefully on the low table while a uniformed hostess serves green tea in small bowls. The reception room, which overlooks the gardens of the Imperial Palace, is decorated in muted tones of grey. Dai-ichi headquarters occupies an office tower constructed atop the stone building that housed U.S. General Douglas MacArthur's occupation authority in the immediate postwar years.

The PR man at Itoda's side hands me a copy of the firm's annual report. With assets of more than ¥24 trillion ($350 billion [CA]), Dai-ichi is Japan's — and the world's — second-largest insurance company. Mami Saito, my interpreter, translates my first question: Itoda-*san* (the suffix *san* added to the last name is a token of respect), how are international bond market decisions made? First, comes the translated reply, our assets are divided into main categories: marketable securities, loans, real estate, and cash resources; bonds are then allotted by country. My next question: What are the criteria for choosing countries for investment? "It is difficult to give a simple answer: we consider the reliability of the issuer, which we evaluate in terms of the country's financial policies, and the size of the market. The second factor, which influences us a lot, involves interest and foreign exchange rates measured against the yen." Do you rely on American benchmarks for distribution by country? "Yes. The J. P. Morgan index." And in evaluating credit, how much importance do you attach to the New York rating agencies? "We purchase national public bonds. For the time being, we do not really make use of the information published by Standard & Poor's and Moody's."

Dai-ichi has trimmed its foreign bond portfolio by 60 percent over the last three years, to 5.3 percent of total assets. The answer to my question on the regional breakdown of foreign bonds is as lengthy as the translation is curt: "Unfortunately, I cannot provide you with many details. Overall, 70 percent of our bond holdings come from the dollar bloc — the United States, Australia, and Canada. The rest are from Europe."

Bond holdings are heavily weighted toward the dollar bloc for two reasons, Itoda continues. Dai-ichi has traditionally held "many" dollar-denominated bonds. But should it decide to sell in the interests of a better portfolio balance, it will take *endaka* (strong yen)-induced losses. Current interest rates indicate that "nowadays it is more interesting to buy dollar-denominated rather than European bonds." Would he be so kind as to tell me the percentage of Canadian dollars in the dollar bloc? I ask, attempting to pin him down. "I am so sorry; we cannot provide you with more details." Mr. Itoda pleads precedent. A competitor who admitted publicly to selling Australian bonds touched off a media frenzy and irritated the Australian government. Using a combination of politeness and reassurance I try again. A waste of breath.

A few days later I obtained a detailed list of Japanese insurance company foreign currency holdings from an investment dealer named Nomura. Opposite the Dai-ichi entry I noted that Canadian dollars accounted for 3.5 percent ($841 million [CA]) of the firm's holdings. The matching figure one year later had dropped to 0.0 percent, not including small change of less than $10 million. The same list showed that 68 percent of all foreign securities were denominated in U.S. dollars (a drop of 4.2 percentage points) and 0.5 percent in Australian dollars. For the same period, the Deutschmark's share climbed from 4.3 to 9.3 precent, and the French franc's from 6.4 to 9.4 percent, while the sterling pound held steady at 6.5 percent.

Back to the interview with Itoda-*san*. What are your criteria for allocating assets inside the dollar bloc? My interpreter scribbles furiously away, but once again the answer is a brief one. I get the irritating feeling that I'm missing something — perhaps because I'm so accustomed to hearing translations from English to French, where the French versions are always longer and more detailed. Allocation, he explains, depends on the interest rate cycle. But Canada's case is a particular one. "I've just come back from Toronto, where we had several discussions with investment dealers and people from the Bank of Canada about the February budget. It is important for us to know how governments are cutting down their deficits. The second subject is Quebec independence; we also need to know which way the Parti Québécois is headed. Unfortunately, because of the Quebec issue, our opinion of Canada has changed. Of course Quebec independence would come about peacefully and democratically, but even so, when Quebec occupies such a large part of the country, we must pay heed. We must be more cautious when we invest in Canada," he says. No one could accuse Mr. Itoda of excessive candour.

Dai-ichi holds federal bonds exclusively; provincial securities were sold off because they offered less liquidity than federal borrowings. My host has some difficulty remembering which Canadian provincial paper the firm used to hold; politely he asks me to remind him of their names. Ah yes, Ontario and Nova Scotia, he confirms, adding that the loan department still deals with the provinces. Later, as I skim through the Dai-ichi annual report, I note that in 1984, for the first time, the firm led a yen loan syndicate, which funnelled ¥12 billion to Hydro-Québec. A bit further along the report adds that "yen-denominated overseas loans are a fixed-interest asset impervious to currency fluctuations, and, for this reason, Dai-ichi has in recent years been expanding its volume of such loans." Japan's insurance companies are large-scale lenders. In tandem with the trust companies, they financed the country's industrial expansion, working along government-established guidelines. The Japanese commercial banks finance only corporate working capital.

The impetus for Dai-ichi's move to sell off its Canadian bonds came from the rise in the yen, says Itoda. The large exchange rate differential between time of purchase and the present was the decisive factor. "There was no good reason for us to keep them," he says, in a typical understate-

---

JAPAN'S 15-PERCENT RULE

Japanese regulations oblige insurance companies to "realize" their foreign exchange losses when they exceed 15 percent during the fiscal year. If the theoretical value of a portfolio's foreign bonds declines by 15 percent because of yen appreciation, the theoretical loss must be shown on the bottom line. The foreign exchange loss on a bond denominated in Canadian dollars held during fiscal 1994 was 19 percent.

---

ment. Since the beginning of the decade, the Canadian dollar has lost three-quarters of its value against the yen. Itoda adds that he sold off his American bonds for the same reason.

At Dai-ichi, 1995 doesn't look like a banner year for Canadian bond acquisition. "We've come to an equilibrium in terms of our foreign bond percentage. If it goes up, the increase will be slight." What would convince you to buy Canadian again? I ask. "We believe Canada is an excellent investment destination. Canada is a reliable country," he says, explaining that the Canadian market follows U.S. trends, only more abruptly. But "what disturbs us about Canada is the deficit problem, and the political problem of separatism." At the end of the interview Itoda-*san* asks for my view of Quebec independence. My answer is as evasive and non-committal as his own.

••••••••••••••••••••••••

Today's edition of the *Nihon Keizai Shinbun*, with a circulation of three million, the world's most widely read financial daily, features a report on the G-7 finance ministers' meeting in Toronto in the run-up to the organization's summit in Halifax in June 1995. The first half of the article explores the peso crisis. The second half, in the dry, just-the-facts style of the Japanese media, concludes: "Canada is heavily dependent on foreign creditors. On the impact of the Mexican peso crisis on the fall of the Canadian dollar, Mr. Martin pointed out that: 1) although a volatility crisis happened in Mexico, it couldn't possibly happen in Canada and 2) the Canadian economy is much stronger and more diversified. Mr. Martin appeared confident to reach his goal of reducing the deficit from the current 5.9 percent of GDP to 3 percent in fiscal 1996 and urged the markets to remain calm."[1]

Visiting the investment dealers

TUESDAY, FEBRUARY 7, 1995

As Japanese shoppers flock to the department stores of the Nihonbashi, the Tokyo stock exchange district, they collide with the thousands of hungry traders who crowd the narrow side streets at lunchtime, wolfing down bowls of noodles in stalls or slurping eel soup in restaurants. Eel is prized as energy food; some marketeers believe that eating the slithery fish can send share prices upward. Just around the corner from Bank of Japan headquarters in the heart of the Nihonbashi district stands the Nomura Securities Investment Trust Management building. This branch of Nomura specializes in mutual funds sold to small savers, corporations, and other financial institutions. A good-natured, easygoing man named Sachio Hori, a veteran of seven years in the trenches in London and two in Boston for Goldman Sachs, heads the bond market division.

Hori's division manages assets of ¥11 trillion ($157 billion [CA]), two-thirds in fixed income instruments (split evenly between money and bond markets). Nearly $7 billion (CA) is invested in foreign bonds distributed in different proportions among a wide range of balanced or specialized funds. A small fund set aside entirely for Canadian bonds has shrunk from $350 million (CA) three years ago to $25 million (CA) today. Generally, foreign investment has dropped on the heels of foreign exchange losses, as depositors sell off their shares in foreign currency funds.

The international bond portfolio is distributed in a "very orthodox" way, explains Hori. Specialists develop interest, exchange rate, inflation, and growth forecasts for each principal market; scenarios are analysed, and a computer program optimizes the geographical distribution. The Salomon Brothers index is used to compare performance, but hardly at all for weighting, which varies by fund type. Nomura's world is divided into currency blocs. Within the dollar bloc, Canada and Australia are seen as complementary to the American dollar. "We go to those markets if there is a good reason," he says, meaning that the dollar position is determined by the American market. Last year, Nomura cut back its dollar holdings as insulation against rising U.S. interest rates. (Remember: any increase in interest rates reduces the value of bonds held in a portfolio.) Normally, when the weight of the dollar bloc declines, Canadian and Australian dollar securities are the first to go. If the bloc is being beefed up, they are the last to be bought.

"Canada is a little harder to figure out than the United States because of the Quebec situation and political uncertainty," Hori explains. "We have a Canadian specialist, and he is quite clever, but the Fed-watcher is the number-one guy. Tomorrow we have a meeting. We'll start with the Fed-watcher, who will tell us what Clinton said last night, blah blah blah . . . and the likelihood is that interest rates will go fifty points higher. He speaks for about ten minutes. It's an hour meeting, and the chair will tell the young guy who follows Canada to make a quick point about the Canadian dollar. He will speak two minutes, and the older and more experienced guy will ask him questions on foreign exchange. Then we go to the German guy who is leading the European market, who will touch on three or four points during ten or fifteen minutes. Other countries are seen as spreads against the German market. The U.K. is a little bit different, and the U.K. guy will also make some remarks." For Nomura management, the American and German markets are where the action is, leaving precious little time for Canada.

Aside from political uncertainty, what are the risks of investing in Canada? I ask. Hori keeps close tabs on the budget issue, but he seems unconcerned. For him, the Quebec situation is more puzzling than it is distressing. "The major concern of our customers is how international bond funds perform against yen-based investments, like the 2.5-percent interest rate they would get for a bank deposit. Because they are buying the fund in yens, not with dollars or Deutschmarks," he adds. Since Nomura's clients adore stable income and are extremely sensitive to currency fluctuations, the company systematically hedges its foreign investment risk. It's a lesson the Japanese have learned the hard way. "About ten years ago, Japanese insurance companies bought a lot, a lot . . . a lot of Canadian bonds without any currency hedging. They started at ¥200, now we are at ¥100. Halved. It's tremendous what they lost!" As I left Hiro's office, I was experiencing vague pangs of guilt myself.

WEDNESDAY, FEBRUARY 8, 1995

Public hearings on sovereignty are getting underway in Quebec: the CBC report broadcast on CNN International shows cars refusing to start because of the cold. Outside my hotel room, the Tokyo weather looks like spring. I haven't eaten breakfast yet, but the man I'm scheduled to meet has already been at work for an hour. Nick Bonellos, a trader specializing in Canadian bonds, makes his office in the new Nomura Securities building in the Otemachi district, one of the last Tokyo structures built during the "bubble era," the term the Japanese use to describe the speculative fever that swept over the stock and real estate markets in the late 1980s. Nomura might be the world's largest investment dealer, but the firm lacks the scope of the great New York houses.

The centrepiece of the atrium, finished in almond tones, is an impressive modern sculpture stretching several stories upward. When I reach the thirteenth floor, Bonellos shows me into a capacious, high-ceilinged trading room where more than three hundred people are hard at work: traders wearing white or pin-striped shirts, and, young, attractive, female "non-professional employees" dressed in green knit jackets and sea-blue skirts. These women handle the secretarial chores. The handful of professional women dress as they please; gender equity is not yet a rapid-growth phenomenon in Japan.

This is the room where JGBs (Japanese Government Bonds) and other fixed-income instruments are traded. Stocks change hands in an identical room a few floors up, he tells me. Banks of wall-mounted screens flash the latest financial data: interest rates, which are stable in Japan; the Tokyo stock market index, still sliding downhill; and the American dollar rate, which has taken yet another tumble as Japan has announced a new, record trade surplus. Seven digital wall clocks give the time in the world's major time zones. Traders occupy the tiered seats at the rear of the room; beneath them sit the salesmen in straight rows. The room is quiet now, but in the afternoon, when a JGB issue is in progress, pandemonium breaks out. For ten minutes they are all on their feet, gesticulating, telephones glued to both ears, in an attempt to place a few zillion yen.

The foreign bond section is off to one side. Here, traders and salesmen work side by side. Bonellos is a Canadian who paid his way through the

University of Western Ontario by working part-time on the floor of the Toronto Stock Exchange. Later he went on to Shorcan, a specialized broker that handles anonymous transactions between dealers. Nomura signed him up and brought him to Tokyo, where his job now is to maintain contact between the main trading room and the company's Toronto office. In theory, Bonellos is a market maker for Canadian bonds. In practice, Japanese clients have all but deserted the Canadian market, and Bonellos has been transferred over to the Euromarket to keep him busy. Ontario is the only Canadian name on the list of the sixty busiest Euroyens.

Back in his office, speaking in a mixture of Japanese and English, he fields a call from a major insurance company asking for prices on five- and twelve-year Canada bonds. The client apparently wants to sell, but says nothing about quantity. Bonellos estimates his current holdings at nearly $1 billion (CA). "Canada is rallying and Japanese institutions sell on uptake. They sell every time there is a big bid for Canada." As a rule, Japanese investors hold fire until operations begin in London (4:00 p.m. in Japan); they then check prices on offer, assuming that increased liquidity on the European market is working in their favour. For big transactions — those of $100 million and more — they are more likely to wait until business opens in Toronto, the deepest source of Canadas. Nomura is well connected. A bid sweetened by one or two cents will give the firm an excellent shot at closing the deal.

The Campeau incident

Did I see what Campeau said last night? Bonellos asks me, pointing to a Reuter's dispatch from Ottawa on his screen: "Canada's Finance minister Paul Martin dismissed comments made by Quebec's Finance minister that an independent Quebec might refuse to pay its share of the Canadian debt if doing so would undermine the new country's economic development. 'Quebec is not going to separate and people know it, but what is particularly ironic about that kind of statement is that it really calls into doubt the integrity [of the Parti Québécois] and therefore it will have an effect on Quebec bonds,' Martin told reporters." Another dispatch reports that Jean Campeau's statement, "later denied by the province's premier," touched off a sell-off of Canadian dollars for a few hours. The Canadian bond market skidded off the tracks and the loonie lost half a cent. "When people at insurance companies read that, they don't like it," says Bonellos. But in the six-line daily commentary he prepares for Nomura clients, Bonellos has the minister stating that "with separation the province will not repay its share of Canadian debt." Full stop.

Whatever Campeau may or may not have said, the market reaction is as short-lived as it is skin-deep. Japanese dealers are not the kind of people who sell at the first alarmist headline that comes along; today, they haven't even blinked. Back in Canada, the loonie quickly moved back upward and the bank rate dropped by thirty-one basis points, with the Bank of Canada stepping in to cool down an overheated market. While Japanese investors remain unimpressed, the Americans are buying on the favourable spread. Bonellos hands me a copy of the *G7 Daily Briefing*, an American financial newsletter that says the Canadian rally took place in anticipation of the upcoming federal budget: "Sources believe that Martin will introduce a budget that at least reaches and potentially exceeds his stated goal of a deficit-to-GDP ratio of 3 percent by fiscal year 1996–97. The Canadian dollar will reap most of the fruits of the new budget before Martin even presents it."[2]

The Japanese press did not even pick up on Campeau's statement, but a source outside Nomura tells me that a few days later Quebec government representatives paid a call on the Tokyo brokerage community to brief them on the political and economic situation, assuring them that the minister's declaration did not represent government policy. Quebec is in a hurry to complete its borrowing program for the year: the province must locate $2 billion (CA) by the end of March. European investment dealers are noticing a lack of appetite for Canadian dollars, and are looking at the possibility of a borrowing of U.S. dollars, French francs, or Deutschmarks, while in Japan Quebec is borrowing heavily in yen. In early 1995, Yamaichi organized a private ten-year placement of ¥10 billion ($143 million [CA]) at 5.05 percent. In late January, Nomura put together two other operations totalling ¥4.1 billion ($58 million [CA]) maturing in seven and ten years at reasonable rates. In Japan, an investment is considered private when investment dealers canvass fewer than fifty institutions. The Tokyo rumour mill also has Nippon Life granting an additional loan of $150 to $200 million (CA).

Low-key canvassing

Bonellos leads me through the ranks of black, chauffeur-driven limousines drawn up in the underground garage to the minibus shuttle service that will take me to my meeting with Kanju Sugimoto, Nomura's "*gaijin* handler," the man who specializes in dealings with foreigners. Sugimoto, an "adviser to the board," greets me with a handshake instead of the usual bow, although we exchange business cards all the same. In excellent English he asks me if his friend Gérald Tremblay, the former Quebec minister of Industry and Trade, is any relation. Sugimoto, considered one of Japan's most skilled *gaijin* handlers, has friends in high places around the world; his white hair testifies to years of experience.

We meet in a spacious, wood-panelled room furnished with comfortable leather chairs. For once, in Japan, I am served coffee instead of green tea. I ask Mr. Sugimoto to explain how he canvasses for mandates from foreign issuers. "We try to see those potential borrowers and keep them informed about recent developments in international capital markets. It is very important to see people at various levels, starting from junior officials to, if not the prime minister, at least the finance minister. We try to find out what are their current or future potential needs." And ideally, he tries to ensure that Nomura will be their investment dealer on the Japanese market. Regrettably, adds Mr. Sugimoto, Canadians tend to look at the American dollar market first; if that's not enough, they try the Germans; and then, if they still need money, they borrow in Japan. But things are changing slowly, he admits. People are more and more open to yen borrowings.

There's no such thing as a single borrowing style. For some issuers, the numbers are everything: how many bonds can Nomura sell, at what interest rate? For others, long-term confidence is the primary concern: they want to know their banker's strengths and services. Sugimoto has a soft spot in his heart for relationships of the second type. Sure, an issuer can usually find a good price at auction, he admits, but "the pricing of a bond issue is not just a deal between the borrower and the banker. In addition, both the banker and the borrower face the general market, and the market reaction is very quick and very severe. If the borrower obtains terms that are too generous, the market will say 'No.'"

117

This might happen when an issue is made at par, at its face value of $100, and then it slips rapidly to $95. "This failure damages the name of the borrower and also, of course, the banker will often suffer a loss. The borrower should always remember that he is not just a one-time visitor to the market. He might need to come back to this market many more times." A bit of generosity can help create a good reputation in the investment community. Canada has a positive image, Sugimoto assures me. Canadian issuers have held onto their relatively better credit ratings, in spite of recent downgrades. And that sends a strong signal to investors. "Canada is generally known as politically stable and peaceful. Canadians complain about their economy, but from the Japanese viewpoint the country is very, very rich in resources and the economy is generally stable."

Back in the trading room, Bonellos is on the phone; the London and Paris offices have just opened. Normally a rep from the Hong Kong branch joins the day's conference call, but he is tied up in a transaction. A Tokyo colleague brings the Europeans up to date on recent developments in the JGB and U.S. Treasury markets; Bonellos chimes in with a Euro update. London reports on the new markets in Bulgaria, Russia, and Hungary. And all the while, Toronto is fast asleep: it's 2:30 in the morning. Bonellos usually stays on the job until the Canadian market opens, meaning frequent twelve-hour shifts. In the afternoon he deals with Asia, Australia, and the Middle East, a showcase of contrasting styles. The Hong Kong Chinese have a much stronger speculative bent than the Japanese, he tells me. Naturalized Canadian Chinese in the crown colony provide even Canadas with a solid retail client base. Australian banks like to play the rate and forex spreads between Canada and Australia. The Arabs have hung onto their Quebec bonds, and they're not likely to do anything rash. There is some American activity in Asia but, Bonellos says, the "flavour" of the last three months has been Australia. "It would be Canada if not for the debt and Quebec." But the only Asians interested in Canada right now are the Hong Kong hedge funds.

THURSDAY, FEBRUARY 9, 1995

Japan has a compartmentalized financial system, modelled on that of the United States. Investment dealers, banks, insurance companies, and trusts are not formally affiliated with one another. At one time, borrowers wanting to issue yen-denominated bonds had to deal with one of the four top Japanese investment dealers, but after a recent loosening of regulations, institutions can now invade new fields of activities through subsidiaries. In 1972, Quebec became the first Canadian name to solicit Japanese savings; since then, Nomura and Yamaichi have maintained close relations with the province and with its electric utility. Manitoba followed five years later, with other issuers crossing the Pacific during the second half of the 1980s. In 1994, six provinces issued bonds denominated in yen, but in more than two thirds of the financing arrangements American brokerage houses took the lead role. My two interviews at Yamaichi made clear how much Japanese borrowing methods are changing.

....

Shoko Izumi is a young foreign currency bond saleswoman.

Izumi-*san*, I ask, if you call a Japanese institutional investor this afternoon and offer to sell him Canadian bonds in Canadian dollars, what will he answer?

"The truth is that we haven't handled any investments in Canada for some time," she tells me through my interpreter. "Last year, investors lost money on the exchange rate, and not only on account of the Canadian dollar. Japanese investors have become wary of foreign bonds. But we see interest in yen bonds picking up again. In the specific case of Canada, people are sensitive to the country's political and financial problems."

But haven't some investors begun to buy U.S. Treasuries again?

"Yes, since late 1994. But Canada will have to wait until we've seen how well our U.S. investments fare. We're also waiting for the February budget to clear things up somewhat. Still, the problems of the deficit and of Quebec independence haven't been settled. These days, investing in Canada is speculative investing."

Does this also hold for yen-denominated bonds issued by Canadians?

"Not quite, because the risk is less. But investors are aware of the financial deficit problem, the credit rating, and Quebec."

Are Japanese investors still trying to get rid of their Canadian-dollar bonds?

"Almost all of them were sold last year."

A fluent English-speaker named Hiro Hayakawa is deputy general manager and head of the Americas section of Yamaichi's International Finance Department.

Has the situation Ms. Izumi described forced Canadian issuers to change their borrowing strategy? What would be your advice to them concerning borrowing in Japan?

"There are two approaches. One is a retail type of bond. A retail market emerged in 1994. The yield curve steepened and short-term interest rates obtained at the bank were low. Individuals started to diversify their investment in yen bonds issued by Japanese electric power companies. This market, less sensitive to ratings, is booming. The other thing I might be able to say [to the borrower] is that securities houses have started to find little pockets of institutional investors who have particular needs for coupons, maturity. Beforehand, big public issues were the only way. Now the MTN products are particularly designed for one or two investors. This is not only in Japan but is also happening globally. Those bought by Japanese institutions are fairly simple products, not complex or highly leveraged."

How do you sell bonds retail?

"Through the retail network, recommended by investment dealers with good disclosure. We sold U.S. and Australian dollar bonds this way."

Did you sell any Canadian names?

"Some part of Nova Scotia might have gone to individuals, but this ["samurai" deal] was not primarily focused on retail. We may do it in the future."

For Canada, are you looking at securites in Canadian dollars or in yen?

"Yen-denominated. The retail investor is like my grandfather, mom, and pop — when it comes to a product with foreign exchange risk, they might be interested in U.S. or Australian dollars. But when it comes to other currencies, the Canadian dollar is still a new frontier. Maybe later, but not at this moment. To sell Canadian names we need more PR, we need to disseminate the true story of Canada, to explain the value of investing in Canada."

A "samurai issue" is the traditional method of tapping the Japanese bond market. "Samurais" are yen bonds issued on the local market by foreign borrowers. In August 1994, Nova Scotia inked a ¥35-billion issue led by Yamaichi, the year's only samurai. Samurais are infrequent; Japan's tightly regulated domestic market has the effect of nudging borrowers toward the more accessible, cheaper Euroyen market. In 1994, in order of magnitude, Ontario, Quebec, British Columbia, Alberta, Nova Scotia, and Hydro-Québec issed ¥318.5 billion ($4.5 billion [CA]) worth of Euroyen bonds, 80 percent of which were sold to Japanese institutions. Each issue took the form of public MTNs, with the exception of a ¥100-billion Ontario jumbo in ordinary bonds. Maturities ranged from two to twenty years at rates of from 3 to 5 percent. Yamaichi-organized private investments totalled ¥113 billion ($1.6 billion [CA]), not including yen loans granted by insurance companies, which are not covered by the statistics. Liabilities were estimated by the Canadian Embassy at more than $5 billion (CA) in March 1994, up $2 billion from the previous fiscal year.[3]

Soon after I left Japan, Yamaichi published a quarter-page ad in the *Nikkei Nihon Shinbun* announcing the sale of yen bonds issued by Quebec, bearing 3.55 percent interest and maturing in 1998. Denominations began at ¥100,000 ($1,460 [CA]). Interested persons should contact their investment dealer. The ¥50-billion ($712-million [CA]) issue was the first to be placed on the retail market by a Canadian borrower.

The bureaucrats

FRIDAY, FEBRUARY 10, 1995

This strange place must be a pen-pusher's paradise. Doors open onto offices crammed with desks, each topped with stacks of documents that seem to defy gravity. There is not a computer in sight. A small army of clerical workers, shoehorned so closely together they can hardly move, pores over files. The door at the far end of the corridor leads to a large room with cracked walls and peeling paint. Behind a glass barrier I spot traders at work at their desks. On the near side of the barrier stand solid wooden tables covered with green plastic, barely shielded from the din of the room by modular acoustic panels. I have stepped into the heart of the Japanese bureaucracy. We take a seat at the last table. Space is at a premium; every other seat in the room is occupied.

The man sitting across from me is polite but firm. I may use neither his name nor that of his organization. Through my interpreter I argue for twenty minutes. Finally I give up the struggle, agreeing not to attribute the information he will provide to me. But I put him on notice that I will be writing about his organization. There is nothing quite like the Japanese Postal Service and its network of 24,000 substations, the agency whose financial services department is the world's largest pool of private savings. It probably holds the largest number of Canadian securities outside of Canada.

In preparation for my expedition to Japan, I sent all the financial institutions I intended to visit an outline of my research project, including a general list of the questions I wished to ask. My host is looking at a translation of the question list, whispers the interpreter. Worse yet, the answers are already written out. The man reads questions and answers; the interpreter interprets; I jot down notes. When I dare a follow-up question he holds up his hand for silence. Only at the end of this extraordinary encounter do I open my mouth, and only then to thank him politely. I've never seen anything like it in my career as a journalist. Most astonishing of all, nothing the bureaucrat told me was either interesting or useful. Nothing but hot air, and every word of it off the record. Not the end of the world. Public documents exist, and many of the people I met were happy to talk about the much-feared, much-criticized Japanese Postal Service.

First, let's start at the beginning. When Japan built its first railroad in 1873, it was obliged to turn to London bankers to raise capital. Vowing never to repeat the experience, the government of the day set up the Postal Savings Bureau, called Yucho, which has since financed public infrastructures, via loans to the ministry of Finance. But since 1987, a portion of total savings has been diverted into a special Yucho-managed fund, which was set up to yield more than meagre government interest payments. This fund has now reached ¥25 trillion, 9 percent of which is held in foreign bonds. Yucho's big sister Kampo, the Postal Service life insurance subsidiary, boasts assets of ¥74 trillion, 6 percent in foreign paper. Together, Yucho and Kampo manage assets of more than $1 trillion (CA) (or $1,115 billion [CA]), including $389 billion (CA) in foreign securities, almost twice that held by Canada's six largest chartered banks. Now we're really talking big money. The Japanese Postal Service has strong hands, holding onto the securities it purchases until maturity, which doesn't stop

Wall Street from lying awake nights wondering what it might or might not do with its American bond holdings. Imagine what might happen to its Canadian securities . . . ?

Of the foreign securities held by Yucho in March 1994, 21 percent were issued by Canadian borrowers, and 18 percent were denominated in Canadian dollars. Kampo's most recent annual report publishes no figures, but the 1993 edition indicated that 22 percent of its foreign bond holdings carried Canadian names, with 17 percent denominated in Canadian dollars, all rated A or higher. These are phenomenal percentages, especially when we bear in mind that Canada accounts for only 3 percent of the world bond market. A Canadian Embassy survey of eighty-nine Japanese financial institutions revealed that a group of seven public and quasi-public agencies (dominated by Kampo and Yucho, but also including the Norinchukin Bank) held, as of March 1994, nearly \$15 billion (CA) worth of Canadian bonds. Only a handful of Canadian institutions can boast holdings of this magnitude. More than a third of the portfolio is devoted to federal government securities; the remainder consists of provincial and hydro utility paper. In fact, this small group held almost as many Canadian securities as the twenty-five life insurance companies that answered the questionnaire combined.

Several sources indicated that the Postal Service continued to strengthen its position in Canadian bonds through the end of 1993. It has only recently begun to sell, but in small amounts. The government has also recently loosened regulations, allowing it to hedge its foreign exchange risk; losses in Canadian bonds have been huge. Japanese financial circles have been critical of Yucho and Kampo for what they say is unfair competition with private-sector firms, but few are prepared to make their views public. In Japan, the bureaucracy is still king of the hill.

Canadian investment dealers

MONDAY, FEBRUARY 13, 1995

The fastest way from point A to point B is the Tokyo subway system. This morning, the Mita line is jammed with teenagers in uniform on their way to school at a private institution. The boys are dressed in stiff-collared blue jackets, white shirts, and ties; the girls are wearing pleated skirts, blouses with lace trim, blazers, and hats with ribbons. Boys' and girls' black shoes are polished to a high gloss. Businessmen in well-cut dark suits are engrossed in their newspapers, or hidden behind a thick volume of one of Japan's popular, grotesquely violent comic books; a few are snoozing quietly in their seats. Tokyo's women, more elegantly dressed and better groomed than their Parisian counterparts, tend to read novels: *Akaje no Ann* (Lucy Maud Montgomery's *Anne of Green Gables*) is a perennial favourite in Japan. It's not hard to understand the terror that must have swept through this peaceful throng of commuters when the Aoum Shinri Kyo sect attacked the subway system with sarin gas a few weeks later. We get off at Hibiya Station. My guide pulls out her city map: as most Tokyo streets have no names, we must navigate by landmarks.

Nobukatsu Nishimura is Wood Gundy's man in Tokyo. The Toronto-based investment dealer first opened an agency here in 1973 and finally earned the right to negotiate directly with Japanese financial institutions in 1990. Next door is Wood Gundy's owner, CIBC. Nishimura sells mostly Canada-related products and services, but he has managed to nail down a few mandates from Japanese firms looking to borrow on the Eurocan market. "The life insurance companies are very, very cautious about the country risk, the credit risk," he says. When they picked up huge quantities of foreign bonds in the late 1980s, "they wanted high coupon, but quite low risk. For them, Canadian and provincial bonds presented very low risk." Credit ratings were higher then. With their enormous financial reserves, the insurance companies could easily take on the foreign exchange risk. At the peak of the cycle, Canadian names accounted for nearly 15 percent of all foreign securities in their portfolios, a huge percentage compared to Canada's weight on world markets. When the speculative bubble burst, they scaled back their position in a disciplined, gradual way. "But if you look at the total Canadian credit, including yen bonds and loans, the total outstanding balance declined very little."

Aside from the foreign exchange risk, what other risks are there involved with Canadian names? I ask. Selling corporate paper has become tougher following the Olympia & York fiasco, he explains, adding: "The

124

rating done by Moody's and Standard & Poor's is very important for government and public utilities. As long as they maintain AA, it's super, no problem. Single A, case by case. Triple B: have to sell."

Quebec is a large borrower with a single-A rating. How do you deal with that? "It depends on the investor. Some say: no more at this moment. For others, it depends on the interest rate. The biggest problem with Quebec is political. Institutional investors always make their investment decisions based on the worst-case scenario. The worst-case scenario is the separation of Quebec from Canada. Although they believe that the worst scenario will not happen," Nishimura says. Budgetary problems are also a cause for worry. "Japanese investors are very concerned about the issue of deficits, because it is one of the reasons the Canadian dollar is so weak."

Nishimura is not optimistic about the short-term future for foreign currency securities. The yen is expected to rise further; foreign exchange hedging on positions in the billions is costly business. The huge trade surplus that has been driving the yen to record highs will not be eliminated by American pressure to force Japan to open up its markets. The social cohesion built into Japanese culture means that consumers will continue to seek out local products. People are willing to pay more to keep their compatriots at work.

....

Kazuhide Tanaka speaks unaccented English. Before joining ScotiaMcLeod as vice president of their newly opened Tokyo office in 1985, he worked two years in Toronto for Yamaichi. No one these days is buying Canadian securities in Canadian dollars, so Tanaka devotes most of his time to Japanese borrowers who come to the Eurocan market where, surprisingly, after a swap, they can nail down a lower interest rate than in Japan. Tanaka also organizes private investments in yen for Canadian borrowers.

Institutional investors "stay away from the Canadian dollar right now," he says. For one excellent reason. Tanaka shows me a chart comparing 1994 ten-year bond yields for different countries. The chart breaks down the yield figures by the investor's currency of reference. All figures are presented in parentheses, indicating negative yields. The general increase in interest rates has driven world bond markets down. Canadians who held

Canada bonds lost 9 percent. Japanese who held JGBs took a loss of 7 percent. But Japanese or Germans who happened to hold a Canadian security ended up poorer by 23 percent! The costly exchange loss hastened the collapse of the market in Canadian bonds. That's certainly worse than the 16 percent lost by the Japanese in U.S. Treasuries.

The loonie has depreciated because of Canada's political and fiscal problems, says Tanaka. "There is a consensus view on that around the world." Does that mean the Japanese have given up on Canada? "I think that because they have been bitten so badly with forex losses over the last ten years, I can't see them going back in huge size. But as part of portfolio diversification, I think it would be prudent of them to consider Canada." Nevertheless, he's not about to play the forecasting game. "Their decision-making process is sometimes quite difficult to understand. They keep their cards very close to the chest. Unlike institutional investors in North America, for instance, you don't have an idea of their holdings on an issue-by-issue basis, so that we can recommend certain trades to assist them. They just take a sit-and-hold attitude with their portfolio. It's frustrating for us."

Luckily, the Japanese continue to buy Canadian Eurobonds denominated in yen. Large British Columbia and Ontario issues have gone very well. Most Canadian provinces have been able to take advantage of looser Japanese regulations to make private investments, including several under EMTN programs. Quebec was the first among the provinces to set up such a program, followed by Hydro-Québec, Ontario, British Columbia, and, more recently, Alberta and Saskatchewan. "From the credit perspective, I don't think there is anything wrong with Canadian names. Most are still in the AA category." Besides, he adds, not all investors pay the same attention to credit ratings. "The broadest stroke that you can draw is that they like AA or better. But obviously there are exceptions. What has been disconcerting is that a lot of Canadian names have faced downgrades in the last three years, especially Ontario." Tanaka hopes the situation will right itself; investors become more rapidly saturated with lower-rated securities than with better quality paper, meaning he will have to work harder to sell a single A, such as Quebec.

Risk, you say?

TUESDAY, FEBRUARY 14, 1995

With assets of ¥44 trillion ($636 billion [CA]) the Norinchukin bank is one of Japan's largest. It is also the central bank for a system of agricultural, fishing, and forestry cooperatives that has long since outgrown its original role, and so the bank now operates offices in many of the world's financial capitals. I meet Takahiro Komatsu, international bond investment manager, in a lavish reception room decorated with Miró and Braque lithographs. The low table between us displays a crystal cigarette box, with matching ashtray and lighter. Komatsu compares his institution with the Caisse centrale Desjardins, which he visited for three days a decade ago on a fact-finding mission on interest rate management in an age of deregulation. Interest rates were liberalized only in 1994 in Japan, and the process is not yet complete.

Because Japanese banks are authorized to borrow in foreign currencies, their foreign bond investment strategies are radically different from those of the institutions we've visited thus far. Norinchukin does not convert yen into foreign currency for investment abroad, Komatsu explains through my interpreter. The bank prefers to borrow those foreign currencies from foreign banks. "The difference between the financing rate and the investment rate is our profit." Financing is short term, while investment is long term, he explains. "For us, finding the right moment is the key consideration." Bonds are bought when dropping rates and rising values can be forecast, usually after analysis of the three- or four-year interest rate cycle. Because the yen value of the foreign currency purchased varies in proportion to the value of the currency it must repay, Norinchukin avoids foreign exchange risk. But the bank is exposed to interest rate risk. A rising yield curve with short-term rates lower than long-term ones is vital. If the curve turns downward, if long-term rates fall below short-term rates, the bank will lose money.

Despite my polite insistence, Mr. Komatsu declines to provide me with hard data on the size of foreign bond investments, which other sources have described as considerable. He will admit that U.S. securities make up a significant segment of his portfolio, the rest being divided among bonds from other G7 countries, with Canada slightly ahead of the rest. The quantity of the Canadian bonds held by the bank has changed little over the last three years, he adds. Meaning: he has not sold.

Credit ratings are not a significant factor in the choice of securities, "since we purchase from public agencies." Most of this paper is rated AA, "but we don't apply any strict criteria here," says Komatsu. What risks do you associate with Canadian bonds? I ask. "I don't see any specific Canada-related risks. If there are, would you please point them out to me?" Well, the deficit, and the Quebec question . . . "Many countries have a deficit problem. And the question of ethnic independence exists in other countries as well; it is certainly not unique to Canada."

A loud, clear message

On the ground floor of the new Nippon Life headquarters in Tokyo's Hibiya district, three impeccably uniformed young ladies rise to greet me with gracious smiles — a welcome change from the usual gruff security guard growling in his granite bunker. By the time I reach the eleventh-floor reception desk, where four more young ladies dressed in the same uniform welcome me with smiles, I'm ready to switch insurance companies here and now!

With assets of $495 billion (CA), Nippon Life is the world's largest life insurance company, ten times larger than Canada's biggest, Manufacturers Life, and twice as large as the American giant, Prudential. Its 80,000-strong sales force taps the savings of 20 million customers, who view insurance products as a way of earning a few yen over the meagre interest rates paid by the banks. One of the four smiling hostesses guides me to Room 12, where I meet Jun Sakazaki, deputy general manager, international investment department. The interview takes place in English.

The groundswell of investment in foreign securities began in 1977, Sakazaki tells me. Interest payments from Japanese bonds were inadequate to cover the cost of guaranteed dividends to policy holders. Capital gains could not be used to pay dividends; using interest income was the only option. "The wide interest rate differentials between Japan and the

United States became quite attractive, even though we had to take a foreign exchange risk." It was an era when insurance companies could readily compensate for foreign exchange losses with capital gains on Japanese shares. Japan's quirky accounting standards mean that corporations hold huge hidden reserves called "unrealized gains." The value of shares held in a portfolio is not readjusted as share values rise on the stock market, as happens in other markets. Nippon Life holds nearly 3 percent of all the shares listed on the Tokyo stock exchange. Many were purchased following the war and reflect the complex web of interlocking stock ownership that still characterizes Japan's industrial and financial groups. These corporate shares are still listed at their historic cost. To register a capital gain, a bank need only sell several such shares, then buy them back. By posting a new purchase price much higher than the first, it can nail down a capital gain to compensate forex losses on foreign bonds. "It can be rationalized as a kind of conversion of capital gain into income gain," Sakazaki explains. At the peak of the wave, in 1989, nearly 18 percent of assets were denominated in foreign currencies; 70 percent was invested in countries offering high interest rates, meaning those belonging to the dollar bloc. Canada alone accounted for almost 20 percent of foreign currency investments, nearly $7 billion (CA), one of the largest positions in Canadian bonds ever held by a foreign investor.

But "we have been reducing our total foreign exposure for the last five years, mainly because of yen appreciation against the U.S. dollar," he says. There were other factors behind the decision. Three years ago, restrictions governing use of capital gains in paying dividends were abolished, and the dividend rate was lowered to reflect Japan's weak interest rates. And when the speculation-driven "bubble era" of the 1980s finally burst, the collapse of the Japanese stock exchange let most of the air out of the "unrealized gains" balloon. New regulations have instituted stricter capitalization ratios to underwrite risky investments, like those denominated in foreign currencies. In the new context, says Sakazaki, "I don't think that from now on we will have a drastic increase in foreign bond investments."

Nippon Life reduced its position by setting up selling priorities: first, the Canadian dollar, followed by the Australian dollar; then the American dollar, where it maintained a certain level. From March 1993 to March 1994, the firm shed fully a quarter of its foreign bond portfolio, with

Canada's share slipping from 14.5 percent ($3 billion [CA]) to zero. Australia was also erased, while the weight of the U.S. dollar dropped from 38 percent to 36 percent. At the same time, investment in the principal European currencies was diversified. "Now we are much more active to reallocate and rebalance the portfolio content than in the past," he explains. Nippon Life now hedges its exchange risk more aggressively and is even considering the use of American indices for weighting its international bond portfolio.

According to Sakazuki, the firm sold off Canada and Australia because the Canadian and Australian dollars proved weaker than the American dollar in relation to the yen. A close examination of current accounts and capital flow volatility in and out of Canada shows that the Canadian dollar is more fragile. "It does not mean that we completely gave up or abandoned the Canadian market, but it is not an appropriate market for long-term buy-and-hold type of investments. Rather a kind of hit-and-run type, depending on the interest rate differentials and the outlook of the currency." Ditto for the Australian market, he adds. And for Nippon Life to move back into Canada? "Well, some solution for the Quebec political problem, action on the deficit." Then, after a few seconds' hesitation, he adds that he hopes the Bank of Canada will hold down inflation when growth resumes. "Of course, the strength of the yen compared to the American dollar is the main consideration."

How important are the credit ratings? The bank keeps an eye on Moody's and Standard & Poor's, "but when we take a foreign exchange risk we don't also take a credit risk. We concentrate on government bonds bought on the secondary market." It is a policy that eliminates Canadian-dollar provincial bonds, despite the fact that Nippon Life used to hold a handful. The company accepts higher credit risks in yen-denominated paper, with the AA rating as a cutoff point. Anything lower calls for strong persuasion. Sakazaki has bought several provinces on the Euroyen market, but in small sizes. The company did not participate in the provinces' recent yen sale, but it did lend them funds. In spring 1994, North America accounted for 20 percent of syndicated yen loans ($3.8 billion [CA]). These loans are private deals that are rarely discussed. Nippon Life's list of the continent's largest borrowers contains only four names: Quebec, Saskatchewan, Manitoba, and New Brunswick.

The Americans

WEDNESDAY, FEBRUARY 15, 1995

As a matter of policy, this New York–based investment dealer prohibits its employees from talking with journalists on the record. We strike an agreement: I'm allowed to describe the firm as one of the most influential on world markets, the Canadian bond market included. The man I'm talking with is an American who has worked in New York, Toronto, and Tokyo. The Americans were generally takers when the Japanese liquidated their Canadian securities portfolio in 1993 and 1994; my source, like most American intermediaries, had a ringside seat on a round of wheeling and dealing that his Canadian competitors never witnessed.

But the movement of capital, which gained momentum in the spring of 1994, was no fire sale. Each deal was carefully organized into large blocks of $1 billion (CA), then distributed in tranches of $200–$300 million. Each operation could either be drawn out over a month or completed with a brief telephone call. The firm combines solidity with a high propensity for risk. But it is also reluctant to take on more than $100 million during Tokyo business hours because of the difficulty of reselling such a position on the Asian market. Customers are encouraged to wait for New York markets to open, explains my source; if they do not, the dealer's price simply won't be attractive, since it will include an additional risk premium justified by the absence of liquidity. As this vice president put it, "it was not a vote against Canada, it was a vote to get back into yen. It just so happened they had very, very large positions in Canada." The country was simply overrepresented in their portfolio. The same thing happened to Australia and Europe; the Americans suffered less.

Today, the Bank of Canada is auctioning off $3.7 billion (CA) in five-year Canada bonds. Neither this investment dealer, nor four others I queried in Tokyo, expects to see a single client purchase a single one of the securities. But, says my source, "I hear there is interest for Canadian names in yen, particularly for Quebec." From here, the province's spreads look good. "Quebec is a very good global name," well known, with large issues, strongly backed by investment dealers. As far as politics are concerned, the Japanese read the same polls as everybody else; a No victory is taken for granted here. Ontario shares many of Quebec's qualities, but it hasn't had a very high profile on the Japanese market. Quebec enjoys some real advantages. The variety of issuers on the Japanese market is limited: aside from JGBs, investors can pick up five-year paper issued by the banks, and a handful of corporate paper, leaving the yield curve full of holes, particularly in the long term. Quebec issues, EMTN in particular, are tailored to fill those holes. Since Eurobonds are not listed on the stock exchange, investors are not obliged to adjust book values to reflect market value.

In Japan, a country where appearances must be protected at all costs, cooking the balance sheet — known as "window dressing" — has become an art form as esteemed as the traditional Ikebana school of flower arrangement. Managers are shifted frequently to new positions, and thus find it to their advantage to conceal problems that they will probably never have to solve themselves. In applying the 15-percent rule for exchange losses, some inventive insurance companies purchase even more foreign bonds before the end of the fiscal year on March 31, in order to bring down the average cost and to slip in under the 15-percent limit, as happened in 1993. If the limbo dancer cannot clear the bar and must absorb the loss, he might decide to sell before the end of the fiscal year, or at the beginning of the next. This is what happened in 1994, at the start of the new fiscal year. For the month of April alone, net sales of Canadian bonds held by Japanese amounted to $2.2 billion (CA), doubling the preceding month's volume; compare that to the previous fiscal year, in which they'd eliminated a total of $8.7 billion (CA) from their portfolio. Some Toronto observers attributed these massive sales to Bloc Québécois leader Lucien Bouchard's foreign excursions. The reality is more prosaic: for the Japanese, spring is the decision-making season; the devastating effects of the *endaka* were uppermost in their minds.

Insurance companies now employ more complex risk-management strategies to distinguish between currency and bond-market decisions, each of which are made by a separate department. Policies can vary from one firm to another, but in most cases the hedge on foreign exchange oscillates between 30 percent and 80 percent. A firm with $1 billion in Canadian bonds with a 50-percent hedge is said to have a net position of

$500 million in Canadian dollars. A 100-percent hedge can be costly, eliminating the entire interest differential between Japanese and Canadian bonds. Japanese traders "often see Canadian debt as a high yield version of U.S. debt." An advantage, notes my source. If the Japanese return to the American market, they'll return to Canada . . .

Visiting a fund manager

FRIDAY, FEBRUARY 17, 1995

Tomoo Sato, a man with a perpetual smile, manages to be timid and forthcoming at the same time. We've settled into a small room just off the trading room where, as portfolio manager for Yasuda Trust, Japan's fourth-ranking trust company, Mr. Sato supervises non-yen investments. His division administers ¥4 trillon ($57 billion [CA]) for private pension funds; another division manages public sector pension funds.

Of this capital, 6 percent is invested in foreign bonds and another 11 percent in foreign shares, he explains. Shares are preferred over bonds because their higher long-term yield better compensates for the exchange risk associated with an overseas investment. Stock markets are also less synchronized in their ebb and flow than bond markets, which makes for better risk diversification. The international bond portfolio is weighted on the Salomon Brothers index, minus Japanese securities and those of countries that are too small to capture the attention of fund managers. Yasuda invests in the United States, Canada, the United Kingdom, Germany, France, Italy, and Denmark. For the last two years the trust company has awarded an overweighted position to Germany and France, but has underweighted the United States. Now Mr. Sato, who is bullish on the American dollar, contemplates reversing that position. "The yen is much overvalued against any currency," a position mirrored in a very low foreign exchange hedge: 30 percent of the dollar position is protected against a fall, compared to only 20 percent of the Deutschmark position.

What does he think about Canada? For the last two years, Canada's weight stood equivalent to the modified index, at 4 percent, but it has recently been overweighted to 5 percent, which represents $140 million (CA).

"But probably too early," he says with a nervous laugh. "My only concern is the currency." He pulls out a chart, indicating that the Canadian dollar rate is at a historic low, making our loonie a bargain. But Mr. Sato hopes it will slide no further. Why is the dollar so weak? Public debt, of course; and the political uncertainty created by the Quebec issue. "I was a bit puzzled," he admits, "to see the strengthening of the Canadian dollar after the Quebec election." And on the question of the debt, he remains cautious: "Are the governments really doing something about the debt? Can we trust them?"

Using Bloomberg's charts, Mr. Sato plays the yield spreads between Canada and the United States, buying Canadian securities when the spread is wide and selling them when it narrows. In other words, he buys when Canadas are cheap relative to their historical average and sells when they are relatively expensive. Using this method, he bought securities in the spring of 1994, which he sold in the aftermath of the Quebec election, but in small amounts. Mr. Sato likes bucking market trends. He chooses government paper on the Canadian market, but leans toward provincial borrowings on the Eurocan market; these are easier to trade because the time difference with Europe is less than with Canada. Yasuda is sticky about credit, settling for nothing less than AA. When Quebec was downgraded to A, approval from top management was needed to keep the securities. Mr. Sato is saddened by the decline of provincial credit ratings, and irritated by the uneven liquidity of their paper.

Finally, says my host, not enough information about Canada is available, outside of investment dealer research and Bloomberg dispatches. "It is very difficult to follow the economic indicators," he says. A few years ago there were five Japanese journalists stationed in Canada; today there is only one. And Canada has absolutely no journalists in Japan. But today is an exception. Information on Canada is abundant. The country's second-ranking daily, *Asahi Shinbun*, has covered Finance minister Paul Martin's Washington press briefing. Its lead reads: "With Canada's serious deficit, the Canadian dollar fell to a nine-year low when the Mexican peso faced a crisis in January and the dollar moved in connection with the currencies of other emerging markets." The reporter notes Martin's disagreement with the Canada-Mexico analogy, going on to attribute the decline of the Canadian dollar to the country's financial problems, exacerbated by the referendum on Quebec independence. "The markets' vague concerns were just activated by the Mexican peso crisis," the article concluded.[4] Mr. Sato will be no more reassured when he reads in the evening edition of the *Nihon Keizai Shinbun*: "Moody's considering downgrading Canadian bond rating; Agency concerned about medium-term deficit outlook."[5]

A reporter's notebook

On the long flight home I skim over my notes. Tokyo's fashionable shops have English names; its chic boutiques, French ones. In spite of mind-boggling prices, the Japanese are inveterate consumers, from the humble Big Mac Trio at ¥600 ($8.55 [CA]) to Debailleul iced pastries imported from Brussels at ¥1000 ($14 [CA]) a shot, and small cakes at ¥5,000 ($71 [CA]). In Japan, prices are astronomical.

The Japanese do not have Europe's long experience in foreign investment; the learning process has been a painful one. Forced to recycle the capital from their huge trade surplus, and to augment the slender interest income available on the domestic market, they have accumulated vast quantities of North American bonds. In the second half of the 1980s, the generous coupons attached to Canadian bonds became irresistible. Exchange risk hedging was then forbidden by regulation; a rising yen cost people their fortunes. Of the eight largest insurance companies, each of which held more than $1 billion worth of Canadian securities denominated in Canadian dollars, only two still possess significant blocks. The Canadian Embassy's annual survey of Japanese financial institutions reveals that the sell-off of Canadian paper hit the federal government hardest. Meanwhile, investors purchased provincial securities denominated in yens and increased their yen loans. In all, the Canadian names portfolio dipped more than $8.4 billion (CA) in fiscal 1994, reaching $45.6 billion. The Canadian dollar portion of these assets slipped from 69 percent to 60 percent; that denominated in U.S. dollars dropped from 18 percent to 16 percent, while the yen portion jumped from 12 percent to 23 percent.[6]

Japanese managers prefer to buy and hold their securities. Their decision-making process is group-based, and too slow and deliberate to allow them to pick up on fleeting arbitrage opportunities. But the trend is

135

toward more active and refined portfolio management. Institutions still behave gregariously, but less so than in the past. As a whole, however, managers remain a cautious lot; they are not paid well enough to assume risks. They might be well acquainted with the crucial facts, but ofttimes the homogeneous nature of the business culture does not allow them to develop a more personal, North American take on market developments. Only a handful of Japanese financial analysts keep abreast of the Canadian scene. Portfolio managers read the research from New York and Toronto investment dealers, of course. But several of the people I met admitted that their principal source of information was the Canadian Embassy in Tokyo, indicating a naiveté that would draw giggles from American or European financiers. Constant rotation of responsibilities within firms is another obstacle to building up solid Canada-related expertise. No one I met had a clear understanding of the deficit and Quebec issues. The Japanese are poorly informed on the PQ's political agenda; for this homogeneous people, the idea of secession is incomprehensible. They continue to monitor the situation, but they feel that Quebec independence is unlikely. If they turn out to be wrong, they might be more distraught than other foreign investors. In short, our fate depends on people who know us very little. It doesn't help matters that we know them no better.

The Japanese believe their bond investment opportunities are limited. Obsessed with the strong growth of their Asian neighbours, they build factories and purchase equity there. But in none of these countries does the bond market have sufficient depth. Confidence in Europe is tempered by apprehensions of Russia, narrowing their choice to countries like Germany, France, and the United Kingdom. So, in spite of their losses, the Japanese still prefer the dollar bloc. Nonetheless, a return to the Canadian dollar is unlikely before the greenback stabilizes or appreciates relative to the yen. While they wait, Japanese investors purchase Canadian securities denominated in yens. They may not like the loonie, but they still trust the creditworthiness of Canadian governments.

Chapter 6

ADAM SMITH STRIKES BACK

OTTAWA, MONDAY, FEBRUARY 27, 1995

TWO DOZEN PEOPLE in dark suits are lined up in front of me in the basement of the Ottawa Congress Centre. Check your weapons at the door, security staff warn: cellular telephones are duly surrendered. The $26.90 admission price — tax included, no change provided — gets each participant a grey packet of documents and a cup of coffee. Documents in hand, the suits file into the windowless room, take a seat at one of the round tables, arrange the documents in front of them, and pull calculators from briefcases. At 3:00 p.m. sharp the door swings shut; latecomers may filter in, but no one can get out: the economists' lockup is underway. One and a half hours before Finance minister Paul Martin brings down his budget in the House of Commons, my studious group of bank economists, investment dealers, analysts, forecasting agency experts, and research institute policy wonks learns the magic number: $32.7 billion, next year's forecast deficit. Jeffrey Moore, analyst for Dominion Bond Rating Service (DBRS), has brought his computer along. Opening the thickest booklet, he begins keying statistics into a spread sheet. This evening, back in Toronto, a four-person committee at DBRS will slog its way through the data to produce a preliminary judgment on the budget.

A few moments later David Dodge, the deputy minister of Finance, makes his entrance, surrounded by a flying squad of high-ranking civil servants. Calm, cool, and collected, he outlines the budget, flitting from highlight to highlight. The message is simple: mission accomplished. The government's economic hypotheses are conservative; substantial reserves have been set aside for unforeseen eventualities. The sales pitch goes down like cold lemonade on a hot day.

Christopher E. Rude, deputy research director at Swiss Bank Corp., has flown from New York for the occasion, armed with a one-page chart entitled "How to read Canadian federal budget headlines." The items listed in the first column leave no doubt about what Mr. Rude is looking for: deficit, dollar deficit reduction, ratio of expenditure reduction to tax increase, a detailed plan for the coming years, debt/GDP ratio, ratio of tax revenue to interest payment, and, finally, growth, inflation, and interest rate hypotheses. The next three columns are labelled "good budget," "expected budget," and "bad budget." After a quick scan of the documents he hazards a snap judgment. "It falls mostly on good," he says. "The minister actually cuts expenses for the first year," notes Andrew Spencer, senior economist for Citibank Canada. "It's a very, very good start. I think the market will react positively." Tom Courchene, of the John Deutsch Institute for the Study of Economic Policy at Queen's University, is jubilant. He reads the budget as a swing toward decentralized federalism. But his colleague Monique Jérôme-Forget, president of the Montreal-based Institute for Research in Public Policy, remains sceptical. The budget seems to have little to offer for Quebec.

Upstairs, in a much larger room, the tension is thick enough to slice. Nearly six hundred print and electronic media journalists and technicians have been sequestered since 11:00 a.m., poring feverishly over the same documents. It's a simple enough job: discover what the minister has up his sleeve, nail the key details, and get the numbers right, all in time for the evening news or tonight's deadline for tomorrow's first edition.

Dr. Sherryl Cooper, first vice president and chief economist at Nesbitt Burns, Canada's largest investment dealer, is one of the handful of financial analysts working the hall. Cooper, a former assistant to former Fed potentate Paul Volcker, is one of the most respected commentators in the financial community. Cooper has been gearing up for the budget for several weeks. "To be honest, we have already determined what the market would like to see. We tell the market what would be good versus not good. And we make those assessments based on our analysis." She has Ottawa's ear, too; she sat in on several pre-budget consulting sessions with high-ranking civil servants and politicians. "The business community was lobbying the government very, very hard. And of course we had the currency crisis in January and the Moody's threat of a downgrade. I was just convinced they understood. This government has been quite good at sending up trial balloons," she says. When she walked into the hall, she was already expecting a $10–$12 billion reduction in the deficit over two years, due primarily to reduced spending, significant reserves, and moderate economic assumptions.

The lockup is only a few minutes old and already Dr. Cooper is digging into the two-hundred-page budget document, ignoring Martin's speech and the sheaf of press releases. "I knew what I was looking for. When I open the budget document, I go to the page that has the net effects of this budget. That gives you any changes in taxes, or cuts in government spending, generated by this budget alone. It also gives you the deficit financing requirements and the contingency reserves. The minute I saw it, I knew it was a good budget. Then I turned to the page of economic assumptions [which support the budget forecasts] to confirm that, then read the details of what were the spending cuts and tax increases." But Cooper's efforts to draft an analysis are foiled by the journalists; before day's end she will have given a good thirty interviews. Luckily, she can turn for support to senior economist David Rosenberg and an assistant. Rosenberg plows through the fiscal fine print. The assistant types in data that he will use to generate presentation-quality graphics. Cooper, meanwhile, focuses on what she calls the architecture of the budget. "I don't get involved with minutiae because I am not an accountant," she says.

A few moments before the lockup ends, Cooper and a handful of journalists climb into a special bus, under close escort, for Parliament Hill. As soon as Martin's budget speech begins, the police allow the passengers to leave the bus and rush into the lobby of the House, where a television set has been installed especially for budget night. As Cooper delivers her first impressions, live, to CTV's Lloyd Robertson, Rosenberg is on the line to Nesbitt Burns's Toronto headquarters. A few moments later he faxes budget highlights to the firm's Canadian subsidiaries, and to its New York, Chicago, and London offices. Her TV stint ended, Cooper jumps into a taxi and heads straight for the airport. But the return trip to Toronto turns out to be longer than expected. A blizzard has swept across southern Ontario, and flights have been cancelled or delayed. When she finally arrives, at 9:00 that evening, she still has a good five hours of work in front of her.

Congratulations, Mr. Martin

TORONTO, TUESDAY, FEBRUARY 28, 1995

The breakfast of scrambled eggs, bacon and sausage, croissants, Danish, and coffee is hardly spectacular, but it will have to do for the several hundred stock brokers and investors who have slogged their way through the fresh snow at the crack of dawn to the Metropolitan Toronto Convention Centre. Still rubbing their eyes, they scan Sherryl Cooper's report. Its title reads: "Congratulations, Mr. Martin!" The diminutive woman with the jet-black hair and the crimson dress strides up to the lectern: "I have unmitigated praise for this budget," she proclaims, in a piercing voice. Finally, "a seminal change that will put us on the path to debt reduction." Using economic assumptions slightly less pessimistic than the minister's, Dr. Cooper predicts a \$10–\$13 billion deficit for fiscal 1996–97, the equivalent of 1 percent of GDP, well below Martin's 3-percent target. Allowing for growth, the federal debt will account for 72.5 percent of GDP, a slight decrease from its current level of 73.25 percent. The next speaker, her colleague David Rosenberg, picks the budget apart one line at a time. It will be a tough one, he concludes, flashing slides on a screen: "Increasingly, we will all be required to pay more, and receive less, on the road to fiscal balance. Over the next two years, Canadians can expect to receive just 78.5 cents in government services for each tax dollar sent to Ottawa, compared with 95 cents in the fiscal year that is about to end. This ratio will slip below 72 cents in fiscal year 1997–98."

Was such a tough budget really necessary? I ask Dr. Cooper after her presentation. Her response: Debt cannot be allowed to go on growing faster than the economy; we must turn back. "Why would foreigners hold that debt if they believe that the currency is going to plunge? There is a huge risk in being as indebted as we are and in being reliant on foreign capital for funding." Like Mexico, Canada has a current payments deficit, meaning it consumes more than it produces. To finance the differential

140

"we are critically reliant on hot money." To lure this kind of very mobile money, we are forced to offer high interest rates, much too high for the health of the Canadian economy, argues Cooper. "Mind you, that's not to say that if the debt were domestically held it would be a whole lot easier, because Canadians aren't stupid and they aren't going to hold it either if they believe it is too big a risk."

What she calls the "tremendous volatility" of the markets worries Sherryl Cooper. Ever since the Americans were "brutalized by the Mexican debacle," she notes, "the sensitivity of international investors to debt risks is just enhanced." Second question: is there such a thing as a "debt wall," a kind of absolute borrowing barrier? "It exists," she answers, "in the minds of the investors. It's a psychological phenomenon. If the market decides to repatriate, we are in serious trouble. What would trigger that? I don't know. It is not black and white. This is shady grey. And I don't foresee that we are going to have a crisis in the next year. But can it happen? Absolutely. I spend 50 percent of my day talking to these foreigners. I travel the world extensively. I know what concerns them. They could in a flash reduce their Canadian debt exposure because, let's face it, it's 3 percent of their port-folio." Sure, there's an interest rate that would bring investors back. "But is it a price you can afford to pay? If it is 15 percent, the economy collapses and our deficit gets bigger and bigger." Still, she concludes, "I think the budget has taken us on a big step out of that risk, but it is not over. It could be three, four years before we feel we've truly turned the corner."

The budget speech has touched off a public relations extravaganza, with politicians, analysts, and commentators competing to shape reactions and perceptions in the financial community. After this morning's breakfast, Dr. Cooper will be speaking to 140 Canadian and foreign investors by con-ference call. In the room next door, the auditing firm Price Waterhouse is laying out the tax implications of the budget to its clients. At 9:30, the Finance minister holds his own telephone conference with some 400 Canadian, American, and European financiers. In Tokyo, Trade minister Roy MacLaren has presented the budget to a select group of 100 Japanese investors; his speech was relayed to Hong Kong via a special phone link. In London, Industry minister John Manley is spreading the good news. Doug Peters, secretary of state for International Financial Institutions, covers Frankfurt and Zurich. Yesterday, at the Canadian Consulate in

New York, Transport minister Doug Young watched the budget speech alongside financial analysts and portfolio managers, preparing the ground for Martin's speech this Friday at the Plaza Hotel.

•••••••••••••••••••••••••

A handful of Nesbitt Burns traders were still hanging around in the trading room when I finally got there late last night. A few were talking sports — feet propped up on their desks, hands behind their heads, ties loosened — but most had finally gone home. Head trader Mark Wisniewski, just back from a home-cooked meal, was bouncing his five-year-old daughter Laureen and her toy monkey Curious George on his knee. Even without the snowstorm I could never have made it to Toronto fast enough. The show was over. Thanks to Wisniewski, though, I was able to piece together what had happened.

Most of the day's action had come from buyers, insurance companies and chartered banks in particular, along with a handful of international investors. The activity centred on short-term paper, but the day's largest deal, worth $125 million, involved five-year Canada bonds. Wisniewski was bothered: the firm had been expecting a good budget and hoped to be long in order to profit from the anticipated rise in values. Instead, responding to strong demand, it was forced to sell off securities, finding itself short to the tune of $155 million. A few minutes before the minister opened his mouth, at 4:30, it successfully hedged and fought its way back to long. A good thing, too. During the first ten minutes of the budget speech, bond prices rocketed upward by 50 cents. No sooner had the lockup ended than the highlights of the budget were being disseminated by agencies and analysts; no need to wait for the applause from the government benches. In fact, the good news had been expected, adds Kush Handa, Nesbitt Burns's short-term paper market maker. Here was the evidence: this segment of the yield curve had gained $1.75 since the fall two weeks earlier that had been touched off by Moody's announcement that Canada's rating would be revised.[1] By the end of the day, further stimulation of demand had come from short investors, the people who had bet on a bad budget, attempting to cut their losses. Yesterday's performance by the Canadian market eclipsed its American cousin. As T-bill rates dropped, the tiny Laurentian Bank stole a march on its big sisters, lowering its base rate twenty-five points to 9.25 percent. For the first time in two weeks, the loonie had clawed its way back over the $0.72 (US) level.

When markets opened this morning, traders went on a selling spree to take profits. But as soon as prices showed signs of levelling off, others moved in to buy. Still, despite the constant electronic chirping of telephones, transaction volumes for the day have not been exceptional. A computer screen near Wisniewski's desk displays the firm's position in bar graph form. Each red bar represents a segment of the yield curve: the first two indicate a neutral position in short-term paper; the third, a long position; the next four are neutral; the following two show a short position; and the last indicates a long position in long-term bonds. Wisniewski's job is to make sure that all positions have been set correctly and that risk is kept to a minimum. Nesbitt Burns claims to handle Toronto's largest business volume, which puts its chief trader in an enviable position to read market trends. If the firm contacts one hundred or so investors, most of whom are in the market for five-year paper, Wisniewski can be all but certain that the price of such paper will go up, and he will attempt to buy in as well. But if the firm has talked to only a few dozen clients, Wisniewski's view of the market risks being skewed, or even false. Dealing with a substantial business volume provides a clear advantage. "Our job is to procure liquidity and make money at the same time." To do so successfully, clients need good prices and smart deal proposals. But if a firm like Nesbitt Burns spots an anomaly on the market and suggests an arbitrage that might work to its clients' advantage, it might find itself short on the recommended paper, a position that can be expensive to correct. Worse yet, the client might end up liking the idea so much that he asks a competitor to offer a better price to do the same job. In short, head traders wear the risk manager's hat.

Four traders share the work of setting buy and sell prices for Canada bonds; each one is responsible for a segment of the yield curve, from short to long term. In front of them sits the institutional client sales group; behind them are the traders who deal in provincial securities and Eurobonds; off to the left are the specialists in corporate paper. In all, perhaps one hundred traders deal in fixed-income instruments here, in the old trading room. In a few months, the Nesbitt Burns traders will be moving into a new facility, alongside the firm's sole shareholder, the Bank of Montreal. The new trading room, Canada's largest, will accommodate

150 people who will not only deal in bonds but will trade shares, money market instruments, forex, and derivatives. There are no women employed as market makers by either of Toronto's investment dealers. Except in sales, it's still primarily a man's world. The dealer's job calls for nerves of steel, just the kind of work that young males with high testosterone levels seem to be most adept at. The four Nesbitt Burns Canada bond market makers have their eyes glued to a bank of monitors. This morning one of them stages a tantrum, dredging up every obscenity in the book. The cause: a technical glitch that has interrupted communications with the Montreal sales office. Burnout is the norm; the atmosphere snaps, crackles, and pops with tension. Most traders last for only a few years before moving on to sales. After all, most institutions prefer to deal with more mature, experienced people.

At 11:25 a rumour that has ScotiaMcLeod leading a $200-million issue for Nova Scotia or New Brunswick has everybody in the room speculating at the top of their lungs. "How about a refreshing long deal?" shouts the provincial bond market maker. Three minutes later, the screen in front of him has New Brunswick offering five-year bonds at 8.454 percent, twenty-nine basis points higher than Ontario. It's the Maritime province's first issue on the Canadian market in two years. The dealer curses. Institutions are looking for ten years, not five. New Brunswick has not listened to Nesbitt Burns's advice. But it's too late to complain. Suddenly the trading room springs into action. Salesmen, on their feet in front of their desks, chatter into their telephones, calling out clients' names and price to the market makers as they sell off the merchandise. Within five minutes everything is gone, its attractive price overcoming a lack of enthusiasm for the five-year maturity. Even though Nesbitt Burns's exact market share is a well-kept secret, the firm has placed between 10 and 20 percent of the New Brunswick issue. Its good offices have earned it about 30 cents per $100 of bonds sold, for a total of around $200,000. Unlike the federal government, the provinces do not auction their bonds, paying their syndicate a commission instead. Ironically, notes Wisniewski, there are not enough new provincial issues to meet current demand. Several provinces have cut back on borrowing, and some has taken place on overseas markets. But now Canadian institutions, which are generally underweighted in provincial securities, are buying, and provincial spreads are narrowing.

After lunch I sit down for a chat with Frank Van Veen, a salesman who handles nearly two dozen institutional investors. Two, perhaps three, of these are active in the market every day; five, twice a week, and the rest, twice a month. Van Veen, whose daily volume is upward of $100 million, is part of a sales team consisting of eight salespeople in Toronto, five in Montreal, three in Vancouver, and a handful in Chicago, London, and New York. "Our job is to reflect to traders what our clients want, and our job is to unwind our traders' positions." Part of his job is finding a compromise between what look like contradictory interests. "Traders tend to bend over backwards for good clients," he assures me. If that doesn't work, the salesman will fall back on street savvy. He'll tell the client: "Listen, old chap, I'd love to do it, but my trader just isn't listening to me today." Van Veen makes out a ticket for each deal; the most common run in multiples of $5 million, up to $20 million. Larger transactions fall into the $25–$100 million range, while the biggest ones might hit the $250–$300 million mark. Anything bigger is on a workout basis, he adds. In such cases Nesbitt is no longer a dealer, but becomes a broker, a middleman between several parties, and demands a commission instead of entering the position in the books and hoping for a profit at resale. In recent days, Van Veen has been busily filling out tickets for insurance companies with excess cash on hand. Normally this money gets plowed into mortgages, but right now the real estate market is dragging its feet, and the insurers are buying five-year bonds to offset their liabilities over the same term. The banks are also strong buyers. The RRSP campaign has left them swamped with hard-to-lend funds.

In the late afternoon, Wisniewski sums up the day: a yawner, not one single "plain vanilla" transaction of more than $100 million. The total value traded in the Nesbitt Burns trading room topped the $3-billion mark, with profits close to the half-million level. What looks to me like an astronomical volume is just another ho-hum day for Wisniewski. When the market heats up, Nesbitt Burns can churn out as much as $5 billion in bonds, all to professionals and institutions. Meanwhile, the 1,200 stockbrokers who work in the firm's roughly one hundred branch offices — the people Mark Twain called the "social workers to the rich" — negotiated a piddling $25 million with private individuals. Once again, a predictable event had made its impact on the market well before the event had occurred. The day after a budget favourably received by the financial community — the Dominion Bond Rating Service confirmed its rating for Canada — the value of federal debt had, ironically, declined by approximately 75 cents for the long term, 50 cents for the medium term, and 30 cents for the short term. Meanwhile, the loonie had once again slipped beneath 72 cents (US). Bay Street celebrated with a spate of profit taking.

Abroad, Canada's budget has not exactly set tongues wagging. The *Wall Street Journal* hid its account on page A10. Business press headlines around the world are monopolized by the sudden collapse of Barings Bank, brought down by the wild-eyed speculation of a twenty-eight-year-old trader named Nick Leeson.

Canada's international investors

The low-key offices at OMERS are all but deserted on this early evening. But the assertive personality of Bob Silcox expands to fill the empty space. Silcox, the robust, silver-haired, clear-eyed, and articulate senior vice president of the Ontario Municipal Employees Retirement Board, manages Canada's third largest pension fund. OMERS manages $20 billion on behalf of 1,120 municipalities, local councils, and school boards.

And what does Mr. Silcox think of yesterday's budget speech? "It was an excellent budget, masterfully crafted. But it will take about five more budgets, certainly as strong and as tough, to bring the debt problem in Canada under control and give us some flexibility to deal with recessions." Why should the debt problem concern a pension fund manager? I ask. "It raises the cost of Canada's borrowing," Silcox answers. But rising rates work to the advantage of pensioners, don't they? The answer is no, and Silcox tells me why. To pay out pensions, OMERS must be able to obtain an overall yield of 4.25 percent, after inflation. Allocating capital by asset category becomes the crucial decision: how much in bonds, how much in shares. "That pays about 85 percent of your returns," he notes. If, in 1926, you had invested $100 on the Canadian bond market and reinvested all interest, in 1994 you would only have $4,732, not even enough to keep pace with inflation. But if you had invested the same $100 in stocks, reinvesting all dividends, you would have made $63,000. "We don't think the relationship will be hugely different in the future." After more than ten thousand computer simulations, OMERS has set the ideal long-term composition of a portfolio at 55 percent equity, 33 percent bonds, and 12 percent real estate. Current percentages are 58 percent, 33 percent, and 8 percent. Pensioners adore high rates, of course, but they stand to pocket more when the stock market is performing well; that, in turn, depends on corporate profitability.

Silcox moves on to the second half of his demonstration. Normally, when an entrepreneur invests in a project, he expects a post-inflation return of about 6 percent. When Conrad Black buys Southam Newspapers, he expects 10 percent. A rate of 15 percent would be an extraordinary figure, but it's rarely seen. Equity itself usually represents only a small fraction of the total investment; the rest is borrowed. But if capital costs you more than 4 or 5 percent in real terms, you will never be able to attain projected profitability levels. If real interest rates reach the 7 or 8 percent range, your return on equity will probably be negative. Foreigners have imposed a real rate of 8 percent on Canada, the highest in the industrialized world. If real interest rates remain above 4 percent or 5 percent, the Canadian economy will gradually be ground into dust. If return on bonds exceeds return on shares, "lenders will end up with all the wealth and the owners will be bankrupt. If the bonds become the thing to hold, then all of the capitalist system will be destroyed. Jobs are created when there are profits."

"We're in business to pay pensions," says Silcox. For managing the risks of the trade, two golden rules apply: diversification and discipline. At OMERS, management styles and portfolios are both diversified. It invests in Canada and around the world; that portion of its assets that may be legally invested abroad is composed principally of equity, which is more profitable than bonds. Silcox did not like the 10-percent ceiling on foreign investments brought in by the Liberals in 1971, and the Conservative government's 20-percent ceiling, enacted in 1991, is still too low to suit him. "Canada accounts for only 3 percent of the world capital market. If we were truly diversified, we would have only 3 percent of our investments in Canada." As a matter of practicality, though, he admits that "it's natural to invest in your home market." His simulations point to 35 percent as the optimum figure for overseas portfolio investment. The OMERS board of directors recently gave the green light for the percentage to be bumped up to 25 percent, using derivative instruments like swaps as a way around the legal limit, a practice that is becoming more and more widespread in the industry.

Silcox invites me to meet Ian Lee, his fixed incomes specialist, who explains that bonds are divided into three baskets: a half-billion dollars in foreign paper, one and one-half billion in a portfolio partially indexed to a market index, and one billion in an actively managed portfolio, with a turnover rate of three or four times a year. The third-basket strategy is to register yields forty basis points above the RBC-Barra index by using frequent arbitrages. Lee overweights those sectors of the bond market (Canada, provinces, and corporations) that seem relatively cheap and underweights those that look expensive. The relative values are gauged by yield spreads in the light of past fluctuations, the credit picture, and anticipated events.

One year ago, Lee threw most of his weight in the direction of the provinces, reasoning that they had shown greater fiscal discipline than the federal government. Furthermore, he adds, foreigners who hold bonds in Canadian dollars are more inclined to hold Canadas than provincial offerings. "If they start selling, chances are they'll start with Canada." The RBC-Barra index gives a weight of about 65 percent to Canada, 25 percent to the provinces, and 10 percent to corporations, meaning that OMERS has pulled back 5 percent from the Canada segment to buy provincial bonds. It was a happy decision, since spreads between provincial and federal yields have narrowed in the meantime, a sign that the relative value of provincial paper has appreciated. Within the provincial segment, Ontario is generally overweighted, even though fluctuations are frequent. Lee is particularly fond of these highly liquid bonds for his arbitrage operations. He would like to overweight Alberta and British Columbia, but has been unable to lay hands on a sufficiently large number of bonds. "Of course we underweighted Quebec, almost to nothing." That decision was made in early 1994, "because of the referendum situation, and, even more important, because the financial situation has deteriorated." Last spring, Lee decided not to bet on the short-term impact of political uncertainty on Quebec spreads, because "we didn't understand the whole political picture that well." But the outcome worries him. If Quebec votes Yes, "it is anybody's guess what the stock will be. Because it would take a long time for the rating agencies or anybody else to make an assessment of what their credit really is," says Lee, adding, "There is a wide range of things that could happen."

TORONTO, WEDNESDAY, MARCH 1, 1995

As my subway rattles toward the Toronto suburb of North York, I skim the *Wall Street Journal's*[2] attempt to make amends for a recent ill-advised comparison between Canada and Mexico. This morning's edition of the voice of the U.S. financial establishment lavishes its praise on the Canadian government for a responsible budget, while it deplores American president Clinton's lack of courage in his own budget. What a marvel of consistency.

Leo de Bever has just been named vice president for research at Ontario Teachers', the provincial teachers' pension fund. He was previously senior economist for Nomura, one of the few analysts — perhaps the only one — who scrutinized Canada for Japanese investors. He has not been replaced. His new employer, with assets of $35 billion, is Canada's largest pension fund.[3] Dr. de Bever's job is to recommend asset allocation and to evaluate the risks of derivatives, which are heavily used by Teachers'. Until 1990, the fund held only Ontario government nontradable bonds — useful for financing the province, but not the best method of providing teachers with pensions.

Teachers' strategy assigns two-thirds of assets to equity and a third to fixed income securities. Meanwhile, the original Ontario bonds are slowly melting away as they arrive at maturity. But to speed the diversification process, the pension fund has made use of sophisticated swaps. Fixed-rate incomes drawn on Ontario bonds were traded for floating-rate incomes in a first series of interest rate swaps; a second round of swaps traded such floating-rate interest incomes for share incomes equal to the yield of stock market indices such as the Toronto Stock Exchange's TSE 300, the New York Exchange's S&P 500, and the EAFE, an index derived from European, Australian, and Far Eastern shares. Teachers' also traded some floating-rate flows for fixed-rate incomes linked to international

---

DURATION

Duration is a measure of risk of a bond or bond portfolio. The longer the duration, the greater the sensitivity of the price of the bond (or of the portfolio's value) to interest rate variations. While the measure approximates the average maturity of the bonds held in a portfolio, it is more accurate as it measures the average maturity of all payments to be received, interest and capital, at present value.

---

bond indices, lessening its portfolio's sensitivity to Canadian rate fluctuations without having to give up a single one of its Ontario bonds. Fully a quarter of the portfolio is traded in this manner.

Investment strategy at Teachers' is a variation on the modern financial theme: you can't beat all the traders all of the time; caution and diversification are the wisest policy. Not surprisingly, the fund sticks close to the indices. "If you make bets based on so-called insight, they'd better be fairly small and extremely well thought out, because the track record of these things isn't very good," says de Bever. Managers have little leeway; they must limit themselves to tactical adjustments. If they believe that interest rates are going to rise, they can shorten the duration of the portfolio by transactions on the futures and options markets.

Use of derivatives has opened the door to wide diversification of investments, geographically speaking. Fully a third of assets are linked to foreign yields. It was "the best call we made, given what has happened to the Canadian dollar. It's kind of sad when you think about it," de Bever admits. Revenues from outside Canada are not hedged for foreign exchange risk because "a lot of the research shows that predicting currencies is a fool's game." But there are times when Teachers' will get involved in a partial hedge.

De Bever doesn't believe that investing outside of Canada heightens the country's dependence on foreign capital. It's a red herring, he maintains. Canada's overall dependency on foreign capital is a result of our current accounts deficit. "If you don't fix that problem, you're lost right there." The arithmetic of the deficit means that a foreigner must include in his portfolio a claim on Canada's future production. The only question remaining is the form: equity or bonds. "The case is often made that we should buy back the debt from the foreigners. You can't do that, because the money that now goes to finance corporations wouldn't go there any more; it would go into government debt instead. Then the corporation would have to go abroad; somebody has to go abroad." Big businesses can do it, he notes, but not small businesses, which would be starved of the capital they need for development (assuming savings remain constant).

THE CURRENT ACCOUNTS AND DEFICIT FINANCING

The current accounts include the trade balance — the balance of international trade in merchandise — and what are termed the "invisibles." The "invisibles" are principally international tourism and investment income, that is, the interest and dividends paid to non-residents, or collected by Canadians on their overseas investments. For the balance of payments to be in equilibrium, Canada's current accounts deficit must be financed by net capital inflow in the form of direct investment, such as the construction of factories or the purchase of Canadian securities by foreigners. These securities may be equity, Treasury bills, or bonds. In accounting terms, the current accounts deficit is also equivalent to the deficit of all public administrations, less the private savings that are not used by corporate investments. In a nutshell, financing Canada's public debt would take increased private savings, reduced corporate investment, more foreign investment, or a combination of the three. Of course, government deficits can also be reduced.

"I hear a lot of complaining about how bond-holders are getting rich off us. We didn't have to borrow that money," says de Bever. "It was our decision to run deficits. And if we run enough of them and the debt gets big enough, people start asking a premium because they worry about getting their money back." Those foreign investors are "ordinary folks who do what we are doing here, that is, the best we can for our pensioners, who are, most of the time, very ordinary people." His view is that with a smaller deficit, and minus all the uncertainty over Quebec's political status, Canadian interest rates would be closer to those in the United States. "It's not an academic issue. It affects the population as a whole, because the interest rates for the government are the level on which all interest rates are based. So it imposes a burden on everybody."

. . . .

RBC Dominion Securities keeps its views strictly to itself — and to its clients. Its analysts are rarely quoted in the newspapers; its traders even less. In the Commerce Court building I meet Jim McGivern, vice president and head of institutional sales. There is not a hint of chrome in the trading room, but RBC will be polishing up its image when it amalgamates its forex, money market, and swap activities in a brand new trading room shared with the Royal Bank.

Canadian financial institutions might turn up their noses at government paper on a day-to-day basis, McGivern explains, but over the long haul they are heavy consumers. "To be a bond salesman, you don't come in in the morning and ask your desk what is for sale, you phone your clients and find out what their view on the market is, what they're doing as a result of that, and then you turn to your traders to tell them what kind of a product you can move. Your traders buy it from somebody else, who has a different point of view or wants to move to another product area." Clients have different needs, depending on the nature of their activities and their management style. Some look for liquidity, others for yield or quality of credit. Will McGivern draw me a profile of Canada's main institutional investors? I ask.

The insurance companies are the "best customers of the bond market, because they all have a natural need to buy fixed income" to match their liability commitments: a five-year commitment is coupled to a five-year bond, and so on; scheduled compensation payments will be paid out of bonds of identical maturity. Insurers purchase primarily borrowings whose maturity varies between one and five years, and generally open from 5 to 8 percent of their portfolio, which they manage actively, to the search for profitable arbitrages. Styles vary from one firm to another. Manufacturers Life buys only top-quality credits, while Mutual Life analyses risks one at a time and makes private investments. Some, like London Life, favour an active portfolio management style, while others, like Great-West, are more passive — a simple offset is enough for them. Generally, insurance companies try to balance their policies and their investments in each province.

Banks are also big, but less regular, players. When they do play, they seek liquidity and lean toward federal debt. What's more, the Canadian government's high credit rating is less of a drain on their capitalization ratios, which are adjusted to account for the risk level of assets. Banks purchase bonds to invest their reserves and to park surplus liquidity. They also use bonds to right imbalances between maturities of borrowings and deposits such as arise, for instance, when clients invest their money in one-year GICs and ask for five-year mortgages. Their swap desks also use bonds to hedge their commitments. All the banks tend to behave in similar fashion, though ScotiaBank has a reputation as a more aggressive dealer.

A fund manager's reputation often depends on his investment style, which is generally the first thing a pension fund will look at. Leyton, which purchases no corporate paper and only a handful of provincial bonds, relies mostly on pinpointing market turnarounds to make a name for itself. T.A.L. is a heavy corporate paper buyer, rotating investments from one sector to another. Lincludden favours a five-year investment horizon, unusual in the industry. Still, none stray very far from the duration of the index they use, meaning that bond performances tend to cluster around the median. In-house managed pension funds also have their own particular style; overall, they tend to shuffle their portfolio less frequently. But the huge public sector funds behave more like the insurance companies, setting aside a portion of their portfolio to be managed using a more active approach.

Foreign investors . . . seen from Canada

T.A.L. Investments, a wholly owned subsidiary of the CIBC, is Canada's second-largest fund manager — after Quebec's Caisse de dépôt — with assets of $13 billion drawn from corporate pension funds and mutual funds. Stocks are managed in Montreal while fixed income is handled in Toronto, where first vice president John Braive manages a portfolio valued at $7 billion.

Braive, a veteran of more than twenty years in the trade, is a seasoned observer of international investor behaviour. "What has changed," he says, "is that ten or fifteen years ago, Canadian investors set interest rates on their own, based on the trends they saw developing in the United States. Today, not even the Caisse de dépôt and Manufacturers Life are big enough to set trends. Instead, they are set by marginal buyers of Canada's debt, who happen to be foreign investors. These are the people who are not obliged to buy the country."[4] But even though, in theory, Canadian institutions, like T.A.L., must buy the country, they are making use of loopholes in the law to invest more and more abroad. "A year ago we thought Canada was risky on the bond side," Braive tells me. So T.A.L. switched over to foreign paper, buying half a billion dollars' worth of World Bank and Asian Development Bank, bonds that are foreign currency denominated, very liquid, of high quality, and considered Canadian in tax terms, meaning they don't count as part of the 20-percent limit, he explains. Just a few weeks ago the position was wound down when Braive concluded that "the Canadian dollar had been severely beaten up, that it was representing fairly decent value vis-à-vis the U.S. dollar." Canadian institutions can still throw their weight around, he admits. They build up enormous cash balances which they then move into the bond market, as they've done recently.

Braive believes he's pinpointed a cycle in the way foreign investors behave. In the late 1980s, when interest rates were high, inflation was falling, and the dollar was rising, they had a crush on Canada. But when the loonie started to nosedive, they picked up their marbles and headed home. "The Bank of Canada seriously missed the fact that we need stability of the currency to attract foreign investors." Still, Braive is optimistic that dependence on foreign capital will ease substantially over the coming two years. Not only will government borrowing decrease, but corporate profits will be expanding savings. Individual savings can't deteriorate any further. "Canada is improving a whole lot," and the bond market will follow suit as soon as the players realize what is happening. The only cloud on the horizon is a possible United States recession in 1996.

T.A.L. likes to overweight the corporate bonds in its Canadian portfolio, where they account for 20 percent, against 10 percent on the Scotia-McLeod index. But Braive remains underweighted on the provincial side, with only 15 percent against 25 percent on the index, due to a weak profile in the two biggest provinces. "I don't like Ontario; this province is spending money like crazy." Today, DBRS has put Ontario on credit watch. "Well done!" he exclaims. But the threat of political uncertainty in Quebec doesn't seem to bother him. Braive is a man who likes to buy at generous spreads when everyone else is selling. He thinks that the upcoming referendum has made Jacques Parizeau put off until later the hard fiscal choices that have to be made. Perhaps he'll be able to learn more when he goes to Quebec next week, part of his policy of visiting each province twice a year. T.A.L. likes investing against the grain: "When everyone hated

Saskatchewan a year and a half ago, that is when we bought them. We met with Roy Romanow, we liked his story. The Saskatchewan NDP is very different from Ontario's. They're fiscal conservatives." Unfortunately, Braive admits, they sold their bonds too soon; the spreads keep on shrinking.

A few weeks later . . .

MONTREAL, MONDAY, APRIL 24, 1995

Jean-Luc Landry, president of Bolton Tremblay, can barely conceal his pride. The view from the forty-second-floor corner office in the IBM Building on René Lévesque Boulevard is breathtaking: a 180-degree panorama overlooking the St. Lawrence River and all of southwest Montreal. And best of all, the expensive wood panelling didn't cost Landry a cent. The lavish quarters used to belong to Bertin Nadeau, former CEO of Unigesco and briefly king of the Provigo grocery empire, before the entire house of cards collapsed, proving that governments aren't the only ones who can get drunk on credit. Bolton Tremblay, one of Canada's oldest pension fund management firms, was founded after World War II by Hamilton Bolton — a Francophile, member of the Saint-Denis Club, author of several books on technical analysis, and the first Canadian president of the American Society of Financial Analysts — and Maurice Tremblay, a bond salesman by profession who had won the confidence of Quebec's influential religious communities. Today, the twelve-person firm manages a total of $2.3 billion out of its Montreal, Toronto, Calgary, and Moncton offices. Most Bolton Tremblay clients are pension funds and foundations, but they still include several religious communities and a handful of wealthy estates.

As an economist, Landry brings a long-term, general overview to portfolio management. Colleague Pierre Garceau, vice president responsible for fixed income, brings his own perspective, focused on short-term market behaviour. Two-thirds of the portfolio is in bonds, the other third in equity. Pension funds normally issue the firm two kinds of mandates: do better than the industry with the lowest possible risk, or increase the value of a certain type of portfolio as determined by the clients.

The shop's philosophy, explains Landry, is to invest when its expectations are different from the prevailing view in the market. "If there is no difference, there's no reason to act, because the market will point to the right price." Last fall, for example, everybody was saying that the American economy was on the verge of overheating and that rates were going to go up. Bolton Tremblay took the opposite view, that there was no reason to fear inflation. In that kind of context, bond yields looked too high. So to derive more profit from the anticipated slackening of rates, they extended the average maturity of their portfolio, Garceau explains. Duration, which had been lower than the index, now rose above it. The longer a portfolio's duration, the greater the capital gains arising from a decrease in interest rates. Subsequent events were to prove them right.

Frequent arbitrages to gain two or three basis points are not part of the Bolton Tremblay style: more substantial inducements, on the order of fifteen or twenty points, are called for. But the firm does not hesitate to buy — after careful study, of course — new, complex instruments such as mortgage bonds backed up by a collection of residential mortgages. In addition to duration, the firm relies on a finely tuned sector-by-sector allocation of its portfolio, which contains a striking 40 percent of corporate paper, 35 percent Canada (including 5 percent in CMHC mortgage paper), 20 percent provinces, and 5 percent municipals. At the start of the recent economic recovery, the firm took the view that corporate prospects would improve more rapidly than those of the provinces. Bolton Tremblay got out of Quebec and Ontario as early as 1992, fleeing unbalanced budgets. It was a premature move, Landry now admits. "The market did not prove us right. The spreads kept on shrinking due to big international market appetite; they took those securities at spreads that surprised us. Today, the market is anticipating that all the provinces will improve their credit, Quebec and Ontario included. But as far as we're concerned, it's not that certain." No one at Bolton Tremblay wanted to speculate on the short-term effects of political uncertainty in the spring of 1994. "Playing political risk is like rolling dice, and I don't like it," says Landry. "How could anybody predict that the PQ would come in with such a small margin? I had no idea. And no one else did either."

When Bolton Tremblay buys foreign-currency-denominated bonds, they are always either Canadian names or those recognized as such by the tax department. Clients like familiar names. But at present, the entire portfolio is invested in Canadian funds, reflecting Landry's optimism concerning the exchange rate. In 1994, "the Bank of Canada attempted to keep interest rates as low as possible compared to American rates, which drove down the Canadian dollar artificially. Today, the governor has realized that policy simply doesn't work; he won't attempt to repeat it. You can rule out the possibility of another drop because of excessively tight spreads." And besides, "our overall perception over the last two years is that Canadian credit is improving. The more the public feels that the situation is deteriorating, the more pressure it puts on politicians. To the public, things are getting worse; but in reality, things are getting better." Landry gives me several reasons for his optimism: inflation is dead, and monetary policy will stay the course; government spending and taxes have levelled off as a percentage of GDP; governments are cutting back their activities, slashing their deficits, and gaining popularity. "It's like a supertanker: you hardly notice when it begins to turn, but when the turn is completed, it's really noticeable."

But, adds Landry, we can't stop now. Rapid developments on the swap market mean that governments can borrow in a variety of foreign currencies with no foreign exchange risk. "Every borrower now has more rope to hang himself. You can always find someone, somewhere in the other hemisphere, who knows a little bit less about your credit and will lend to you at a narrower spread." Even if the debt keeps on growing, rates are rising at a slower rate than they would if we were not borrowing abroad. "We've simply postponed the inevitable." But the inevitable is lurking: a point at which rising rates will simply take off. "The problem is that it always hits you just when you need to borrow the most," he says.

WATERLOO, WEDNESDAY, APRIL 26, 1995

Since 1912, Mutual Life, Canada's fifth largest insurance company, has occupied the same stately red-brick and grey-stone building, worthy of an Ivy League university. But additions to the structure have chipped away at its understated charm; today, the venerable building is overwhelmed by the corporate office tower that looms over this quiet, southwest Ontario town. Paul Reger is Mutual's vice president for investments, a thirty-five-year veteran who, along with two deputies, manages a $5-billion bond portfolio made up of 80 percent public debt, with the remainder in corporate paper. Reger's team also administers a $1.1-billion mutual fund. With the exception of a half-billion U.S. dollars, paired with an American subsidiary's liabilities, everything is in Canadian currency.

Reger is a "tekkie." "I believe a lot in technical analysis," he says, pointing to the colourful charts on his computer screen showing the historical structure of bond spreads.

TECHNICAL ANALYSIS

Technical analysis is a market analysis method that uses graphics to show the evolution of prices and volumes of a given financial product. Analysts attempt to isolate recurring patterns in order to identify current trends and to forecast when these trends are likely to shift. The technique is used primarily to predict short- and medium-term movements, even though certain analysts use it to predict cycles of several years. It is a controversial approach, ignoring conventional factors such as supply and demand, and postulating that prices include all information relevant to decision-making. Technical analysis is more often used as a supplementary tool, particularly for isolating the most opportune moment for a transaction dictated by the fundamentals.

"We're sitting not too far from the ScotiaMcLeod Universal Index," notes Reger. One of the particularities of the Mutual portfolio, he adds, is its underweighting of the provinces, counterbalanced by an overrepresentation of mortgage paper. The provinces are too expensive, and it's been twenty years since spreads have been so tight. "The market has swung from extreme pessimism over provincial deficits only twenty-four months ago to what might be extreme optimism." Ten-year Saskatchewans offering a yield 120 basis points higher than Canadas were available; now the same paper is trading at 40 basis points. It was one capital gain that got away from Reger, because of his provincial underweighting for the last eighteen months. But he made up for it with his mortgage paper, he insists.

He remains cautious about provincial finances, especially those of Ontario, and expects little from tomorrow's pre-election budget, to be brought down by provincial NDP Finance minister Floyd Laughren. The next government will bring down the real budget. Reger is hardly flummoxed by the Quebec referendum: "I don't think it's a problem. The rest of Canada is not going to put up with what it did in the early '80s. The sentiment has definitely changed. It is going to be a non-event. Quebec will vote with its pocketbook." In fact, Reger has already played the impact of political uncertainty on the Quebec spreads three times, and he claims he's ready to do it again. But he admits to some concern over the huge provincial maturities coming up over the next three years. How will the debt, most of which is held offshore, be refinanced? Worse, he is convinced that the market is turning bearish, which could drag on for two or three years. The pressure on government financing costs promises to be substantial, he predicts.

Reger is an active manager, turning the portfolio over two or three times a year, not hesitating to shorten or lengthen duration depending on rate patterns. Investment allocation is keyed to premiums paid in each province, an approach he describes as a social responsibility. The fund manager is a busy man: dealers keep interrupting our conversation, offering advice on arbitrage tactics. Today he has bought $40 million in real yield Canada bonds, which this afternoon's Bank of Canada auction delivered at 4.578 percent.[5] It's Mutual Life's first foray into a product that is relatively new to Canada, but in wide use in the United Kingdom. Reger sees inflationary clouds gathering on the horizon; the new securities, whose rate is indexed to the consumer price index, should provide better performance. Still, it's not iron-clad protection. "If the government of Canada is going to try to inflate itself out of its problem, does that mean there won't be instability in the other sectors of the economy? The answer is fairly obvious. There is no place to hide."

The only solution is a string of tough budgets. "You cannot take your eye off the ball," he says. "What happens if we hit a recession? What happens if interest rates go back up to 10 percent or 11 percent? I don't think it will be pleasant." Money at that price causes a massive transfer of wealth from taxpayers to bond-holders, and many bond-holders are foreigners. If the United States slides into a recession and Canada's exports collapse, the current accounts deficit will shoot right up. Sudden movements of capital could make our life miserable, he adds. "The difference from twenty years ago is that there are so many desks around the world that trade for their own account and try to find weak links in the environment that they can exploit. And right now they do a pretty good job of exploiting the U.S. dollar. But when the focus shifts to something else, Canada could come under the microscope again. You can't hide from computer screens that are trying to make a buck." So, what's in store? "I wish I knew. I don't know, Miville. The big picture is changing, and we don't know where Canada fits. At the end of your research you're going to have more questions than answers." I've got a hunch he's right.

TORONTO, THURSDAY, APRIL 27, 1995

Behind Pat Palmieri hangs an immense painting of the Rockies — a perfect image for someone who likes stability. Palmieri isn't an art critic, though. He's a CFA and vice president, fixed incomes, at BIMCOR, BCE Inc.'s financial arm. BIMCOR manages the cash reserves of the powerful communications group, and the pension funds of its subsidiaries Bell Canada and Nortel. With assets of $8.5 billion, it weighs in as Canada's eighth largest pension fund, and the only private entry in the country's top ten. The equity side of the BIMCOR portfolio is managed out of Montreal; the bond side is administered here in Toronto. The two groups meet once a month. At BIMCOR, everything is handled strictly in-house, except for a small portfolio of European and Asian shares farmed out to a certain Barings, now a subsidiary of Holland's ING Bank. Nope, we didn't lose a thing, Palmieri assures me.

"Our clients are the type of people who would rather sleep well than eat well," he laughs, describing the firm's risk-aversion policy, which builds on the fundamentals and seeks out promising securities. Constant performance is the goal, measured against the SEI median, the yield figure that divides Canadian pension funds into two equal groups as evaluated by a private firm.[6] "We play the relative performance game. So I wouldn't take any undue risk, no matter how strongly I might feel about a particular viewpoint." On the stock market you can always make up for a bad year; not on the bond market, he notes.

Palmieri has set up a small portfolio, faithfully reproducing the Scotia-McLeod Universal Index, for purposes of comparison. But he manages the bulk of his securities to capitalize on his anticipation of rate shifts. "In 90 percent of cases, that's where the money is made or lost," he says. The technique is to break the curve down into smaller segments, each of which is then analysed separately. Bonds are then concentrated in those segments where rates should either be decreasing the most or increasing the least. In late 1993, to ward off the inflationary threat from the United States and its possible effect on Canadian interest rates, he drew up a defensive strategy, shortening the duration of his portfolio to 4.5 years, as against the index's 5.2 years. Mr. Palmieri is proud to have lost less than his fellow bond managers in 1994; at year's end he re-extended duration, lifting it above the index level. "I became very bullish on Canadian bond and dollar markets."

After securities have been distributed across the curve, allocation by segment can also improve yields, though only slightly. Mr. Palmieri is allergic to constant arbitraging; he prefers strategic decisions. Before buying a province he will examine its debt, its deficit, its growth, and its spending reduction plans, in an attempt to evaluate the risk of its credit being downgraded. In this area, his company's policy is among the strictest in the industry: "We cannot buy any credit below single A." Not even a weak A can do the job. If a name slips down to BBB, it must be sold, which wipes Newfoundland off the list. In reality, BIMCOR has held not a shred of provincial paper since the start of the year. "I didn't like their spreads," says Palmieri, although he does admit that some provinces have performed quite well since then. But a successful portfolio restructuring, along with purchase of federal-government-guaranteed mortgage paper, made up for their absence.

What concerns him the most is what he sees as the lack of vigorous measures by Ontario and Quebec to reduce their deficits. Quebec's failure to hedge its risk in all its foreign currency borrowings is another source of irritation. BIMCOR's clout has won it a place alongside institutional investors at the Finance minister's pre-budget consultations, in Ottawa. Palmieri is quite up-front about his views: "As professionals, I think we have to be vigilant. I think it's our responsibility as fund managers to reward those that are making the effort in terms of cleaning house, and to punish those that don't. The message has to be clear. If I don't like what Ontario is doing, or any of the other provinces, that should be known." If

Mr. Palmieri has earned a reputation as the fastest mouth east of the Rockies, well, "it's for the well-being of Canada."

A stern mistress

Stung by the back of Adam Smith's invisible hand,[7] the federal government finally seems to have heard the message from financial markets and begun to put its fiscal house in order. In his February 1995 budget speech, Finance minister Paul Martin managed to please two publics. Politically, the budget came in on target with a deficit equal to 3 percent of GDP, as promised by the Liberals' Red Book. Financially, the budget conveyed a clear message to market participants: If you do your figures carefully, you'll see we intend to do better still.

No surprises here. Canadian financiers are unanimous: governments must eliminate their deficits and reduce the size of the debt. But above and beyond generalities, my Canadian tour indicates less than perfect unanimity among the men and women who play the financial markets. People have their own ideas and behaviour patterns, as in any market. What is fascinating is that public and private pension funds tend to think alike. They might be optimists or pessimists, they might like the provinces or dislike them, they might be buyers or sellers — but as a group, Canadian financial market players have a much more negative image of their own country's fiscal situation than foreigners do. Is it because they have so much more to lose given a collapse of the Canadian market, where they've put most of their eggs? Or perhaps it's because they have a much more extensive knowledge of Canada's problems? Could it be that they are so close to the action that they lack critical distance? Everyone I met oozed sincerity. But the same people have specific interests to promote — to maximize yield and minimize risk. Sometimes, unconsciously, they slip from argument based on facts and objective constraints into an ideologically driven mantra, where preconceptions replace thought.

Foreigners are not the only ones who shift capital in and out of Canada, that much is clear. Canadian insurance companies, as well as private and public pension funds, also speculate on Canada; they even speculate on foreign speculation in an attempt to profit from shifts in attitudes toward the country. Canada's international investors still depend on the local market, but they are no longer its captives. The 20-percent limit can be easily circumvented by purchase of foreign currency bonds signed by Canadian or supranational names, or by swaps in which Canadian yields are traded for foreign yields. In this type of transaction, Canadian institutional investors continue to finance a Canadian borrower (except when they purchase supranational paper), but they have widened the field of risk and yield by adding foreign exchange rates and foreign bond markets.

Canadians also play a vital role in shaping the perception of the foreigners who read their research and newspapers. On some occasions, as in the spring of 1994, Canadian pessimism has become contagious. The alarmist remarks of some financiers actually turned potential foreign investors away.

Governments are learning that the market is a stern mistress. Not only is she continually clamouring for more, but she will walk out at the drop of a hat, and come waltzing back later as if nothing had happened. Ah, but when she kisses you, and whispers sweet nothings in your ear . . .

Chapter 7

IN UNCLE SAM'S BACK YARD

MONTGOMERY, ALABAMA, TUESDAY, MARCH 21, 1995

MONTGOMERY'S FIRST SKYSCRAPER, a gleaming, white-stone structure, towers over a plaza and fountain. At each corner of the plaza, beneath lavishly ornate lamp standards, workers are putting the finishing touches to a logo carved in the granite, superimposing the letters "RSA" over a stylized map of Alabama. A billboard proclaims: "RSA Tower Plaza. An office complex built by public employees to save dollars for Alabama taxpayers. Dr. David G. Bronner, Chief Executive Officer."

In fact, except for the state capitol, virtually every major building in this sleepy Deep South government town is Dr. Bronner's handiwork. The gilded RSA logo can be seen everywhere, beginning with the headquarters of Retirement Systems of Alabama, another monumental white shrine to the *nouveaux riches* of American capitalism. The David Rockefellers of this world might give the stirring speeches, but men like Bronner wield the power. Big money in the United States is in the pension funds, and the people who run them know it.

Of this select group, a handful of public pension funds stand out in terms of their overall clout. The administration of government employees' pension funds varies widely from state to state. In Pennsylvania, assets are divided among several funds; in Alabama and Colorado they are consolidated. California and Texas have set up both large groups and small, freestanding funds. In Virginia and Mississippi, fund management is left to the private sector, while California and Minnesota manage a portion in-house, the rest outside. In states such as New Jersey and Alabama, fund personnel handle all the money.

Bronner slumps back into his leather armchair and lights up a fat cigar. For the last twenty-two years this unlikely "civil servant" has headed the Alabama state employees' pension fund, the same outfit that employs Tom Milne. Milne, you will recall, is the man who gave me the story behind RSA's decision to unload $700 million of long-term Quebec and Hydro-Québec bonds in October 1993. "I used to go out with a girl from Winnipeg," Bronner laughs. "I think I know you guys as well as I know anybody in the world." RSA began investing in Hydro-Québec bonds in the mid 1970s, when the utility was raising funds for the James Bay hydro development project. As most American power utilities depend on nuclear or coal-fired facilities, the Hydro-Québec securities, denominated in U.S. dollars, meant risks could be diversified. And while legislation prohibits pension funds and life insurance companies from purchasing foreign securities, Canada is an exception.

Bronner shrugs off my pointed questions about investment criteria. "It's all academic! We don't do that. We are interested in where we can stick money." Bronner takes one look at a bond and asks, "Is it cheap? Is it expensive?" Then he compares the risks. "Is there going to be somebody doing something off the wall? And then you forget about it and go on to the next thing." When the market turns bullish, "we buy everything that crawls in our direction," including the odd BBB-rated paper. One thing Alabama State won't touch are the "munis," the tax-free bonds issued by American states or municipalities. Those bonds, which are designed primarily for individuals, pay low interest because of their tax-free status, so they offer no advantage to pension funds, which pay no income tax.

How risky is it to buy Canadian-government-issued bonds? "Canada has overspent its mind just like the United States has," he says, but "Canada is a hell of a lot better and stabler than all of these three-legged chairs in the rest of the world."

Would an independent Quebec be just another one of those three-legged chairs? "Only if the separatists in Quebec start to shoot at each other. Then we'll have the feeling we are in Bosnia." An unlikely scenario, notes Bronner, who believes that Canadians are even more conservative than Americans. The country has been through several rough patches, politically speaking, and nothing terrible has happened. But if the Parti Québécois wins its referendum "what would happen is like anytime you have a big political change. Everybody would stop. They may not pull funds right away, but a few would. Everything in the pipeline would stop and that hurts any country because funds stop for two or three years."

Alabama State's decision to sell $700 million (CA) of Quebec bonds and $250 million (CA) of Ontario bonds in late 1993 had nothing to do with political uncertainty, contrary to the rumour mill. Markets had been nervously anticipating the rise of the Bloc Québécois, which became the official Opposition following the October 25 election. Still, the transaction was an unusual one for a pension fund. For starters, it was RSA's first excursion into paper that was not U.S.-dollar denominated. At the time of purchase, at the beginning of that same year, explains Bronner, "the U.S. market wasn't interesting and we had plenty of money to invest." Another fact made it unusual: the bonds were sold after a few months, and not held until maturity, the normal practice at this pension fund. But when interest rates fell, "the market went nuts and we had this huge profit," he adds. It was crucial to take the profit before rates headed off in the other direction. The daring move impressed the board of directors, who promptly gave Bronner the green light to explore United Kingdom and Australian bonds.

A record-setting transaction

Moving down the hall to investment manager Tom Milne's office, I patch together the day-by-day story. At the start of the decade, he explains, Alabama State's $13-billion assets were invested entirely in American dollars. "To get our feet wet, we looked at Canada as an initial spot" in a foreign currency. The idea was to stay in the dollar bloc and start out with familiar credits. Milne leafs through his files looking for the exact figures. On January 29, 1993, he bought from Merrill Lynch $200 million (CA) worth of Hydro-Québec bonds maturing in 2022 with a $9\frac{5}{8}$ percent coupon, part of a global issue valued at $1.2 billion. On February 6, he bought $250 million (CA) more, in twenty-year Ontario bonds this time, from Goldman

Sachs. Two days later, he picked up $100 million in twelve-year paper issued by the City of Montreal as part of a private placement set up by Salomon Brothers. Finally, on February 17, he bought $500 million of thirty-year Quebec bonds. It amounted to a cool billion in Canadian dollars, concentrated at the long end of the yield curve, not hedged by foreign exchange risk. "A fairly aggressive stand," as Milne describes it.

The bet turned out to be sound, as long-term rates dropped by more than 1 percent over the ensuing months, pumping up bond values. But by September the slackening trend had run its course, and Milne decided to shorten the duration of his bond portfolio, which held no long-term American government securities (seen as too stingy in terms of yield); American corporate paper is hardly notable for its liquidity. In mid September Milne phoned the RSA salesman at Goldman Sachs to offer the provincial bonds. Just as the sale was about to be finalized, the Canadian market dropped. Milne cannot remember what had happened, but he does remember that the broker's price wasn't attractive. The project was put on ice.

In fact, the news that shook financial markets on Tuesday, September 14, was the announcement that Quebec premier Robert Bourassa, who had been diagnosed as suffering from cancer, had decided to resign. The news compounded existing political uncertainty. The federal election campaign had begun the week before, and the Bloc Québécois was expected to end up holding the balance of power. On that day, the Canadian dollar lost half a cent, and long-term Canada bonds lost $2 per $100 of face value.

For Milne, the behaviour of the American market was an even greater cause for alarm. A month later, on Thursday, October 14, U.S. Treasuries took off with the publication of figures showing that the threat of renewed inflation in the United States was far less acute than assumed. Long rates dropped to 5.85 percent, their lowest level in sixteen years. The Canadian market reacted even more strongly, and Milne moved quickly to sell Goldman Sachs $500 million (CA) of thirty-year Quebec bonds. Others picked up on the imminent shift as well. The next day Milne read in the *Wall Street Journal*'s "Capital Markets" column that a Fidelity Investments manager had begun to sell his long-term bonds. That same day, new inflation figures underlined price stability. This time, the American and Canadian markets took off in the opposite direction. Correctly concluding that rates had bottomed out for this cycle, Milne sold the same investment dealer his remaining $250 million of Ontario and $200 million Hydro-Québec, keeping only the private investment in the City of Montreal, which was not very liquid.

Before they could gobble up the huge block of provincial paper, the Goldman Sachs traders needed the green light from corporate headquarters in New York; a position of that magnitude would tie up a significant part of the firm's capital, I've been told, by a source who asked not to be named. To hedge bond-market volatility risk, Goldman's trader sold short an equivalent number of Canada bonds. But there was no way for Goldman Sachs to guard against the risk of a possible widening of spreads between Quebec and Canada bonds during the election campaign. The traders checked with the Quebec Finance department and the Hydro-Québec Treasury department. A decision by either to issue new paper would have created excess supply and depressed prices. The Goldman operation had all the makings of a large-scale issue, the kind of work normally handled by a multi-member syndicate. In Quebec City, Finance department officials' first reaction was one of surprise, then concern.

The resale was handled both in the firm's Montreal office (for the Quebec paper) and in Toronto (for the Ontario bonds). To Goldman Sachs's surprise, the street was quick to learn that it was sitting on a huge chunk of Quebec; the rumour mill was working overtime. Figures like $1.5 billion (CA) were in the air. Milne protests that he was the soul of discretion, but he does admit letting traders in on his intentions. Goldman's position quickly became vulnerable, as buyers attempted to lay hands on the paper at cut-rate prices. Goldman bluffed its way through the next week, even purchasing additional Quebec bonds to keep the price up — and to let the market know who was in charge. When the vultures moved on, the investment dealer was able to get a reasonable price for its goods.

Milne has no idea who bought the paper from Goldman, but he remembers being told that it would be knocking at the door of Quebec's Caisse de dépôt. In fact, the Caisse did buy $200 million (CA) worth of Quebec bonds, which it hung on to, reasoning that the price was fair. Toronto investment dealer Nesbitt Thomson also picked up about $100 million (CA) Quebec from Goldman; it clipped the coupons and resold the parts separately on the retail market. Even though it took Goldman more than a month to sell its position on the Canadian market, the firm ended up with an attractive profit in what had become the single largest transaction ever negotiated on the secondary provincial bond market. Perhaps of equal significance was Goldman's ability to demonstrate to the province and to Hydro-Québec that, by keeping the secondary Quebec bond market stable during a potentially troubled period, it made a powerful ally. The American investment dealer had done "an outstanding job," managing to disturb the provincial securities market as little as it did, notes Milne. Curiously, however, the Canadian market did feel the impact when Goldman Sachs sold Canadian paper short to hedge its provincial risk.

On the heels of Prime Minister Kim Campbell's election call, Canada-U.S. and Quebec-Canada spreads widened, reflecting investor nervousness at the prospect of a rising Bloc Québécois and the possibility of a minority government. But one week prior to the elections the polls were pointing to a Liberal majority, an indicator of stability. As Canada-U.S. spreads had become positively generous, investors snapped up Canadian bonds, touching off a narrowing of spreads. Quebec-Canada spreads followed suit six weeks later, delayed by the Goldman Sachs jumbo deal.

After the transaction, Milne made the mistake of reinvesting the proceeds of the sale in Canadian T-bills to be renewed after three months. To his dismay, the fall of the Canadian dollar worked out to a 4-percent loss, bringing his net profit down to 6 percent. "I'm glad that we are now rolling out of those T-bills," he tells me. Milne says he learned a valuable lesson: that provincial bonds are not liquid enough for this kind of massive, short-term investment. Alabama State will be back to Canada, he assures me, but probably in federal government bonds. And when it buys provincial bonds again, they will be denominated in U.S. dollars.

BOSTON, MONDAY, MARCH 20, 1995

"Hot Money!"[1] screams the cover of *Business Week*: $2,000 billion (US) flows back and forth across national borders looking for high yields and rock-solid security. "The dollar is crashing. Mexico is in meltdown. The European currency system is collapsing. One force is driving it all: global money-traders voting thumbs down on deficits," runs the lead. Americans are feeling vulnerable; 20 percent of their debt is held by foreigners. The magazine quotes Nicholas P. Sargen, chief global strategist at the prestigious merchant bank J. P. Morgan, as saying that the United States is learning that "the price of breaching market discipline is much more painful than anyone ever expected." What would he say about Canada, where foreigners hold fully 40 percent of the debt?

•••••••••••••••••••••••••

The harbour view from the thirty-fourth floor of International Place is magnificent. It's a view Jay Leu never sees; the office he shares with a colleague is a windowless cubbyhole stuffed with documents and overflowing waste-baskets. Leu, who boasts a Masters in Finance from the Massachusetts Institute of Technology, is a specialist in quantitative management and vice president at State Street Global Advisors, which manages $170 billion (US) for pension funds, mutual funds, and foreign central banks. State Street handles seven times more bonds than T.A.L., Canada's largest private fund manager.

Leu's answers are dry and laconic — as far as you can get from the cigar-chomping Bronner's down-home style. His specialty is international bond mutual funds, where American investors have placed more than $50 billion (US) within the last five years. Yields have been generally below expectations, as many funds hedged the foreign exchange risk, sacrificing any potential gain from major currency appreciation against the greenback. State Street is an exception, with a fund worth half a billion U.S., whose composition reflects faithfully, and passively, the Salomon Brothers World Bond Index, minus its U.S.-dollar component. The firm owes much of its reputation to its indexed funds.

For investors seeking above-index yields, State Street has created a new, actively managed fund that gives the fund manager a little leeway. Using derivatives, Leu separates investment allocation by currency from allocation by bond market. "For currencies you buy high because it is going higher, and sell low because it is going lower," he explains. Applying purely technical logic, he ends up following market trends passively, without even a glance at the fundamentals. Applying the same approach, State Street is working on a mathematical model that would combine total recent performance with each bond's interest rate volatility to fine-tune by-country bond allocation. Canada now weighs in at nearly 5 percent in the fund.

The Yankees

State Street, like most institutional investors, purchases the bulk of its securities on the immense American bond market; its approach is the traditional one of investing in credits that are staging a comeback, or for a variety of reasons have been too harshly judged by the market. In both cases, the gambit is to bet on a narrowing of yield spreads between this kind of paper and risk-free American government bonds. The spread is an indication of the probability that the borrower will not repay his creditors. It narrows when the risk is felt to be lessening; bonds will thus be worth more. Conversely, the spread widens when the perceived risk increases.

YANKEES

Yankees, U.S.-dollar-denominated bonds issued in the United States by foreign investors, make up approximately 3 percent of the American bond market. Nearly half of these bonds carry Canadian names, with Quebec and Ontario bonds being the most popular. Their liquidity compares favourably with the American corporate paper with which they are most often equated. Yankees are easy to buy and sell in quantity. Canadian Yankees represent 8.4 percent of American corporate paper. Investment dealers assume, rather arbitrarily, that half of global U.S. dollar financing takes place on the Yankee market.

Glenn Migliozzi, a State Street general manager, invests regularly in Yankees. All things being equal, he prefers buying a Manitoba bond, which yields 58 basis points more than an American government bond, to a Wal-Mart bond, which only gives him 42 points more than U.S. Treasuries. And with both bonds rated AA, things are equal enough. His objective is to top the American bond market general index. "I take out the names and try to buy the index cash-flows as cheaply as possible," he says. Sometimes the manoeuvre is extremely rapid. One morning last January, he bought a thirty-year Quebec bond at 117 basis points above the U.S. Treasuries, selling at day's end at 115 above, for a slim but instant profit of two one-hundredths of 1 percent.

The approach presupposes that the fundamentals determining credit quality are moving in the right direction. Should the opposite occur, "it's like a falling knife. You prefer to wait until it hits the floor, then stare at it for awhile before you go pick it up. It is very hard to stick out your hand and try to catch it." A still knife on the floor is like a cheap bond. What does that make Quebec, a falling knife? "I think it's an uncertain knife," says Migliozzi. "When you check the fundamentals: poor, poor, poor." Worse yet, everybody's holding Quebec bonds, State Street included. That makes for a lot of potential sellers. Today, by coincidence, these investors will be reading about the fires of independence burning in Quebec's Saguenay–Lac Saint-Jean region on the front page of the *Boston Globe*.[2]

•••••••••••••••••••••••••

At the tender age of thirty-three, Ford O'Neil manages a bond portfolio for Fidelity Investments, the largest mutual fund company in the United States. A specialist in international relations and a Wharton MBA, O'Neil began his career as a Canada analyst in Fidelity's research department. His job is to buy bonds denominated in Canadian dollars when Canadian yields rise relative to American yields; when the spreads narrow, he resells them.

In the spring of 1994, when spreads widened in anticipation of a Parti Québécois election victory, "we saw that as a dramatic buying opportunity," says O'Neil. "We have always held the view that Quebec will end up receiving additional powers from Ottawa, but that it will not secede." After the vote, the bonds were sold at a profit.

O'Neil describes Finance minister Paul Martin's recent budget as "short-term positive." But he is critical of Martin's goal of a deficit equalling 3 percent of GDP, because of the country's high level of debt. The minister has to be aiming for a balanced budget, but the next recession could stop him from reaching his target. "That is why we are not overly bullish on Canada in the long term."

What did O'Neil think of the recent *Wall Street Journal* piece comparing Canada to Mexico; does he believe that the two countries are really facing the same kind of problems? "I do not," he replies. "Because Mexico was a BB country, clearly an emerging market. Canada is still nominally AAA. What happened in Mexico was a crisis of confidence that is unlikely to happen in Canada any time in the near future." Why? "Because Canada might have to raise interest rates by twenty-five to fifty or maybe one hundred basis points for their debt to clear in the market.

But I don't think that you'll get into Mexico's situation, with investors waking up and saying: I am no longer interested in buying Canada at any price." A Mexico-type foreign exchange crisis couldn't hit Canada as hard, O'Neil explains, since the Bank of Canada doesn't attempt to defend a fixed exchange rate. "What a hedge fund wants to see," he notes, "is a central bank that says: our currency will never go beyond this level, and we have $20 billion to defend it. All you need then is people with $21 billion, and the minute you cross that line, you have nothing but profits. Because no one has any idea of where the next line is gonna be."

NEW YORK, THURSDAY, MARCH 23, 1995

On the banks of the Hudson River, not far from Wall Street, seven hundred people are buying and selling bonds in a huge trading room.. In spite of the goodwill of several of the firm's employees, I have run up against a towering wall of bureaucratic paranoia: I cannot reveal the identity of the person I'm speaking with, unless I agree to let the firm's lawyers vet my book!

My host, a friendly and outgoing person, handles the bond issues steered by the American investment house, one of the most powerful in the world, Canada included. Every day the firm evaluates the cost of borrowing on the world's ten most important bond markets. A provincial government or a crown corporation wishing to make a five-year borrowing is given a chart showing interest rates paid in each market. To make comparison easier, rates are converted into a standard measure such as the LIBOR (London Interbank Offered Rate — a short-term, thus floating, rate in U.S. dollars) or Canadian bank acceptances (a short-term rate in Canadian dollars). If the client wishes, the dealer will handle the swaps, making it possible to convert the debt into Canadian dollars.

Liaison agents in the firm's Toronto and Montreal offices look after direct contacts with borrowers. Should the issuer wish to borrow on the Yankee market, the operation will be run out of New York. Should the issue be a global one in American dollars, the nerve centre will be shifted to the major financial centre where the largest number of potential buyers is to be found. For Euro financings, deals are run out of London, or the country of the borrowing currency. The firm is also well established on the

Canadian bond market; its Toronto trading room is one of the most active participants at the Bank of Canada auctions, and its salesmen are among the most active in placing Canada bonds and Treasury bills both in Canada and around the world.

Yankee buyers are ready to take a calculated risk on an issuer's credit quality, explains my host. They give the provinces with weaker ratings relatively low interest rates, but they are stingy toward those with relatively strong ratings. Small wonder that the best-rated provinces prefer borrowing in Europe, where high-quality credit can bring more attractive rates.

The most daring American investors venture into the Canadian market, where yields are better; however, those who do run the risk of seeing the value of their investment sink along with the Canadian dollar. But the same investors are less inclined to take chances with credit quality. They purchase mainly Canadian government bonds, which they can unload rapidly if the market begins to fall. When their minds are made up about a currency, they put their money on T-bills; if they smell a shift in interest rates, they move into bonds. Yankee market investors generally have longer investment horizons than Canadian market players. But each market has an effect on the other, and whenever Canada has a bad day, Canadian spreads widen on the Yankee market.

FRIDAY, MARCH 24, 1995

This morning's *Wall Street Journal* features an op-ed piece headlined: "Canadian Finances Look a Lot Like Accounting at Barings," referring to the British bank that dealer Nick Leeson scuttled with a few rolls of the dice in Singapore. The author, Reuven Brenner, a McGill University professor, writes: "Unless Ottawa, the provinces, and all Western governments change their ways significantly, their access to credit could be severely limited, if not completely cut off."[3]

••••••••••••••••••••••••

Indian-born, British- and American-educated Ravi Bulchandani, economist and partner at Morgan Stanley, is the dean of Wall Street's "Canada Watchers." His calm, good-natured, considerate manner makes him highly suitable as an analyst whose views help shape the way foreign investors see Canada.

"The only reason that American investors look at any other financial assets apart from U.S. bonds," he explains, "is either additional yield or risk diversification." The typical American pattern is to take their first steps abroad in Canada, a neighbouring country that's easier to understand than the rest. If they want to diversify their credit risks and still not run any foreign exchange risk, they can choose Yankees. But "if you're going to be successful [in Yankees], you have to be able to anticipate rating changes before they occur," as down-rated bonds will be worth less. Bulchandani respects the work of the credit rating agencies, but points to their tendency to react to events. The Mexican crisis, which not a single agency saw coming, will force them to take "a much more aggressive approach to sovereign credits."

If you invest in the Canadian market, he explains, "then you open up the range of risk enormously. You get more diversification, more volatility in your portfolio." In these circumstances, investors are well advised to keep a close watch on monetary and fiscal policy, as well as on political developments that can affect interest rates and the Canadian dollar. In a recent study, Bulchandani reminded his clients: "As ever, the rule for investment in Canada is to buy after the panic."[4] It was a polite way of saying that it is still too early to invest in Canada; the Martin budget, though seen as positive, has not allayed Bulchandani's fears.

Currently, he reports, American investors see Canada as a country grappling with a double-headed dilemma, both fiscal and political. He describes their perception as "negative" when it comes to public finances, and as "concerned" on the issue of Quebec. But is there a way to manage these risks? I ask. "One way to manage the risk is to eliminate it, to just walk away from the Canadian market," he replies. "Mexico is a good example of what happens when markets lose patience: you get cut off."

Sure, he adds, "there is a price to clear the market. At 100 percent, Mexico could borrow easily! But the price would impose such a cost on the economy that you would not want to pay it." Still, despite its current accounts deficit, Canada is "far away from that situation." The deficit, he notes, is heading in the right direction, and "markets are interested in trends."

When the markets sing the same song

Alliance Capital is one of the largest fund managers in the United States. Half of its $120 billion (US) assets are administered on behalf of institutions such as pension funds; the other half consists of mutual funds sold to individuals. Alliance's senior economist and strategist, Selig Sechzer, studies economic conditions in the principal industrialized countries, and recommends allocation by asset categories.

Sechzer thinks he has spotted a pattern among his institutional clients: some are prepared to accept credit risks, but not foreign exchange risks; others can live with foreign exchange risks, but not credit risks. In practice, this means that Alliance buys the provinces on the Yankee market while sticking strictly to federal borrowings on the Canadian market. Each month, Sechzer and his staff run a detailed comparison of the world's main bond markets and lay down recommendations for allocation of the assets to be invested in this category. Alliance's portfolio managers then adapt the recommendations to fit their clients' needs and their own convictions.

A month ago Sechzer, feeling bullish about the Canadian bond market, made up his mind to invest 5 percent of his international bonds, an over-weighting when compared with Canada's 2.7 percent in the index. But he was bearish on the Canadian dollar, suggesting a negative weighting of 6.5 percent, for a net short position of 1.5 percent. Today, as Canada-U.S. spreads have narrowed, he's turned the advisory on its head: nothing in Canadian securities, but a 5-percent position in the national currency.

Sechzer has picked up something else: national markets are all singing the same song. "In the '80s, any time U.S. yields went up one hundred basis points, German yields might go up ten or twenty basis points. Over the last two or three years, you will see that everything else being equal, German yields moved up by seventy or eighty basis points. You have much more integration of world financial markets."

Liberalization of markets has made it possible for fund managers to accumulate huge masses of capital and to move them very rapidly in search of marginally higher yields. The phenomenon has bolstered existing relations among markets, or, to use financial insiders' jargon, the positive correlations are stronger than before. Small markets like Canada move in the same direction as the larger markets but often in a more pronounced fashion. This kind of behaviour weakens the theory of the diversified portfolio, which assumes that some markets rise while others fall, or, in more technical terms, that the component parts of such a portfolio display negative correlations.

For portfolio managers, this means "that you have to be very careful about risk, because your portfolio won't be as diversified as you think it is," he notes. "Because fund managers have money in the dollar bloc, money in Europe, money in Japan, money in the emerging markets, they think they have a very diversified portfolio and their performance will be stable. We found out in 1994 that it is very hard to be well diversified. Everything moved in the same direction. That is a serious problem that made us more cautious about taking on riskier positions. We now have to go back to basics and invest less in risky bonds: shorter duration, better credit rating, fully hedged bonds."

The implications for Canada? Sechzer pauses for a moment, then: "It is one of the elements of the global environment that is placing bigger and bigger demands on policy makers. There is going to be a wider gulf between well-managed countries and poorly managed countries. Canada, I think, is fighting very hard to make sure that it gets included with the group of well-managed countries. The outcome depends ultimately on the successful completion of Mr. Martin's plan and the willingness of the Bank of Canada to keep the Canadian dollar stable."

MONDAY, MARCH 27, 1995

Computer science, art history, and mortgage bonds ought to make strange bedfellows. But not for Michael Lustig, a thirty-year-old vice president at BlackRock Financial management, specialists in the most complex type of securities known to man.

Lustig manages a small mutual fund consisting of North American government bonds. Rules require that at least two-thirds of the fund's securities be Canadian; the percentage currently stands at 75 percent. The fund never hedges foreign exchange risks, which was a bit of a disaster for fund-holders. With the fall of the loonie, over two years this fixed capital fund lost fully one quarter of its value, which now stands at $370 million (US). But the fund did pay good dividends, he adds.

Under American regulations, mutual funds must diversify their investments, which explains why Lustig holds all provinces, from $6 million (CA) in Prince Edward Island to $100 million (CA) in Ontario bonds. But the investment list shows only $10 million (CA) in Quebec bonds. Transactions involving the big provinces are more frequent than those with the small ones, he explains. Earlier in the year he sold $30 million (CA) worth of thirty-year Quebecs. At purchase, four months before, they had been trading ninety-eight points above Canadas; he is happy to have resold them at eighty-five points, for a profit of approximately 2 percent, not counting interest income. "We felt that separation was unlikely, and that the political risk was less than the market perceived it to be," he adds.

While the BlackRock fund holds only $60 million (CA) in Canada bonds, it boasts $85 million (CA) in mortgage bonds issued by banks but guaranteed by Canada Mortgage and Housing Corporation, a crown corporation. These securities are attractive because they yield forty basis points more than Canadas for the same credit quality. In comparison, Albertas yield only fourteen points above Canadas, with inferior credit. Still, provincial spreads are quite narrow at the moment, and mortgage bonds are not as liquid.

TUESDAY, MARCH 28, 1995

Wall Street traders don't always eat in upscale restaurants. At lunchtime most of them line up at delicatessen counters for a Coke and a $1.75 wedge of pizza, which they'll gobble up on the spot or take back to the office. I tag along with a handful of them as they cross Maiden Lane and take the elevator to the twentieth floor, the site of the RBC Dominion Securities trading room. In a corner, two men are puffing frantically on their cigarettes; of the two, the elder seems most concerned with his appearance. Dressed in a blue shirt with a white collar, a canary-yellow tie dangling between his suspenders, Gary Ball is chairman of the board. "I've been in New York since, ah, um . . . 1967," he admits sheepishly. His colleague also has suspenders on, but his tie isn't quite as flashy. He holds down the managing vice president's job, and his name is Steve Ashby.

RBC Dominion Securities, Canada's largest investment dealer, traces its New York roots back to the turn of the century. Since then, it has helped Canadian governments and corporations raise capital on the Yankee market. Tomorrow, Ball volunteers, they're off on an American tour to introduce CMHC to institutional investors and prepare an issue.

There is no retail clientele for the Canadian Yankees, but the bonds attract a large number of institutions, from one coast of the United States to the other. "Canada has a unique and favoured position in the mind of U.S. investors," Ball explains. But, "I've never seen so much bad publicity on Canada. Some of the analysts involved in the U.S. institutions are probably as knowledgeable, if not more knowledgeable, than Canadian analysts." It's an important market for Canadians, he insists. "The Yankee market is the last provider of long-term capital in the world." It also takes on riskier paper. "There have been times when Quebec, and particularly Hydro-Québec, have received a better acceptance in the United States than in Canada."

New York hedge funds

Ashby supervises Canadian bond sales to American institutions. Some of them — such as insurance companies with Canadian subsidiaries — are longtime buyers. But in the early 1990s, Ashby started noticing an increasing number of spread plays between the United States and Canada. Transaction volume at RBC Dominion Securities' New York office is twenty times what it was a decade ago, a growth rate related to the upsurge of the swaps market. The banks and investment dealers who offer borrowers swaps make abundant use of bonds as hedging assets. The availability of swaps broadens the range of plays open to investors attracted by Canadian bonds.

The most spectacular turnabout, however, has been caused by the rise of hedge funds, specialized in short-term speculative investments. These funds pick up their cash from a large number of conservative institutional investors who are prepared to hand over a small portion of their assets in the hope of earning higher yields. Borrowings obtained from investment dealers through repurchase agreements have the effect of multiplying the fund's clout.

Ashby deals with five or six such funds. A New York hedge fund knows the capital markets much better than the average client in Canada, he asserts. "Their technology is phenomenal." With capital in the billions, they patrol the planet on the lookout for quick profits. And nothing can stop them. A few years ago, Ashby recalls, a client decided that the Canadian dollar had become vulnerable, and predicted that the Bank of Canada would raise short-term rates to support it. The fund's strategy was to sell short those assets whose price would go down as rates went up. "He called up and said: where can I short a yard of three-month bills?" (In Wall Street lingo, a yard means one billion dollars.) Ashby went on to explain that the Canadian market was too shallow to sell short one yard of three-months. "Where can I short half a yard of six-month bills?" the client asked. Once again, the Canadian market simply wasn't deep enough to absorb the transaction. The client tried again: "Where can I do a quarter of a yard in one-year bills?" He finally sold short $125 million (CA) worth of two-year bonds. Each one of these positions offered, in terms of risk and volatility, the same financial leverage as $1 billion (CA) in three-month bills, because a rate rise has more impact on long-term than on short-term paper.

Hedge funds can nudge prices. "I have seen a hedge fund come in and buy ten-year Canadas, and in three to five minutes move the market up by close to a dollar," says Ashby. It goes without saying that other investors are anxious to find out what's going on. "They have the feeling that the hedge funds know something they don't know," chimes in Ball. But they'll never know; clients' transactions are strictly confidential. Luckily for Canada, Mexico has been keeping the big speculators busy.

"Canadian clients have to buy Canadian dollar bonds. Foreigners don't have to buy them," notes Ashby. "They will buy the debt if they like it, and they will short the debt if they don't like it. There are several hedge funds out there that have the financing ability to short more than a billion" of Canadian debt. They all know one another, and they like to attack in a pack, like wolves — or sharks. "They can sell mercilessly. They sell it and sell it and sell it. If it keeps going down, they will sell some more. So it is very important that they are on side."

WEDNESDAY, MARCH 29, 1995

From the ninety-fourth-floor offices of Fiduciary Trust International in New York's World Trade Center, I have a nearly aerial view of the Statue of Liberty. But here, where the investment horizon is resolutely internationalist, capital enjoys all the liberty. Fiduciary Trust manages funds for the largest international organizations, wealthy private foundations, and super-rich individuals, a little like the private banks of Geneva. A man in shirtsleeves leads me into a cubbyhole kitchenette, where we each pour watery coffee into large styrofoam cups and then walk down the hall to a handsomely appointed conference room.

My informally dressed host is Warren A. Keyser, Fiduciary's outspoken senior vice president, and a man with an insider's knowledge of Canada. I start the ball rolling by asking him about the recent federal budget. "Progress on the budget deficit is very good. Paul Martin was down here two weeks ago. It was his second big presentation to New York investors. Last year he said: 'You don't really believe me, but this is what I'm gonna do.' I was on the sceptical side. He came in this time and said: 'This is what we've done.' He's a very charismatic speaker. But there were also lots of numbers that were very sound and proved that they are really trying to get a handle on public sector finances. But there is still a good distance to go." In any case, Keyser adds, "it is not necessary to eliminate the deficit, but to show strong progress in the right direction. Paul Martin is moving in the right direction."

On the subject of monetary policy, Keyser bares a few more teeth. "I was an enormous fan of [former Bank of Canada governor] John Crow. Some years ago I even said that the resignation of John Crow would make me eliminate Canada from my bond portfolio. The changeover in leadership during Christmas week, when nobody was paying attention, was extremely well handled. But the benign neglect of the Canadian currency over the next eighteen to twenty months has really soured my taste for the Bank of Canada. I think it was a very deliberate depreciation of the Canadian dollar to make Canada more competitive within NAFTA."

Keyser judges Quebec just as harshly. "Quebec has a special status in the market. They are the biggest Yankee issuer by far. Many of our clients, who wouldn't think of buying a foreign issuer, think Hydro-Québec is a

U.S. issue. They are in almost all our portfolios from time to time." The reason is that "Quebec is probably one of the cheapest thirty-year bonds that is single A," he says, adding that "Quebec is cheap for the single reason that they keep trying to leave the rest of Canada." Cheap for the buyer, but expensive for the borrower. Constitutional uncertainty might well have driven the average cost of Quebec borrowing over the last fifteen years up by half of 1 percent, he estimates. The cost has been just as stark for the country as a whole. Canada accounts for a mere 3 percent of the world bond market, Keyser reminds me. "It is getting to the point where a lot of global investors say the time required to stay on top of what is going on in Canada is increasingly not worth the reward. When you add that to the devaluation of the Canadian dollar that has occurred over the last two years, I think you're lessening the investor base that puts up with Canada" in their portfolios.

TRENTON, NEW JERSEY, THURSDAY, MARCH 30, 1995

In Trenton, a small, unremarkable city about a hundred kilometers south of New York City, the state capitol building is right on State Street. The state's Republican governor, Christie Whitman, was elected on a promise to cut taxes by 30 percent, with public spending not far behind: perhaps that's why Roland Machold's shoes are wearing thin. A department head at New Jersey State Investments, he manages assets of $44 billion (US), including the government employees' pension fund, the state treasury, and several funds set up by the state. New Jersey State might be four times larger than Alabama State, and the same size as Quebec's Caisse de dépôt, but Machold's work space reminds me of an unemployment insurance office.

"I'm such a fan of Canada," he bursts out. "I lived in Quebec for a year; it's a wonderful place." In the 1950s he worked for Alcan. But ties between the New Jersey pension fund and Canada are more than personal; the State has been buying provincial and electric utility bonds for the same period.

New Jersey buys what it considers low-priced bonds on the Yankee market. The basic criterion is a minimal single-A rating, Machold explains as he hands me a copy of his list of Canadian securities: $50 million (US) of Hydro-Québec, including $3 million in the form of a private investment; $32 million (US) from an Ontario global issue, and $2 million (US) of B.C. Hydro, for a total of $84 million (US). "We tend to buy and hold," he says. "We are not traders."

The cornerstone of Machold's management philosophy is investment diversity, which has taken on international dimensions since 1989. Of his portfolio, 12 percent is currently invested abroad, half in equity, the other half in bonds. American equity makes up 54 percent, real estate 5 percent, with American bonds, including Yankees, making up the rest.

The foreign currency bond portfolio is managed along Salomon Brothers index guidelines, minus the American component. The investment list includes government debt only — France, Spain, United Kingdom, Australia, Holland, Finland, Germany, Belgium, Denmark, Sweden — and a certain amount of paper issued by supranational organizations like the World Bank. Not a single Japanese bond. The list also shows $160 million (CA) in Canada bonds allocated among four maturities, representing 7.5 percent of the portfolio, or slightly above their weight in the modified index. The Quebec question and the debt have led them to reduce their weighting by 1 or 2 percent, explains portfolio manager Victor Yu, who has just walked into the room. The position is 40 percent hedged against foreign exchange risk, he notes.

What concerns Machold most is the impact of Québec's drive for sovereignty on the other provinces. "It would be a different economy. How different, I don't know." But he has his doubts about the kind of economic policies that might be adopted. "We would like to see that issue resolved in some permanent way. As long as tensions are there, they create possibilities and worst-case scenarios — and maybe best-case scenarios. We don't know."

Public finances are another worry. In Trenton, the impression is "that the management of government is not in control." When Machold visited Quebec for the 1976 Olympics, he remembers Montreal mayor Jean Drapeau, "a very charming man," who asserted that the Olympics would not have a deficit, but only a gap, which "'would be filled in by more royalties.' How very French!" he laughs.

Easygoing Americans, complacent Canadians

Canadian governments that come to borrow in New York follow a well-worn path; names like Hydro-Québec almost pass for American. Canadians are not really foreigners, just good neighbours. American investors know us well, or, failing that, think they do. The problem is that they tend not to notice that we're different. Even our riskiest borrowers, with their thirty-year maturities that no one else in the world will buy, are welcome on the Yankee market. The Americans are our biggest creditors, as easygoing as we are complacent.

The arrival of American investors on the Canadian bond market is not only a much more recent development, it's also far less stable — although still predictable. The Americans buy Canadian paper when our interest rates are substantially higher than theirs, and sell when the differential narrows. But the movement of capital takes on another dimension entirely when hedge funds join the game. Exchange rates play a role, but much less so than with the Europeans and the Japanese. After all, they reason, the loonie is just a poor cousin of the greenback.

Americans are generally cooler-headed than other foreign investors — and much cooler-headed than traders in English Canada — about our constitutional debates. The Quebec issue has been around for a long time. The Americans might not be as open-minded, politically speaking, as the Europeans, but they are pragmatists, and well informed to boot. Most major American investment dealers have competent analysts; a few, like Merrill Lynch, have excellent ears in Montreal. American brokers are more than American; they are everywhere; and their reading of events is widely disseminated.

Perhaps because my American trip took place after the second Martin budget, perhaps because the Americans themselves are experiencing serious fiscal problems, I came away with the feeling that they are less bothered than the Europeans by Canada's debt problems. As their investment horizon is generally shorter, several told me they could simply leave a situation if it became too risky.

For Canada, the American bond market is more than a significant source of capital. It is a bellwether market that dictates interest rate trends for Canada, and indirectly shapes European and Japanese investors' perceptions of Canadian bonds. Financial technology, from hardware and product engineering to the information networks, the largest distribution channels, and financial theory itself . . . everything is American. There's no way around it: we are trapped in a dependent relationship. The least we can do is to shake ourselves out of our complacency and start making Canada a good place to invest. Just in case the Americans turn a little less easygoing.

THE
RATING
GAME

QUEBEC CITY, TUESDAY, AUGUST 23, 1994

ON THIS BRIGHT, late-summer afternoon Place d'Armes is swarming with tourists, their clicking cameras trained on the Château Frontenac. Kitty-corner across the square, a massive Second Empire edifice with grey-stone façade and green copper roof draws hardly a second glance. Built in 1883 as the Quebec City courthouse, today it houses the province's Finance department. I've come here to meet the deputy minister, the man whose job it is to make a select group of American visitors on a tight schedule feel at home. No camera-wielding tourists these; the visitors are the representa-tives of Moody's and Standard & Poor's, the New York–based credit rating agencies who can turn thumbs up or thumbs down on entire economies.

I have come to Quebec City to learn how the agencies — and the governments they scrutinize — get along. In the spring of 1993, Gérald Tremblay, then minister of Industry, Commerce, and Technology in Robert Bourassa's Liberal government, told me: "Our budget had only one pur-pose: to maintain our rating; and we were not successful." He must have been simplifying matters. Still, I wondered how the government could have so badly misjudged the amount of stiff financial medicine that would be needed to maintain the province's credit rating.

They don't build rooms like this any more. Alain Rhéaume's immense office reminds me of a loft. And today's strict regulations protecting historical sites make subdivision out of the question. In his early forties, the baby-faced Rhéaume speaks with a deep baritone voice. I pinch myself at the sight of a deputy minister with three tiny embroidered rabbits on his shirt pocket. Clearly the man's taste in shirts didn't stop Jacques Parizeau from recruiting him to the Finance department in the first place, nor Robert Bourassa from appointing him deputy minister. Now that the PQ is back in power, Parizeau has asked him to stay on. Nobody here is second-guessing Rhéaume's abilities.

We sit down across from each other at a work table; the interview gets underway. My first question: How do the rating agencies and the government get along? "We have a strictly professional relationship, based on an ongoing exchange of information," he explains. "At minimum we do a complete yearly review of Quebec's financial and economic situation, and we hold additional private meetings when the need arises. The annual review usually takes place after the budget. The rating agencies evaluate government and Hydro-Québec securities at the same time, which means that Hydro and the agencies that review its operations also meet annually.

"We usually spend an entire day with each of the American agencies," he continues. "With the Canadian agencies like CBRS and DBRS it doesn't take as long, usually only a half-day. We prepare a working document giving all our budget and debt-management data, which we hand them a couple of days prior to the meeting."

The document uses information drawn from the budget, but it provides additional details on the economical assumptions and the sensitivity factors used to measure the impact of error in budget forecasts, and the answers to specific questions that the agencies have forwarded to the Finance minister after examining the budget.[1] "We spend the whole day going over the document, answering their questions." A fifteen-member delegation from the department sits in; their job is to provide the details. "But by the end of the day, the deputy minister is the one who's looking for a glass of water," laughs Rhéaume. On some occasions the minister of Finance — or, rarely, the premier — will present a capsule summary of his government's financial, economic, and fiscal policy.

"Afterward, we keep the agencies up to date on our situation," he adds. At the end of each quarter the department forwards new information and, should the need arise, sorts out the odd question by telephone.

Should Rhéaume be passing through New York, he "tries to meet with them for an hour or two, to go over things."

Information exchange aside, how do you get on with them? "There are people who trade bonds based on the ratings. Obviously, the agencies are completely independent; they make their own judgments. Our job is to keep them as well informed as possible, and to present them with the Quebec government's approach to managing the economy, public finances, and the debt. But it's their call!"

After the day's briefing in Quebec City, the agency analysts head back to New York to draft a report, which is then submitted to the rating committee, a group made up of high-ranking people in the organization; it is this committee that brings down the final verdict. "When the marks are negative, they give advance notice. Standard & Poor's has an appeal procedure; at that point you can meet the members of the rating committee, or at least a significant portion of it, and argue that your rating should be maintained, not lowered. With Moody's it's not quite so clear-cut. They give you prior notice, but there is no appeal procedure as such, though we can talk with them informally and try to get our message across. In the past we've been successful on certain occasions, unsuccessful on others. In 1982 we succeeded; in 1993 we did not." In 1984, didn't then-Finance minister Jacques Parizeau successfully avoid a downgrade from Standard & Poor's by travelling to New York to plead his case at the eleventh hour? I ask. "In 1984, as you say, we were successful, but I can't really give you the details on what went on at those meetings," answers Rhéaume.

In 1993, discussions with Moody's got underway on April 14, immediately after the government tabled its spending budget for 1993–94. In his May 20 budget speech, the late Gérard D. Lévesque announced a $4.97-billion deficit for the fiscal year just ended, against a forecast of $3.79 billion made a year earlier; the predicted deficit for the new fiscal year was $4.1 billion. The annual reviews were held on May 25 with Moody's, and three days later with Standard & Poor's. Moody's downgraded Quebec from Aa3 to A1 on June 3. On June 11, Standard & Poor's notified Quebec of its intention to drop the province's credit rating from AA- to A+. On June 17, Rhéaume and Gérard D. Lévesque defended their cause before the rating committee in New York, but to no avail. The decision to go ahead with the change was announced five days later. (Moody's again dropped Quebec's rating, from A1 to A2 on June 15, 1995, after Parti Québécois Finance minister Jean Campeau's first budget; Standard & Poor's maintained its rating at A+.)

Is there a power struggle during these meetings? "I don't think that's the best way to define the relationship," Rhéaume replies. "You can't change their minds unless you have some objective evidence. The party being evaluated has no power, except to put forward its arguments, to show clearly which way its fiscal and financial plans are heading. You can't really call it a negotiating position. What you do have is your own persuasiveness, your credibility and that of the government, and the strength of your financial and fiscal plans."

The agencies are on the lookout for a host of objective, quantifiable variables, dealing with finances and the capacity of the economy to support the debt: things like economic growth, debt ratios, deficit forecasts, fiscal leeway, government spending in comparison with other provinces, etc. They also pass judgment on "the credibility, the seriousness, and the ability of the people who manage public finances, from the premier to the deputy minister of Finance."

The agencies have no precise mathematical formula for establishing a given borrower's rating. For the quantitative side of the evaluation, they compare the financial ratios of several borrowers. These ratios are public knowledge; government officials can calculate them and get a fairly accurate idea of where the province stands. "We try it ourselves," admits Rhéaume. "But the margin for error is too great. In 1993, we thought we would sail right through."

So where did you go wrong? "When we prepared the budget, we had two main concerns in terms of the soundness of public finances. First, we wanted to get deficit and debt growth under control as fast as we could. We didn't need a credit agency to tell us that; it was important for Quebec. Second, we had to come onto the market with our borrowing program, and we wished to maintain our credit rating." Consultations with the financial community made it clear that the province really couldn't afford a higher deficit, relates Rhéaume.

"We later came to the conclusion that even if the deficit had been a few hundred million dollars lower, we would probably have lost our rating anyhow, because our debt level was becoming incompatible with the kinds of benchmarks the agencies use," he adds.

But can't you ask the agencies what would be an acceptable deficit, before you bring down the budget? "Never. They give no prior notice. When we draw up the budget, we do it as responsibly as we can in terms of public finance. If we're serious, if we go about deficit reduction firmly and if our plan is a credible one, then we can probably salvage our rating. But that's all I could tell the Finance minister and the premier when we finished the budget. I couldn't give any guarantees. No one could. We brought down the best budget we could in terms of public finances, without going too far and destroying everything."

Rhéaume and his officials had been aware for nearly a year that a downgrade was a possibility. The agencies had sent out "clear signs" but nothing else; no detailed prescription of what had to be done to maintain the precious rating. "If they did, it would make things easier, but at the same time, I suspect no one would really like it; neither the agencies nor us. We don't want a budget drawn up by financiers. In a democratic society, the government's job is to govern, and to make the choices that must be made in the best interests of society. That's what the people expect. You don't want outsiders dictating your responsibilities." The possibility of a downgrade was "one consideration" among many. "We thought we'd succeeded; it didn't happen. If they had told me, 'You're missing 100 million,' maybe we could have come up with the money. But we certainly wouldn't have changed the budget by billions, or changed its structure and approach."

What about political uncertainty? Isn't it one of the variables the agencies look at? Things have changed, he replies. The rise of nationalism might have been a factor in the 1970s, but "now the agencies look at the willingness and the ability to pay back debt. As far as the willingness is concerned, I think most people believe Quebec is a democratic society that is not going to repudiate its paper from one day to the next." Of course, it's obvious that you're better off without uncertainty when it comes to finance and the economy. But political uncertainty isn't unique to Quebec and the question of its status in Canada, Rhéaume maintains. Anywhere in the world, whenever a new government a little more to the left or to the right, majority or minority, takes power, uncertainty is likely to be the result. The agencies wait to see what will happen, what direction the new government will take in terms of economic, fiscal, and financial policy. The last thing they're interested in is tales from the political twilight zone.

Lower credit ratings do have an effect on the province's debt costs, Rhéaume concedes. The question is: how much? "Our only measuring stick is to compare our debt costs with the Canadian government's. But many things influence the spreads: interest rate levels, the rarity of your own paper, how regularly you go to the market over a given period, foreign investor interest in the Canadian dollar, investor confidence in the creditworthiness of Canada's provinces, particularly Quebec, political uncertainty, and the credit rating. Factoring the impact of each variable into changes in the spreads is a complicated business."

Then there are the guessing games people play. "When your rating drops, have the investors who are running more and more sophisticated analyses already anticipated it? If they have, then the downgrade doesn't mean much; you might have been paying more for a year already. Strange . . . in 1993, right after the drop, our debt costs continued to decrease," says Rhéaume. "Does that mean the investors had anticipated it completely? Or was it because we hadn't been on the market for a while? One thing is certain, though: all things being equal, a lower rating ends up costing you more."

Putting a dollar figure on the cost is tough. It could be an eighth of a cent, or one quarter, he says. Much also depends on how far the rating has fallen: is it a case of slippage within the same class, from AA to AA-, or a fall from one class to another, from AA- to A+?

Rhéaume performs a quick, off-the-cuff calculation. His example is strictly theoretical, but it provides an idea of the powerful impact a downgrade might have on public finances, and how that impact would make itself felt. If a lower credit rating costs ten basis points — one tenth of 1 percent — and Quebec would have to grin and bear it for five years before getting its old rating back, with borrowings of $5 billion per year (the deficit plus debt refinancing) at an average maturity of ten years, the interest bill alone would rise by $5 million for each year of the ten-year life of the new bonds, for a total of $50 million for one year's borrowing. The cumulative effect over the five years of the downgrade would be even more striking. If, in the fifth year, money were again to be borrowed for another ten-year period, the impact would be felt over a period of fifteen years. "At the end of fifteen years, new borrowing for those five years alone would end up costing $250 million. And if we're talking about twenty-five basis points, additional costs would shoot up to $625 million."

The impact on Hydro-Québec debt would be similar if not identical. Hydro cannot have higher ratings than the province, which guarantees its debt. Rating fluctuations also affect the bonds issued by all other public sector borrowers. The financial results of Hydro-Québec and the debt costs of other crown corporations, hospitals, and school boards all feed back on the government's deficit. If the government manages with a pre-determined deficit objective in mind, it will have to reduce expenses significantly, or increase revenues by an equivalent figure, to compensate for its increased financing costs.

"Plus," adds Rhéaume, "there is the capital access issue: you might be able to meet your interest payments even if they cost you more, but you're in a dicey position if no one wants to lend you money." A downgrade dries up the pool of investors prepared to buy Quebec bonds. "A high percentage of institutional investment goes into high quality credits." Capitalization rules and in-house policies govern what proportion of portfolios can be invested in the various classes of bonds whose rating falls below a given level. And "every incremental reduction of your credit places your bonds in a larger pool of paper that investors have even less room for in their portfolios. If you end up with only one banker who's prepared to do business with you, it's going to cost you, and the price won't have anything to do with your credit rating."

At Standard & Poor's

NEW YORK, WEDNESDAY, MARCH 22, 1995

Head lowered, ready to lunge, a bronze bull sculpted by Arturo di Modica peers out from Bowling Green Park, at the southern tip of Manhattan Island, gateway to Broadway and the financial district. Not far away, as if to caution market bulls[2] to check for risk before charging, stands

Standard & Poor's, a subsidiary of the international publishing empire McGraw-Hill.

Standard & Poor's (S&P), along with its sister firm Moody's (owned by financial data behemoth Dun & Bradstreet), has been evaluating borrower creditworthiness since the Crash of 1929, when one American railroad company after another slipped over the edge into bankruptcy. There are other credit-rating services — among them Toronto-based Dominion Bond Rating Service (DBRS) and Canadian Bond Rating Service (CBRS) in Montreal — but the Canadian firms are lightweights compared with the two New York mega-agencies. Not a single Canadian or foreign investor told me that he paused for an instant to consider the DBRS or CBRS ratings before going ahead with an investment. That has not stopped the Canadian agencies from making headlines — perhaps because they are often quicker to downgrade Canadian governments — but their influence over financial markets is marginal. Foreign investors hardly know the two agencies exist, and Canadian investors maintain that they understand Canadian public finances just as well as the Toronto- and Montreal-based agencies. The two firms have a positive role to play in evaluating Canadian corporate paper, but they are facing sharper competition from the big American firms.

In a windowless meeting room I wait for Marie Cavanaugh, director, international finance. As she walks in she apologizes for keeping me waiting: "We've just downgraded Mexico! The press release will be out in an hour." I'm kicking myself: what a scoop for the press agency journalist I used to be! But by the time I'm out of here, it will be too late. Cavanaugh sits on the rating committee that evaluates what are called "sovereigns," the very same committee that has just downgraded Mexico from BB+ to BB;[3] she is the analyst in charge of Canada, the Scandinavian countries, and Turkey. She also works with two analysts from S&P's new Toronto office, who look after Canadian provinces and municipalities (called "quasi-sovereign entities"), the job she used to do when she joined the firm in 1984. Ms. Cavanaugh holds a Master's in Public Policy Analysis from the Kennedy School of Government. And, to tell the truth, she doesn't look like a wicked witch who eats children for breakfast. In fact, she's downright nice.

"Ratings exist to provide information on creditworthiness to the investment community," she explains. The agencies do not measure the market risks (such as foreign exchange risk) that cause the value of an investment to rise or fall; their sole concern is the risk of default, "the willingness and ability to service the debt on time and according to the terms of issue." Any bond issue in the United States must be rated by one of the Big Two; no formal requirement exists on international markets, but in practice S&P rates all major public borrowers, close to fifty countries in all. Investors rely on ratings to make a rapid comparison of risks and yields for a broad range of borrowers.

The rating system

The credit rating scale is divided into two main grades: investment and speculative. Investment grade is subdivided into four sub-groups: AAA, AA, A, and BBB. The speculative grade includes: BB, B, CCC, CC, and C, with the D rating reserved for issuers in default of payment. Under American financial regulations, banks, insurance companies, and trust companies are subject to more stringent constraints when they invest in bonds that are not rated investment-grade. Beyond U.S. borders, institutional investors tend to be even stricter in their criteria, rarely looking at bonds rated lower than A. Speculative grade bonds include "fallen angels," but also paper issued as such, including the notorious "junk" (or high-yield) bonds that financed the surge of hostile takeovers in the 1980s. Shallow in Canada, the trash paper market in the United States is significant.

"Everything from BBB- and above is considered investment-grade rating, which means that in our opinion debt will be serviced on a timely basis. Going from BBB to AAA defines the size of the cushion that the investor has," she explains. Plus and minus signs — "shades," as Ms. Cavanaugh terms them — are added to ratings to point to a given issuer's relative position within the subclass. Moody's uses the numbers 1, 2, and 3 to underscore the same differences. S&P (but not Moody's) also shades its ratings positive, stable, or negative to indicate which way the rating might be heading in the next few years if observed trends continue. S&P did not change its AA+ rating of Canadian federal government bonds following the February 1995 Martin budget, but it did change its outlook from stable to negative.

194

CREDIT-RATING AGENCY LISTINGS

Standard & Poor's	Moody's	Definition of ratings applied to long-term securities
AAA	**Aaa**	Excellent quality debtor, minimal investor risk; extremely strong repayment capacity.
AA	**Aa**	High quality debtor; debt well protected over a long period, very strong repayment capacity.
A	**A**	Upper medium grade; numerous positive aspects but also long-term risks; strong principal repayment capacity but more vulnerable to unfavourable circumstances.
BBB	**Baa**	Medium grade; good chance that debt will be repaid in time, but long-term protection uncertain.
BB **B**	**Ba** **B**	Risky investment of deteriorating quality; interest payments and the investment itself are minimally insured.
CCC **CC** **C**	**Caa** **Ca** **C**	Small probability that debt can be serviced on time and in total. For Moody's, possible delay of interest payments.
D	—	Late by more than one interest payment deadline

"We have a sovereign ceiling policy: with a few rare exceptions, no entity within a country can be rated higher than the sovereign itself. This has to do with the extraordinary powers of the sovereign in foreign exchange, to tax, and so on," says Cavanaugh. At Moody's, the rule is the same; when the agency downgraded Canadian federal government bonds from Aa1 to Aa2 on April 12, 1995, British Columbia, along with a bevy of Aa1-rated municipalities, were swept downhill along with Ottawa, while lower-rated issuers were unaffected.

Debt denominated in national currencies is normally rated higher than that held in foreign currency; sovereign states can tax or print money to repay their creditors. S&P rates Canada bonds in Canadian dollars AAA; its foreign currency securities are rated AA+; Moody's rates them Aa1 and Aa2, respectively. But the provinces enjoy the same rating for the totality of their debt. Default on bonds denominated in national currencies is extremely rare: since 1970, S&P has listed only five countries (Argentina, Brazil, Burma, Russia, and Viet Nam) that have defaulted on their national-currency bonds, but thirty-one that failed to honour their foreign currency commitments.[4] Payment defaults on foreign currency debt occur several years before defaults on national-currency bonds. Defaults are more frequent because debt service is, in that case, guaranteed by foreign exchange reserves, which a recurring balance of payments deficit can exhaust in a fixed exchange-rate system.

Finally, the agencies often slap a "credit watch" on an issuer when they anticipate important developments, but when the information they need for evaluation is not yet available. This is the rule when corporations announce mergers or takeovers in circumstances unknown, or "if a new government comes into office and says: 'We are going to do things so dramatically differently, wait for the announcement in our budget in two and a half months.'" Ratings are not put on credit watch on the eve of a routine budget, but they are reviewed not long after.

Ratings are established, says Cavanaugh, by scrutinizing "a broad range of economic, financial, and political factors. With sovereigns, there are two categories of risk: political risk, which has to do with the willingness to repay; and economic risk, which has to do with the ability to repay. For most of the countries, willingness is not a question. The political assessment focuses more on the various policies of the key parties — what kind of pressures are building for change or resisting change, like the whole debate about the extent of the social safety net. We try to assess the government's room to manoeuvre." Of course, the weight of political considerations in the overall evaluation varies from one country to the next — more for South Korea than for Canada, for instance.

"On the economic side, we try to put together an external balance sheet for the country." Its commitments to foreigners, irrespective of the currency in which they are denominated, are examined by an analyst. When a Canadian-dollar bond is redeemed, the foreign investor can invest the proceeds in Canada, or trade them for another currency and invest the money somewhere else. Debt held by foreigners represents either a real or potential withdrawal on the country's international reserves. "Canada's external indebtedness has grown fairly substantially over recent years; it's one of the key reasons for our lowering of the rating in 1992," Cavanaugh says.

Most of the variables that enter into the evaluation process are measured using statistical indicators and financial ratios, such as GDP growth, the unemployment rate, the interest payment against fiscal revenue ratio, or net foreign debt relative to exports. It is fascinating to note that per-capita debt is nowhere to be found in the agency's statistical compendium: that figure might be the centrepiece of innumerable chamber of commerce speeches, but the agencies pay it little or no heed.

"We do a long-term rating with an eight- to ten-year perspective. We try to be forward-looking through the business cycle; simply to raise ratings during recovery and lower ratings during recessions is not useful to anyone. We try to reflect changes to structural conditions," maintains Cavanaugh. Country is matched with country; province is matched with province, with the German Lands, and with the Australian and American states, with the necessary adjustments made.

In evaluating Canadian creditworthiness, S&P takes into consideration the fiscal situation of the provinces. "We look at the whole country, not just at the Government of Canada," scrutinizing both parts of the balance sheet — assets and liabilities. S&P also analyses capital investment by government, drawing a distinction between countries that take on debt for investment purposes and those that borrow to stimulate consumption. At budget analysis time, Cavanaugh checks whether expenditures and revenues are reasonable, and asks civil servants "what if" questions. "It is our job to look at things from the worst perspective possible." S&P examines results and fiscal commitments in the context of what can be reasonably accomplished. But Ms. Cavanaugh is well aware that "as you cut, it gets more and more difficult" to make progress in cutting back on government expenses.

S&P's SOVEREIGN RATING CRITERIA

Economic risks

The system, economic structure

- Market economy or not
- Resource endowment; extent of diversification
- Size and composition of savings and investment
- Rate and configuration of economic growth

Fiscal policy, public debt

- Public sector finance equilibrium
- Public debt and interest burden
- Contingencies of liabilities, including banks
- Debt service history

Monetary policy, inflation

- Price patterns
- Credit and money supply growth rates
- Foreign exchange policy
- Central bank autonomy

Balance of payment flexibility

- Impact of fiscal and monetary policies on external accounts
- Needs and composition of capital flows

External financial position

- Size and foreign-exchange composition of foreign debt, private and public
- Maturity structure and debt-service burden
- Level and composition of reserves and other asset elements

Political risks

Political system

- Form of government and adaptability of institutions
- Extent of public participation
- Orderliness of leadership succession
- Degree of consensus on economic policy objectives

Social environment

- Standard of living, income and wealth distribution
- Labour market conditions
- Cultural and demographic characteristics

International relations

- Integration into the international commercial and financial system
- Security risks

How it's done

Under normal circumstances, the issuer asks for the credit evaluation and must agree to cooperate throughout the process. The issuer must also pay a fee equivalent to three basis points on all bonds rated; regular issuers pay a preset yearly fee. In other words, in the great nightclub of bonds and credit, the stripper pays for the dance. Ms. Cavanaugh declines to specify what governments pay, though she does let slip that federal government bonds denominated in Canadian dollars are not a part of the equation. These fees are the principal source of revenue for the agencies, whose ratings of borrowers are put simultaneously at the disposition of the media and of potential investors.

A two- or three-person team visits an issuer to review that issuer's files; the rating committee then studies the team's report, in what Ms. Cavanaugh describes as a "very academic" atmosphere. "You're not selling something, you're presenting an analysis, and other people will go over it very carefully and bring their own expertise from other countries." With a downgrade looming, the issuer may appeal the decision. Downgradings are infrequent, and reversed decisions are rare: "More often than not, the first decision is final." But, she adds, "there are exceptions. The difference between AA and AA- is a matter of opinion. The first committee might have been split. It is very unlikely that a committee will be split by more than one notch. There are very well-developed ways to look at things. New information can sway a few people to look at things a little bit differently, and the result can be different by a notch." Still, to plead that a downgrade will entail higher interest charges and will only make things worse does not pass muster as an argument.

Dealing with governments

Did the Quebec government make an error when it structured its 1993 budget to maintain its credit rating? "I think there was some slippage in the deficit, contrary to expectations," Ms. Cavanaugh recalls. In reality, Quebec was $1.2 billion off target for the fiscal year just ended. S&P

RATINGS OF CANADIAN PUBLIC NAMES

At January 1, 1996

Borrower	Standard & Poor's	Moody's
Government of Canada	AAA stable ($CA)	Aa1 ($CA)
	AA+ negative (foreign currency)	Aa2 (foreign currency)
British Columbia*	AA+ stable ($CA)	Aa1 ($CA)
	AA+ negative (foreign currency)	Aa2 (foreign currency)
Alberta	AA- stable	Aa2
Saskatchewan**	BBB+ positive	A3
Manitoba	A+ stable	A1
Ontario	AA- stable	Aa3
Quebec***	A+ stable	A2
New Brunswick	AA- stable	A1
Nova Scotia	A- negative	A3
Prince Edward Island	not rated	A3
Newfoundland	BBB+ stable	Baa1

* British Columbia is the only Canadian province with different ratings for its debt in Canadian dollars and foreign currency, as it is the only one whose credit is restricted by the sovereign state ceiling policy.

** Following Saskatchewan's spring 1996 budget, S&P raised the rating to A-stable.

*** Following Quebec's spring 1996 budget, S&P changed the outlook to negative.

explained its decision in a press release that said: "The downgrade reflects the increase in the considerable tax-supported debt burden, the likelihood of further, albeit modest, increases until the recovery is well underway, and ongoing fiscal pressures that hinder more rapid deficit reduction." The agency went on to note that debt supported by taxation (excluding Hydro-Québec's bonds, which are guaranteed by the government, as well as government equity in the utility) had reached 52 percent of GDP in 1993, compared to 42 percent in 1990. The deficit had risen from 7 to 16 percent of revenues during the same period.

But Quebec would not necessarily have kept its rating even if it had made additional spending cuts. "It is not a question of cutting $100 million. It is not the way we do it. We take a longer-term perspective, we look at ongoing pressures," says Ms. Cavanaugh. "Quebec has a very heavy debt burden and continues to have fairly high deficits." But she does admit that agency decisions can sometimes leave people perplexed. "The most frequent misunderstanding that exists is when people see their deficit going down dramatically and then say: We should be upgraded! We say 'No,' it is just part of recovery. This is what we expect. It is often very difficult to see through a cycle.

"The whole notion of presenting a budget for the rating agencies is probably misguided," she adds. "The governments are elected to serve the people of Quebec, and it is our feeling that this should be their first priority. Our job is not in any way to influence policy but to analyse performance and the appropriateness of policy given certain factors."

Yes, I ask, but do governments ask for your advice when they are preparing their budgets? "We don't get involved in that kind of discussion, with any issuer," she replies unequivocally. "That is not our role. It is not appropriate in any way. We can't be both analysts and advisers."

The agency receives no privileged information before a budget is brought down. But like all interested observers, the credit-raters try to decipher the signals governments are sending, as they did prior to the 1995 federal budget. "I wouldn't characterize the budget as an enormous shock to us or to anybody else; actually, many of the broad outlines were announced the previous year. But we didn't have any prior knowledge of what was presented in the budget."

Canadian traditions are stricter on this point than most other countries', Ms. Cavanaugh notes, but she admits that at times "you might have information that you cannot make public that might be important in the rating decision."

Quebec independence

Finally, I drop the big question: What might Standard & Poor's do if Quebec should vote for independence in the referendum? "Our position has been and continues to be that our concerns would be mostly for the transition period. There are smaller countries than Quebec, and there are worse diversified countries than Quebec, and there is no reason why, in the end, it would not be all right. The difficulty is that both levels of government have substantial deficits, although declining, and we consider continued progress in this area to be very, very important in reinforcing economic potential."

In the event of a Yes vote in the October 1995 referendum, "it would take an extended period of time, perhaps a number of years" to settle all aspects of Quebec's economic relations with the rest of Canada: use of the Canadian dollar, trade, tax law, debt sharing, etc. "We would not expect a sudden or abrupt change. It would be very carefully negotiated," since it would be in the interests of both parties. "Our concern about the transition period is that investors might be somewhat reluctant to invest, not because of the fundamentals necessarily, but just because they don't like uncertainty." Nervous markets would only make things more complicated. "It is difficult enough to reduce your deficit even when everything is going right. There might be a risk that [the transitional efforts] would divert a lot of attention from addressing the fiscal problem. We see that as a risk." For S&P, "there are problems and potential negatives for both sides, although more so for Quebec. A large negative? It is a little difficult to assess that," says Ms. Cavanaugh in response to her own question.

Quebeckers, just like Ontarians, are already financing Canada's debt. "It's not as if there is something new. It is a question of how it is divided." It seems unlikely that S&P would revise Quebec's rating the day after a Yes vote in the referendum, but it could put a credit watch on the province. "We're not talking about 'credit cliffs' here but, again, the rating could change depending on what might happen during the transition period." Ms. Cavanaugh foresees "a range of outcomes that are possible," but she doesn't believe in dramatic upheavals. "Financial management in Quebec is very good." Bearing in mind recent events in Mexico, couldn't market reaction lead to a downgrade? "I don't think so," she answers, "if only because this issue has been discussed for so long." She does admit that she would be surprised if the Yes were to win. But the Mexican crisis is certainly not a telling example; the risks just aren't the same. "Mexico didn't have investment-grade rating," she reminds me.

I had come expecting to hear sharp criticism of federal and provincial government policies from Standard & Poor's, but Ms. Cavanaugh's judgment is a cautious one: "It's been a difficult time for Canada. We view as positive that many of these governments have taken strong actions to cut their spending. The difficulty is to assess what is going to happen when there is an economic downturn; will the progress be maintained? It is a challenging question."

Rating the raters

FRIDAY, MARCH 24, 1995

Salomon Brothers is hardly the most prestigious name on Wall Street, and the firm has had more than its share of problems. But it is still a power-house for bond-market operations, and its reputation for risk-taking is intact. As part of the fifteen-member team that analyses sovereign credit, vice president Peter Plaut spends three-quarters of his time keeping track of Canada. His job is to challenge Marie Cavanaugh's conclusions every step of the way.

"We try to do cross-border analysis in terms of sovereign creditwor-thiness," Plaut explains. "Is the rating appropriate? Can we be a little more forward-looking than the rating agencies when it comes to the political, economic, and fiscal realities? If the rating is not correct, where would we rate it? If it's okay, are there value opportunities in the market?" Where the agencies would never dare suggest a sale or a purchase, Plaut is paid to advise Salomon's clients, in the hope that they will negotiate the suggested transaction with the firm. While Salomon's economists forecast economic conditions for the upcoming year, Plaut's horizons are broader and deeper. Examining a dizzying number of factors, he attempts to determine creditworthiness five or even ten years down the road. It's a tricky assign-ment, but the thirty-something Plaut is long on confidence.

Like everyone else on the street, he is waiting for the verdict from Moody's. The Manhattan-based rating service had announced, two weeks prior to the February 1995 budget, that it would be reviewing Canada's rat-ing with an eye to a possible downgrade.[5] "Will Canada lose its coveted AAA rating on domestic currency? Yes, I believe there is about an 80 to 90 per-cent chance that in the next couple of weeks you will see Moody's downgrade the foreign and domestic rating of Canada by one notch." Plaut rounds out his forecast: he sees a 60 percent probability that Moody's will follow suit with Quebec's rating; for S&P the probability is only 40 percent.

The morning's *Globe and Mail* lays the weakness of the dollar and of the Canadian bond market at the feet of Moody's expected judgment. "So what? Most of it is probably priced in! It's still a very high-rated country." The surprising thing is not the downgrade, he adds, but Moody's decision to act when it did. If the agency had wanted to show some foresight, it could have acted a year earlier. Things have improved following the second Martin budget. "Now, the market doubts the ability of the rating agencies to be forward-looking." Still, "both Moody's and S&P are very sound," and quite similar in their approach, the difference being that Moody's takes a slightly longer-term view, while S&P tends to tilt toward the borrower when in doubt, but pin a negative outlook on its rating.

Plaut feels certain that Moody's likes the latest Martin budget, but, he says, the agency has "put it in its drawer." The concern is that the deficit will still be at $24 billion in three years, while Quebec and Ontario, which account for two-thirds of the Canadian economy, are still up to their necks in red ink. The average maturity of the Canadian debt is short, making it vulnerable to interest rate hikes. Finally, observes Plaut, more than in other OECD countries, Canadian public finances are sensitive to swings in the business cycle. For him, taking the long-term view means gearing up for the next recession: "What is more important is that Mr. Martin has got to meet his targets through the next downturn. That is the true test."

The peso crisis has forced institutional investors to do their creditworthiness analysis homework, and not to rely blindly on the ratings from Moody's and S&P, maintains Plaut. Of course, Canada and Mexico cannot be compared, but people are taking the lesson to heart. It can be seen in market reaction to the Bank of Canada's efforts to relax rates. Each time, the market has replied: "No, no, no. There is a risk premium you must give to us to hold your debt."

Investors, he argues, are doing more and more country comparisons. Moody's has given Italy an A1 rating, and for a few more days at least, an Aaa rating goes to Canada. But both countries are facing major political uncertainty; debt has reached 123 percent of Italy's GDP and nearly 100 percent of Canada's. Still, Italy finances only 10 percent of its debt abroad, compared to nearly 40 percent for Canada. Canada has posted a current payments deficit; Italy, a surplus. Finally, Italy's debt maturities are better distributed than Canada's. Bearing all these factors in mind, can Canada justifiably claim a rating so much higher than Italy's? Plaut wonders.

The Salomon Brothers analyst has been making the rounds of America's largest institutional investors in recent days. No one asked about the Quebec referendum, but people want full information on the province's financial situation. "They want to see fiscal discipline in Ontario and Quebec right now. They want to see it in all countries." For Plaut, "you need a debt profile that is on a more sustainable path." Still, he describes himself as "cautiously optimistic that Canada's credit ratings will be stable for the next two to five years." After the upcoming Moody's downgrade, of course . . .

Minimizing risks

Marie Cavanaugh, with her measured, sensible advice, reminded me of a kindly schoolteacher. But she might not prove quite so generous come report-card time. And Wall Street is crawling with aggressive, youthful Peter Plauts, people who believe she should be stricter — and then some.

Traders are quick to pounce on rating errors by the agencies. Writing about the Mexican debacle, *The Economist* noted that "Standard & Poor's had egg all over its face."[6] Investors have begun to lose confidence in the ratings and are attempting to forecast changes themselves. They know that weak ratings are usually more short-lived than high ratings, that one downgrade usually leads to another. Once bitten, twice shy.

Assigning ratings remains a subjective process; no point in losing sleep over pluses and minuses, or over the 1s, 2s, and 3s that describe them. What counts are the underlying trends: the weight of the debt as opposed to a single year's deficit. Of course, a small deficit can finally make a full cup overflow, and drop a name a grade lower. And in spite of the appeal procedure, there is very little a government can do at the last minute to avoid a downgrade.

Ratings are useful in measuring, grading, and defining an investor's credit risk. As a general rule, less-well-rated governments must pay more to borrow than better-rated ones. More critically still, every downgrade narrows the number of investors prepared to purchase the downgraded government's bonds, and lessens the appetites of those who might still be prepared to invest. While the rating system appears to be a finely graduated ladder, some rungs are farther apart than others, and more solid than others. Still, Rhéaume and Cavanaugh summed it up best: governments must answer to their citizens; it is up to them to put their financial house in order.

Chapter 9

FOUR BORROWERS, FOUR STRATEGIES

TORONTO, FRIDAY, APRIL 28, 1995

TODAY IS "CASUAL FRIDAY" at the Ontario Financing Authority. In the trading room the Authority's eight traders, clad in jeans, sport shirts, and running shoes, look on as the wall-mounted television set broadcasts Premier Bob Rae's announcement of a general election on June 8. "The job of the next government will be to struggle against federal government cutbacks," says the NDP leader. Priority will be given to job creation and "humane, sustainable" deficit reduction.

In yesterday's budget speech Finance minister Floyd Laughren — nicknamed "Pink Floyd" for his leftish sympathies — made public a deficit of $8.1 billion for the fiscal year just ended; optimistically, Laughren is predicting $5.8 billion for the new fiscal year. Already, the budget's highlights have been faxed around the world in the Ontario investor relations department bulletin, and financial analysts at banks and investment dealers have been briefed: "A big yawn!" said one, predicting that the figures would be different after the election. (In fact, the new Conservative government led by Mike Harris would later revise the deficit upward to $8.7 billion, after a $1.9-billion cut in expenditures.)

Carved out of the Finance department in 1993, the Ontario Financing Authority supervises deficit and debt financing, both of which grew substantially after the NDP took power in 1990; previous governments had experienced small deficits, easily financed by non-negotiable bonds invested in the teachers' and civil servants' pension funds, and in the Canada Pension Plan. The Authority also handles infrastructure financing and arranges off-balance-sheet operations, an accounting tactic that the financial community has frequently criticized. The Authority is one of the top three borrowers on international markets, and one of the most sophisticated.

Unlike his jean-clad staff, president and CEO John Madden is dressed in a conservative business suit: he's expecting callers today. Looking more like the financier he used to be than the civil servant he has become, Madden explains that the Authority's investment plan, drawn up at the beginning of each year, is determined by the deficit forecast in the provincial budget, by debt maturity allocation, and by the financial market outlook. The plan is a general one: markets are in a state of constant flux; the Authority must be able to act rapidly and flexibly.

Overall, the objective is to borrow at reasonable costs and risks, year in, year out. Madden, a seasoned professional with street smarts, likes to jump at a tempting opportunity, but not at the expense of his reputation as an issuer. "You need to establish a credible track record" when you're borrowing a billion a month, says the professional; but, adds the street-wise operator, "we usually try to set up transactions in such a way that any time we issue in one market we're also setting up to deal in another."

The Ontario government has developed a hearty appetite for capital. To raise that capital, the Authority must show sensitivity to the specific needs of each segment of the market, and seek out the crossover point where its operating constraints meet market demands. Traders, for instance, are partial to specific bond maturities: five- and ten-year paper is more popular than three- and seven-year; still, when he issues bonds, Madden must pay close attention to maturity allocation. "You don't ever want to concentrate all your financing in any one year. You tend to spread your financing need through various terms across the yield curve; because if it gets too large in one particular year, you have refinancing risks in that year, and it may be in poor markets."

Ontario works closely with a syndicate of investment dealers and bankers. "We used to have a fixed, global syndicate — no more," Madden blurts out. Today's arrangement is a flexible one, shaped by the type of operation: a combination of New York firms (Goldman Sachs, Salomon Brothers, Morgan Stanley), Canadian investment dealers (ScotiaMcLeod, Wood Gundy, and RBC Dominion Securities), as well as Europeans and Japanese. "The mixture will depend on where we think the majority of the distribution will go."

Madden's ties with investment dealers and bankers are based on long-term relations rather than price, he insists. But bankers themselves are divided on the issue; some feel Ontario is not as "loyal" as Quebec. "I have worked hard to develop relations," he counters. "Because of the size of the financing requirements, we are conscious of price, but we don't just take the best price. The reason for that is, the intermediaries are very much marketing in conjunction with us our product around the globe. And to always take, as a philosophy, the last piece that drops off the table is inappropriate." He is on the lookout for bankers who share his philosophy: "We will deal with them during the good and the difficult times," in the hope, of course, that they will reciprocate.

The approach is calculated less to please the financial syndicate than to satisfy the investors who purchase Ontario bonds. "The importance of the relationship for me is that we need, as far as possible, fair and equitable quotes and fair relationships with investors. I am very concerned about spread management, and fair performance for investors. And if we focus on price alone, we can imperil that relationship, particularly during bear markets." In other words, if Madden is too close-fisted with the bankers, they are unlikely to go out of their way to maintain an active secondary market for his paper, and spreads will be in danger of widening, something that would leave a bitter taste in investors' mouths.

The Authority is in constant contact with the principal members of the syndicate. "They provide us with various offers and advice, on anything ranging from private transactions to EMTN, to medium-term notes, to global transactions, to specific issues on an arbitrage basis in various currencies around the globe. There might be many offers in any one particular day, or only a few," Madden says. Employees talk three or four times daily with each of the five managers of the Canadian syndicate

(ScotiaMcLeod, CIBC-Wood Gundy, RBC Dominion Securities, Nesbitt Burns, and Richardson Greenshields). This is the lead group, which absorbs some 70 percent of issues on the domestic market. The remainder is subscribed by the underwriting group (Merrill Lynch Canada, Goldman Sachs Canada, T-D Securities, Midland Walwyn, City Bank, J. P. Morgan Canada, Casgrain et Lévesque Beaubien Geoffrion) and the distribution group; contact with these investment dealers is daily.

The Authority's vantage point gives it an informed overview of Canadian market receptivity. If Madden believes the time is ripe he phones a member of the lead group, they discuss a specific project — amount, maturity, and price (formulated in terms of the spread above Canadas) — for a few minutes, and then he gives the green light. The investment dealer becomes syndicate leader and immediately contacts the other members; within ten or twenty minutes, the issue will be complete. The Authority provides no advance warning; rumours of an upcoming issue can widen the spreads; dealers might be tempted to lighten their Ontario holdings, knowing that they will have to purchase substantial quantities in the underwriting operation. The price is set for quick sale, creating the impression that Ontario bonds are in demand, and ensuring narrow spreads. But caution is in order: selling at cut-rate prices would mean expenses financing for the province. Fine-tuning prices is a delicate art.

Choosing a market

The Canadian bond market is the natural market, the market of reference for Canadian public issuers. But it is often cheaper to borrow on foreign markets. To make an opportunity really interesting, Madden explains, "there have to be two factors. The market has to be what I call constructive: good distribution and price performance. Then there has to be the arbitrage opportunity" to bring those funds back into Canadian dollars, at low cost. Investor appetite for Ontario securities is the first criterion; the second is the cost of the swap itself. "It is an important distinction. There can be an arbitrage opportunity in yen, but nobody wants the paper." The opposite is also possible.

Ontario will issue foreign-currency bonds on a foreign market if, converted into Canadian dollars through a swap, it is cheaper than a similar issue on the Canadian market. For the Authority, the transaction becomes doubly attractive, as a broader cross-section of investors is drawn to the Ontario name. "Most often, we get cheaper costs. There are times when it's very close and we decide to go for the diversification. In truth, it is very difficult, sometimes, to measure, especially for larger transactions. It's a theoretical measurement. Frankly, if we did try to do two or three billion in one shot in the Canadian market, it could be quite expensive." By borrowing abroad, Ontario contends, it is helping the domestic market; if the province handled all its financing needs in Canada, spread performance would be poor.

The Authority has a fondness for U.S. dollars, which it can borrow in very large sums. These issues attract Canadian investors, who purchase paper denominated in U.S. dollars to diversify their market risks while respecting the 20-percent foreign securities limit imposed on pension funds. Most Canadian institutional investors have few problems with the American bond market — but the outlook changes when other foreign currencies enter the picture. Unfortunately, the Eurocan bond niche, an Authority favourite, has shrunk considerably since 1994.

Ontario's borrowings on public markets vary widely in composition from year to year: in 1990–91, Canadian dollars accounted for 40 percent, U.S. dollars for 45 percent, and foreign currencies for 15 percent; in fiscal 1994–95, the breakdown stood at 13 percent U.S. dollars (a single one-billion-dollar transaction), but 60 percent in Canadian dollars, 19 percent in yen, 4 percent in Deutschmarks, and 4 percent in Dutch guilders. Demand for greenbacks dropped off after the Fed tightened the credit screws in February 1994. The Authority also concluded that its yield spreads had performed poorly as a result of its jumbo issues of recent years. Last year, Ontario shifted its emphasis over to a Euro medium-term note (EMTN) program and managed to profit from Japanese enthusiasm for yen-denominated Canadian names.

Note programs, to be successful, depend on continuous surveillance and hair-trigger decision-making. Institutional investors who are looking for specific yields, currencies, and terms make their needs known to an investment dealer, who then sounds them out on three or four names for credit acceptability. A simple transaction can be patched together in a few hours; a more complex package can take days. The first borrower to match the features sought places his securities easily; the second and third might pay slightly more. The total number of borrowers is determined by demand and by the size of the initial transactions.

No foreign exchange risk

Madden is categorical: Ontario accepts no foreign exchange risk when it borrows in a foreign currency. As a rule, all debts are swapped. But, on the odd occasion, when the swap market is unfavourable, the Authority will negotiate "forwards" with a bank until a swap can be set up. "The hedging is the most complex, challenging, and innovative part of the transaction. It allows you excellent financing opportunities."

The province was the first Canadian borrower to turn to international issues on a massive scale. A January 1993 issue of bonds nicknamed Global III was worth $3 billion (US) of U.S. bonds. The entire amount was swapped in Canadian dollars either on the day of the deal or in the days leading up to it. The mega-transaction mobilized nine banks and took place in three stages: first, the fixed-rate borrowing in U.S. dollars was transformed into a floating-rate borrowing in U.S. dollars, which was then converted into a floating-rate Canadian-dollar borrowing, which was in turn traded for a fixed-rate borrowing in Canadian dollars.

When Ontario began foreign currency borrowing in 1990, the largest swaps would not exceed a few hundred million dollars. The market has soared since, but "you can't do all the swaps on the day, unless you're lucky. You can't do more than a couple of hundred million in fixed Canada at any point in time. So we have to set up well in advance so as to ensure the costs are appropriate." If not, traders will be waiting for you with less than optimum prices. His advice: "You have to disguise your money."

The sticking point is the leap from the floating U.S. rate to the floating Canadian rate. (Whatever the currency swap, it must transit through the greenback.) To nail down the transaction, the bank or investment dealer which has set itself up as a counterparty to Ontario must locate other borrowers who want to carry out the operation in reverse. Symmetry need not be perfect, nor simultaneous, but capital must flow in both directions in order for the swap market to function efficiently. The non-Canadian borrowers who flocked into the Eurocan market had to trade their Canadian dollars for American dollars, then into the foreign currency of their choice. These Canadian-dollar debts generated excellent liquidity and attractive prices on the swaps market. But the decline of the Eurocan — the loonie's weakness has made it far less attractive for investors — has reduced the capacity to make large-scale swaps toward the Canadian dollar.

To get around this obstacle, the Authority has set up a kind of reserve that Madden calls its "warehouse." It works like this: a bank needing to swap Canadian for American dollars for a client calls Ontario with an offer to become a counterparty. If the terms are right, the province takes an option on the swap, but puts off the purchase until later. The bank itself carries the swap for a certain length of time, in the knowledge that Ontario will use it for an upcoming foreign currency financing. By purchasing foreign currency swaps at the request of the banks rather than when the province needs them, Ontario successfully reduces its transaction prices by a few basis points. The price of a foreign currency swap is determined by capital flowing into and out of the Canadian dollar, typically six or eight points.

Depending on the state of the swap market, a borrowing, even at a low coupon price, can be more expensive after the swap than a bond issued on the Canadian market. The risk is real enough, Madden admits. "That is why you must diversify. In the environment that we have had [at the beginning of the year] the arbitrage opportunities did not exist in many currencies around the globe. They come and go very quickly. In this bear market, we have had a substantial currency volatility, and swaps have moved." During this turbulent period, Ontario sold most of its debt on the Canadian market and even brought forward its program to build up a cushion.

Swaps can be risky

Using swaps to eliminate foreign exchange risks exposes the borrower to counterparty risk. In a foreign currency swap, the bank that acts as a counterparty promises to pay all interest and to repay the principal at maturity in the contractually stipulated currency. Ontario agrees to pay the counterparty the corresponding amount in Canadian dollars, at the exchange rate provided at the signing of the swap contract. But if the Canadian dollar depreciates during the life of the contract, the counterparty must absorb the foreign exchange loss, sending the swap into the red. If the Canadian dollar appreciates, the counterparty pockets the profit, and the swap is in the black. The bank manages its counterparty risks within the framework of a diversified portfolio, taking care that its commitments are properly counterbalanced.

But the fact remains that the strength of the bank is the only guarantee that Ontario will be able to honour its bonds in foreign currency without forex loss. Obviously, counterparty risk cuts both ways: the bank might doubt Ontario's creditworthiness and its ability to honour the promised payment schedule. Swaps alter the relationship between the borrower and the bond-holders: the counterparty who underwrites swaps becomes a new link in the credit chain, and its strength is crucial.

Counterparty risk management is a controversial topic on international capital markets. "Our swap policy is to deal only with AA counterparties," says Madden. If the counterparty is downgraded, Ontario might terminate the contract; fortunately for Ontario, the converse is not (yet) true. "We have exposure limits by counterparty and we try to diversify. The biggest risks in terms of size are linked to our Canada-U.S. swaps; they are fairly substantial," he concedes.

"Swap capacity is something that everybody is concerned about around the planet because long-term-basis swaps erode a lot of credit capacity. One way to deal with this is through collateralization," Madden explains. This is done by depositing bonds guaranteeing payment. When a shift in the foreign exchange market creates a substantial theoretical loss for one of the parties, the one assigns to the other securities to be held in collateral. If the party in the red cannot respect its commitments, the other will keep the securities held as collateral as compensation. The World Bank has begun to operate in this manner; Ontario is seriously contemplating following its example. Risk can also be reduced if the party in the black pays the party in the red when the amount at stake exceeds a certain level.

"The issue of swap capacity becomes more exacerbated when credit ratings fall. If the credit rating of the province or any other institution falls down to single A, without collateralization, it becomes more difficult," he says. Since May 1991, when Ontario boasted an impeccable AAA from both New York agencies, the province's name has been downgraded three times, and is currently rated Aa3 by Moody's and AA- by S&P.

Capital sources must be diversified, argues Madden, "because even if the Canadian dollar is out of favour, as long as there is no problem with the credit, swaps allow you immense capacity" for borrowing. If the investor feels comfortable with Ontario's credit, the Authority will provide the foreign currency of his choice — as long as swap conditions are favourable. In the long term, Madden foresees no capital access problems: "The reason I don't, is not that there aren't challenging periods, but I think the access to capital is always a challenge for most large borrowers. I would say that we are, among the large borrowers around the globe, probably one of the most diversified," both in terms of financial assets and in terms of regions solicited. "What would become a problem, to be honest with you, is if the credit rating eroded. Then I think it would be much more difficult. Investors might not be allowed to hold your paper if it erodes. Given that the credit ratings are what they are, I think we can comfortably fund the province."

Hydro-Québec meets the money men

MONTREAL, MONDAY, MAY 15, 1995

In October 1962, a certain F. J. McDiarmid, president of the Lincoln National Life Insurance Company of Fort Wayne, Indiana, was the guest speaker at a business luncheon held at the Canadian Club. McDiarmid was a native of Canada; his firm had invested more than $4 million in Quebec electric utilities. "What you have here is a politician who talks as if his name was Robespierre, and who acts as if the aristocrats should be lined up at the guillotine," he told his audience. "He is hurting the investment climate. I believe this man should be warned!"[1] True enough, McDiarmid's political nemesis had launched the slogan "The people of Quebec against the trusts," shorthand for the English-speaking financiers of St. James Street, members of the Canadian Club. The youthful, impetuous minister of Natural Resources, a man called René Lévesque, had just announced

215

his intention to nationalize the province's eleven privately owned electric utilities (which he successfully accomplished shortly thereafter). McDiarmid could hardly have imagined that thirty-three years later Hydro-Québec would be a crown corporation with assets of $51 billion, with its head offices located at 75 boulevard René-Lévesque ouest, anchoring Montreal's skyscraper row.

A huge, electrically charged "Q" is emblazoned high on the flank of the headquarters building, where I meet Daniel Leclair, who does double duty as the utility's vice president, finance, and as treasurer, and David Blustein, head of the utility's capital markets division. In the 1970s and '80s, when Hydro-Québec's massive dam-building program was in full swing, it was one of the largest bond issuers on world markets, hitting a record $5.7 billion in 1991. Borrowing has tailed off substantially since then, but the utility still has a $37-billion debt to manage.

On financial markets, Hydro-Québec is a strange kind of hybrid, a cross between a corporation and a quasi-sovereign issuer. "We try to sell as if we were a corporation, but with a government guarantee," is how Leclair puts it. As a tradeoff for the guarantee, the utility pays its sole shareholder $174 million in annual fees. Not surprisingly, the two names are frequently confused; when traders talk about "Quebecs" they mean both the provincial government's bonds and those of its electric utility: six of one, half a dozen of the other. The government guarantee also means that Hydro-Québec's rating can be no lower but also no higher than the province's. "Oh well, you can always dream!" quips Leclair. Hydro-Québec might well possess enviable assets, but for Leclair's dream to come true, it would have to double its equity and raise its rates by 30 percent; only then would its financial ratios approach those of comparable American utilities.[2] For better or for worse, the fate of Hydro-Québec is intimately linked with that of the Quebec government.

Hydro-Québec's annual borrowing program is part of its overall five- and ten-year plans, Leclair explains. The annual planning exercise begins in late August and reaches its climax at the beginning of the new fiscal year, January 1. The program covers maturing debts as well as new investment needs: some 30 percent will be self-financed out of the utility's profits; the remainder will be borrowed. The 1995 program is only half the size of the previous year's, for a total of $1.5 billion: $400 million for financing new investments and $1.1 billion for financing debts reaching maturity.

A combination of favourable circumstances on the secondary market also enabled Hydro-Québec to buy back $700 million of its own paper at a high coupon price, replacing it with new paper with lower-priced coupons. In 1994, Leclair reminds me, Hydro-Québec had already surged nearly $800 million ahead of the 1995 financing program, well above its normal cash reserves of $500–$600 million. "Our objective was to get through a volatile market during the first six months of 1995." The strategy worked, but not necessarily for the anticipated reasons: the referendum was not called that spring, but the Mexican crisis shook markets badly, says Leclair.

Now it's over to Blustein, who ticks off the utility's overall objectives: a debt in Canadian or U.S. dollars, along with terms of ten years or more to match long-term assets. "We look for a presence on the largest possible number of markets to give our name visibility to international investors." With these parameters in mind, he draws up a hypothetical program: for example, $500 million (CA) on the Canadian market, $200 million (CA) in Europe, and so on. How close does the plan come to reality? "You can't avoid making adjustments over the course of the year," Blustein replies. The Eurocan market once represented a significant source of funds; this year's Eurocan volumes account for barely 20 percent of 1994 levels, which dropped by 40 percent from 1993, a record year. But when the time comes to swing into action, adds Leclair, "we coordinate things in real time with our friends in Quebec City" to avoid soliciting the same markets all at once. For similar reasons, "it's important to know what our competitors intend to do." The best-informed, quickest issuer enjoys a tactical advantage: he can skim the cream of the market as soon as a specific demand materializes.

Syndicate members are then shown the overall outline of the funding program. "It's vital to have a solid partner network," says Leclair. "They are our eyes, ears, and mouth on financial markets around the world." But Hydro-Québec confidence in the expertise of its partners does have its limits. "Our own people here cover the big financial markets," Australia and Southeast Asia excepted. "Sometimes," adds Blustein, "we don't want the market to know that we're going to do a financing. And since we have specialists who keep close track of markets, we can show up unannounced."

Still, as a rule, "the members of the syndicate know whether we want to borrow or whether we're closed. If we're open, they'll make us offers on hot markets." Like the bond issued in June 1994 on the Yankee market: a bond with a put option that paid 8.05 percent the first year and gives the buyer the right to repayment in the eleventh year, well ahead of the thirty-year maturity. Why? "That product was tailor-made to immunize the portfolios of large investors" against long-term rate increases, notes Leclair. "We started off with $400 million (US), but considering the beauty of the product, we upped the issue to $700 million (US). We reopened it this year, bringing our liability up to $1 billion." The issue — a first on the Yankee market — has now become a benchmark for similar bonds issued by other borrowers. But for Hydro-Québec, there are disadvantages as well as advantages to having its bonds considered as simple commodities: "When times are good, yields shrink fast. But when there's a problem with Canada, or with the Yankee market as a whole, our paper is the first to be sold," admits Leclair.

Well-connected investment dealers and bankers are indispensable in exploiting the small market niches that are continually opening and closing. Hydro-Québec has set up an EMTN program with an objective of $2 billion (US); the utility has already borrowed half a billion. Meanwhile, it has announced a $3-billion (US) note program in the United States, now half completed. Quebec has a note program on the Canadian market, but not Hydro-Québec, which wants to avoid competing with its sole shareholder — for the time being, at any rate, says Blustein. Selling debt on troubled markets is easier with notes, but terms rarely exceed ten years, and the size of each transaction is limited. The majority are yen issues, at fixed rates; the principal buyers were Japanese. Not much in the way of complex instruments, notes Leclair. "When you do an 'exotic' transaction it causes counterparty risk; I never know who's behind it, and it's lacking in liquidity." Hydro-Québec policy is to stick to relatively simple options.

The financial syndicate

Historically speaking, Hydro-Québec has maintained a policy of ongoing relations with the banks instead of calling for tenders for every operation, explains Blustein. "Still, it's not carved in stone; things change as the markets and the banks evolve. You always have some banks coming up, and others that are going down." When S. G. Warburg pulled out of the Euromarket last year, the British bank immediately withdrew from the syndicate. Syndicate makeup must also be adjusted in response to changes on the markets: ten years ago, banks with a retail network in the Benelux countries accounted for three-quarters of all European buyers; today, 85 percent of sales are to institutional investors.

Hydro-Québec and the province both use the same syndicate; together they track the performance of their partners on the secondary market, who, as market makers, ensure post-issue liquidity of Quebecs and the stability of the spread. "Sure, we pay them fat commissions," explains Leclair, "but you realize just how important they are when you run into a problem. They are people with an excellent reputation on their local markets."

When times are tough — Leclair prefers not to give any examples, but it's clear enough that he's referring to political tension — "we've heard people say: 'Yes, the issue will be a hard one; it won't be a success, but we'll support your issue and the market won't know we're the ones doing it.' That's important!" Perhaps more important, Leclair isn't convinced that it's any more economical, over the long term, to sell at auction than to hand the job of placing securities to a relatively stable syndicate. "Right now," he says, "we're paying competitive prices." And in any case, he confesses, it would be hard for an A-rated issuer to go the auction route.

Ratings are a factor, says Leclair. "When we dropped from AA3 to A1, it cut down the sources of savings available to us." The first downgrading took place in 1986. On June 3, 1993, Moody's downgraded the province and Hydro-Québec again from A1 to A2; S&P followed suit two weeks later, on June 22, from AA- to A+. "Today, the investor has the choice. Will you go out and pick up a BBB for 25 cents [extra] yield? When I put on my investor's hat, I don't want to be bothered. I want something solid, with lots of liquidity, something that lets me sleep at night." Leclair demands securities rated no lower than A1 when it comes to investing Hydro-Québec's cash resources, meaning that the utility would rather invest in paper with a higher rating than its own!

THE QUEBEC UNDERWRITING SYNDICATE

(January 1996)

The Canadian syndicate	The American syndicate
Lead	*Lead (alternating)*
Lévesque Beaubien Geoffrion	Merrill Lynch
	CS First Boston
Managers	*Managers (two of three in rotation)*
Merrill Lynch Canada	Lehman Brothers
Nesbitt Burns	Goldman Sachs
RBC Dominion Securities	Salomon Brothers
Scotia Capital Markets	RBC Dominion Securities
Major participants	*Managers (at all times)*
Richardson Greenshields	Scotia Capital Markets *(one in two)*
Casgrain & Cie	Wood Gundy *(one in two)*
	Other regions of the world
Other participants	*(no standing syndicate)*
Goldman Sachs Canada	Yamaichi
Tassé & Associés	CS First Boston
Whalen Béliveau et Associés	Merrill Lynch
T-D Securities	Société Générale
Midland Walwyn	WestLB
	Commerzbank

Managing risks

"Our risk-management policy is a conservative one," says Blustein. And a very sophisticated one, he could well have added. Still, Hydro-Québec is bedevilled by a long-term debt denominated in American dollars. The problem arises from the fact that the utility borrows over the very long term on the Yankee market to finance asset elements whose economic life span is equally long. The catch is that finding swaps for more than ten years is almost impossible; counterparty dealers consider the risk to be too high.

Ever since 1986, foreign-currency borrowing — except for that denominated in U.S. dollars — has been made in shorter terms and has been entirely hedged by swaps. Borrowing contracted before 1986 represents only 2 percent of liabilities, but this non-hedged fraction triggers a foreign exchange loss or gain of $14 million for every one-cent swing in the value of the loonie (if it lasts one year).

Hydro-Québec accounting standards recognize foreign exchange losses or gains on American-dollar debt only upon bond redemption. Theoretically, if the exchange rate remains at comparable levels for the next thirty years, Hydro-Québec will take a foreign exchange hit of $2 billion! Worse still, no one knows how big the loss will be when all outstanding bonds denominated in foreign currencies are finally redeemed.

As a crown corporation, Hydro-Québec is not exactly defenceless. The value of its electricity exports to the United States fluctuates in inverse proportion to its borrowings; U.S. dollar revenues provide built-in, natural protection against the volatility of a U.S.-dollar liability. At the same time, Hydro-Québec no longer enters into long-term contracts of the kind prized by former premier Robert Bourassa. The North American energy market has been deregulated; ultra-short-term spot sales at continuously fluctuating prices now predominate. "We'll have to take another look at our operating methods," admits Leclair. "For the last two years we've been studying the issue." But exports aren't the only source of U.S. dollars, Blustein reminds me: the aluminum smelters that have signed risk-sharing contracts with Hydro buy their electricity in U.S. funds, the aluminum trading currency of choice.

"We really manage a small economy here. We have interest rate risks, forex risks, raw material risks, crude oil risks," Leclair explains. Three years ago, in an effort to bring all the factors that could threaten Hydro-Québec's profit stability under control, its Treasury department set up a model to evaluate total risk, just as bond portfolio managers do. The model rests on the correlations observed between risks. "We can hedge part of our aluminum risks, but unhedge a portion of interest rates": a fall in the price of aluminum usually indicates lowering inflation and interest rates drop; the loss in aluminum revenues will be offset by lower interest rates. To hedge its aluminum risks, Hydro-Québec buys futures contracts on the London Metal Exchange (LME) or over the counter at major banks like the Société Générale or Barclays. It also negotiates futures contracts for commodity baskets in the United States.

The more contracts, the greater the counterparty risk: when a bank like Barings collapses in the space of a single weekend, who can guarantee that even the Société Générale or Barclays will be able to honour their commitments over the long term? Hydro-Québec has painstakingly set up an integrated credit policy structured by currency, duration, instrument type, and quality of counterparty dealer, explains Leclair, a former banker. In so doing, it provides an AAA-rated counterparty a much larger line of credit than it would an A-rated institution. "We do long term with some credits; short term with others. But the risks are reviewed regularly." Leclair knows very well that without a well-diversified counterparty portfolio, the utility's own credit rating could be at risk.

Dealing with investors

A well-structured investor relations program has been in place at Hydro-Québec for the last four years. Among major issuers, only the World Bank can boast anything comparable, Leclair insists. "The main objective is to establish a business relationship with investors and with our financial partners." The program is run by four full-time employees, using a contact list that is kept constantly updated. Department heads spend several weeks meeting investors, either individually or in small groups. "We meet more than one thousand people per year," Blustein says. "Which helps us over the rough patches," adds Leclair. "It is important to be up-front with investors, to make sure that they are not surprised by a bit of news; that's the financial markets' worst enemy." It goes without saying that Hydro uses a similar approach in its dealings with the credit-rating agencies.

Every year, the utility's investor relations department publishes a thirty-six-page booklet outlining Hydro-Québec's financial profile, a document distinct from the eighty-four-page annual report. Each week a select group of larger investors receives a bulletin entitled *This Week in the Press*, which sums up news and articles dealing with Hydro-Québec. Special updates are issued when necessary to deal with important subjects, such as recent changes in upper management. "It has helped us establish really close links. David and I get calls from investors asking us about environmental issues, our relations with the native peoples, and the

Quebec political situation. At the same time, we can sound them out and test their appetite" for Hydro-Québec bonds.

"The feedback has been mostly positive; it has even led us to change some of our financial practices," Leclair says. Institutional investors were concerned over the ambitious borrowing programs of the 1980s and early '90s. "We were falling all over ourselves telling everyone about our $52-billion or $62-billion programs for the next ten or twelve years. The investors told us: 'If you keep on building at that pace, you're going to need a lot of bonds.'" Their apprehensions, and the latest news about the changing energy market in the United States, were passed on to the people who were in a position to take action: "We told our board [of directors] that we couldn't keep on borrowing as we had during the '80s."

The era of the trusts that René Lévesque once fulminated against may be over, but Hydro-Québec must still court the institutional investors who furnish three-quarters of the utility's capital. The discipline of the marketplace might not be quite as severe for crown corporations as for private enterprise, but it is discipline all the same.

Betting on the Canadian market

OTTAWA, FRIDAY, JUNE 2, 1995

The twin, white-stone towers of Esplanade Laurier soar skyward at the corner of Laurier and O'Connor streets. As I exit the elevator on the twentieth floor, I spot a poster advertising the 1995 Job Fair. It depicts a curtain rising on a better world, and three civil servants about to discover the delights of the private sector: "Get ready . . . over 200 firms confirmed." Sponsored by several federal government departments, including Finance, the fair is for civil servants only. No doubt about it, times are changing.

Bill Mitchell's office decoration is a bit more prosaic: large Scotia-McLeod charts showing Treasury bill yields since 1945 are pinned to the wall. Three computers are crammed onto his desk; the telephone rings constantly. Mitchell is head of the financial markets division at the Finance department, a man whose only concession to humour is to speak of Canadian, American, French, and British dollars.

The main objectives of federal debt management are to minimize and attempt to stabilize borrowing costs, to diversify capital sources, and to promote development of Canadian financial markets.[3] In the great federal scheme of things, the Finance department makes the decisions and the Bank of Canada carries them out; in practice, the two agencies work hand in hand. Debt program planning follows the budget cycle, Mitchell explains. He and his colleagues kick off the planning process in October, handing the minister his options in January; all major decisions are announced in a press release issued in early March, shortly after late-February's budget speech; the fiscal year begins formally on April 1 and ends March 31. If the forecast deficit is respected, the gap between plan and execution is minimal.

Such has not always been the case. In fiscal 1982–83, then-Finance minister Marc Lalonde had budgeted a deficit of $8 billion; recession quickly puffed up the figure to $24 billion. "Obviously the financial planning was based on early budget planning and had to adjust to significant changes in the financial requirements." The shortfall was financed by issuing a greater number of T-bills on the Canadian money market, whose flexibility and capacity is greater than the bond market; "the bond program is more locked in," Mitchell says. In fact, most deficit overruns were financed in a similar fashion, which drove up the floating-rate portion of the debt. Since T-bills are renewed at a different interest rate after only a few months, they are seen as a source of floating-rate capital. At the time, floating rates seemed less costly than the fixed rates attached to bonds.

"In 1989, we began to get some feedback from the market, and our own internal analysis began to suggest to us that we had a problem with the proportion of floating-rate debt. And we began the change." Why? I ask. "Clearly, the concern was interest rate volatility, which caused, in one year, quite a large fiscal hit," replies Mitchell. "It was Minister Wilson at the time, and he said we can't have such a large change in the fiscal position of the government from the debt financing." Now, reducing vulnerability has become a priority. "The market is fast-moving. Performance-driven investment managers all over the world are moving money around; we expect events to affect us, whether they are internally generated or externally generated" by interest rates. The budget is particularly sensitive to these pressures: in 1995, a 1-percent increase in rates (if it lasts one year) will mean a $1.5-billion increase in the deficit.

In 1990, the floating-rate debt percentage exceeded the fixed-rate one, by 53 percent to 47 percent. Today, the fixed-rate debt accounts for 55 percent, with 65 percent as a target for 2005. "Every year we pushed it up a percent or two." Mitchell calls it a "big shift in our strategy." The exact figure is immaterial, he adds. It could be 67 percent or 75 percent. Even though short-term rates tend to be higher than long-term rates, "when we do a twenty-five-year analysis, the cost of fixed and floating are not all that different." In one sense, he explains, the premium priced into long-term rates is the cost of avoiding the impact of short-term rate volatility.

Then why increase the percentage of fixed-rate debt so deliberately? "We only grow the bond program in a very measured, careful way. We don't want to force the bond market; we always ask ourselves: what is the capacity, and is there a constraint?" Bond-market traders like regularity and clarity, Mitchell maintains. Ottawa does not modify its issue schedule, which is well known to all market participants.

The Finance department and the Bank of Canada hold regular consultations with the industry on this subject. The central bank coordinates a committee of jobbers, made up of Canada's main chartered banks and a select group of investment dealers, with which it holds quarterly discussions on the money market. The Finance department handles contact with the Capital Market Committee of the Investment Dealer Association of Canada (IDAC). The second group, which overlaps the first, looks after the bond market. The deputy minister of Finance and Mitchell sit in on IDAC's fall meeting and sketch out the coming year's financing program. Both groups are intended to foster market growth and efficiency, and to act as policy incubators.

IDAC committee members have persuaded Ottawa to increase the average size of benchmark issues on the Canadian bond market. In most countries, benchmark maturities are two, five, ten, and thirty years. (A five-year bond becomes a four-year bond one year after issue, losing its benchmark status. As they mature, bonds cover the entire yield curve.) But the kind of concentrated borrowing that IDAC was suggesting created a cash-flow problem for the government. The solution finally chosen was to reopen benchmark issues and to issue additional paper bearing the same maturity and coupon characteristics. These bonds provide substantially greater liquidity with their volumes outstanding in ranges of $4 billion to $9 billion, depending on maturity. At the same time, increased volumes have led to the disappearance of three- and seven-year issues. Participants raised a hue and cry, and three-year paper was reintroduced, though at reduced volume. Thirty-year government debt — riskier for the lender and more expensive for the borrower — is also a delicate proposition. Volume outstanding has been reduced, but the term, essential for matching insurance companies' long-term liability, has been conserved, enabling the government to manage interest risks by extending the average maturity of its debt.

Meanwhile, the Finance department promised to respect a quarterly schedule for two-, five-, ten-, and thirty-year issues. Each quarter it also issues thirty-year real yield bonds; five- and ten-year bonds may also be issued twice quarterly.

Why tie your hands with a rigid issuing schedule? Wouldn't it be to your advantage to borrow at two years when two-year rates are low, and at five years when five-year rates are low? I ask Mitchell. "On this question, we are agnostics," he says. "We don't say it's going to be cheaper in the fall. Our job is to be cheaper over ten years. We've got to be in all the segments of the market in a somewhat even-handed fashion, so that all those segments work efficiently." The department estimates that its efforts to boost market efficiency have reduced the government's debt expenditures over the last ten years by some ten basis points, or nearly $500 million yearly. And, he adds, "Who's to say, over a long period of time, that 'I'm sure the five is gonna be cheap in the fall,' and wait. If we started to behave like opportunists, the market would counterbalance that, because they would see what we are trying to do. We do not try to play games in the market. We take the price."

The Finance department "strongly encourages financial innovation to make the market more efficient": futures markets, stripped or reconstituted bonds, repos, and more. After considerable head-banging, the department and the Bank of Canada have convinced the major traders and inter-brokers to bring together on a single electronic page the best bid and ask prices, making the prices displayed on traders' screens more transparent. As Mitchell puts it: "We need all the attributes of a well-developed market."

Borrowing more from private citizens

Net federal government debt (total debt less financial assets) stood at $546 billion at the end of March 1995. "You want money from everywhere you can get it," Mitchell tells me. "All borrowers want a diversified investor base." Perhaps 20 percent of net debt is financed internally, primarily in the form of accounting entries indicating monies due to the government employees' pension fund. The remainder is borrowed on financial markets in the form of negotiable bonds, Treasury bills, and savings bonds.

Foreigners now hold one-quarter of the federal debt financed on the markets,[4] meaning that three-quarters of all debt is sold to Canadians, broken down as follows: the Bank of Canada, 8 percent; public administrations, 7 percent; insurance companies and pension funds, 24 percent; banks, 21 percent; and other financial institutions, 20 percent. Individuals hold a mere 16 percent, compared with 40 percent ten years ago. The government wants to stop, then reverse the process of erosion; mobilizing private savings has emerged as a strategic objective.

There are two reasons for the relative decline in retail placement: the debt has grown much more rapidly than household savings, and financial institutions have offered citizens products that have proved far more attractive than savings bonds. In last February's budget, Finance minister Paul Martin announced a new retail bond placement program. The idea is not so much to sell more savings bonds but to offer a wider product range. Small investors can already invest in T-bills via mutual funds set up by investment dealers. Mitchell believes it will be possible to sell the same small investors negotiable bonds of the kind currently purchased by financial institutions, beginning with denominations of $1,000. New financial products are in the planning stage, in response to the new needs of different classes of savers, whether retired or preparing for retirement. And to smooth out the distribution process, the government has set up the Canada Retail Debt Agency, which will now assume some of the responsibilities originally entrusted to the Bank of Canada.

Borrowing abroad

Mitchell is definite: caution dictates that the Canadian government not borrow abroad to finance current operations. If we were to swap foreign currencies for Canadian dollars, it would be more expensive than borrowing in Canada, where the federal government can command the lowest possible rates. "The generally accepted view is that countries that have big financing requirements should develop a well-functioning domestic market." Among the industrialized countries there are really only two exceptions: Australia, which has begun to build up its own bond market after borrowing abroad, and Sweden, which has frequently changed its policy. The government of Canada borrows in foreign currencies on foreign markets only to rebuild its international foreign exchange reserves. In May 1995, for instance, it issued a $1.5 billion (US) global five-year bond at a spread of only twenty-five basis points above U.S. Treasuries. But debt of this kind represents only 4 percent of net debt.[5]

By keeping its foreign-currency paper relatively rare, Ottawa can pin down highly advantageous rates. Still, when federal agencies and crown corporations regularly solicit foreign markets, they must fully hedge the foreign exchange risk, unless they already possess assets in the particular currency. This foreign borrowing capacity has proven its worth, as foreign investors have purchased their bonds at much narrower spreads than Canadian investors, setting up a creative tension between markets — the upshot being that neither is free to set prices.

Investor participation

Despite fears expressed by several commentators, the federal government has been successful in financing its operations with comparative ease, even though it must occasionally pay a higher price. Dealers offer at least two dollars for each dollar the government wishes to borrow at every bond or T-bill auction. "They've been there through thick and thin," confirms Mitchell. Small investor behaviour — as shown in the massive buying sprees at RRSP time — is not significantly less volatile than that of institutional investors, but the volatility is different, another factor lowering overall risk. The government is well aware of investors' sentiments, and the judgment of foreign investors is not the only one that counts. Concludes Mitchell: "If you have inappropriate policies, the domestic investors will be the hardest on you."

Halifax builds a golden bridge

HALIFAX, THURSDAY, JUNE 15, 1995

When Douglas Stratton came east to join the Nova Scotia Finance department, the transplanted Albertan was astonished to see his taxi driver pull up at a toll booth. "How come they charge seventy-five cents for this bridge, it's so old? It must be paid off!" Not necessarily, even though the Angus L. Macdonald Bridge has spanned Halifax Harbour since 1954.

A few kilometres along, vehicles must pay an identical toll to cross the Murray MacKay Bridge, built in 1969. To build the MacKay, and to pay off the balance due on the Macdonald, the Halifax Bridge Commission borrowed $25 million in Deutschmarks. In 1973, when the loan came due, the Commission replaced it with another loan, in Swiss francs. Up until then, foreign exchange losses had been limited, and offset by low prevailing European interest rates. But the first oil shock, in 1973, turned the entire international monetary system on its head, touching off a foreign exchange loss of $15 million.

The loan, in Swiss francs, would be discreetly renewed year after year. Hopefully the losses would simply evaporate on their own. The illusion lasted until 1981, when the authorities finally bit the bullet and renegotiated the loan in Canadian dollars. Today, the two bridges are saddled with a debt of $75 million! True, the Commission borrowed an additional $20 million to improve access roads. Nonetheless, the depreciation of the Canadian dollar vis-à-vis the Deutschmark and the Swiss franc had the effect of doubling the initial debt. Halifax drivers might just as well have thrown fistfuls of Swiss francs and Deutschmarks from their windows for twenty-five years as they crossed the two bridges!

Stratton is director of liability management and treasury services, and second-in-command to Richard McAloney, director of investments, pensions, and treasury services at the provincial Finance department. Within less than two years, the two young CFAs have taken charge of the province's troubled debt financing operations. Their predecessors, who are now sampling the pleasures of early retirement, bequeathed them a legacy worthy of the Halifax bridge saga: 72 percent of the province's $10-billion debt is denominated in foreign currency, without the slightest hedge against foreign exchange risk! Last year's foreign exchange losses on the debt stood at a half-billion dollars, close to the size of the deficit. True, the losses can be paid off over the long term and do not account for the entire deficit, but they dangle like a Sword of Damocles over the Nova Scotia budget.

Finance minister Bernard Boudreau has just returned from a road trip that took him to Montreal, Toronto, Vancouver, and New York, Stratton tells me. There, Boudreau dotted the "i"s and crossed the "t"s of his action plan: that portion of the debt exposed to foreign currency risks will be brought down to 30 percent in from five to seven years; the percentage of the debt at a floating rate — traditionally close to zero — will be upped to between 15 percent and 35 percent; finally, the province's credit rating — A3 according to Moody's, A- with a negative outlook, according to Standard & Poor's — will be stabilized by the complete elimination of the deficit by fiscal 1997–98; in fact, the Conservative provincial government plans to begin paying back its debt.

"When you look at foreign exchange losses, keep in mind that in practice they are smaller because they are offset by lower borrowing costs. There might be 6-percent difference on a yen loan. On $100 million, it means you've got to lose more than six million on forex to be worse off," McAloney explains. At issue is less the cost of borrowing in foreign currency than the risk that the debt will knock the government off the rails as it attempts to bring spending under control. Stratton chimes in: "The rationale to go into foreign exposure is the lower coupon. It enables you to carry the debt at lower cost. It makes a lot of sense, but there is a limit." Nova Scotia has already left the limit behind.

McAloney explains that his strategy will be to reduce foreign exchange risk by swapping, picking the right moment by estimating future foreign currency movements and analysing interest rate differentials between Canada and the currency's country of origin. These differentials determine the cost of the swap. Nova Scotia might decide to swap all new debt, or to put a swap on any of its old yen, U.S. dollar, pounds sterling, or Swiss franc debt. The objective is the same: reduce overall portfolio risk.

Nova Scotia faces another problem: maturities are badly distributed over time. The lack of floating-rate debt has extended the average debt maturity, which now stands at $13\frac{1}{2}$ years, compared to $4\frac{1}{2}$ years for the federal government. In fact, Halifax's problem is quite the opposite of Ottawa's. Says McAloney: "The safe assumption is that it is very difficult to time the market and know when to borrow short and when to borrow long." He agrees that the yield curve generally rises, making the short term cheaper than the long term. On the other hand, too short a term makes for volatility. Stratton sees the ideal compromise as being close to 30 percent of the debt in floating rate. In an effort to speed up the conversion to floating rates, Nova Scotia has begun to use interest rate swaps.[6]

One distinctive feature of the province's finances is a sinking fund. Each year, a part of the amount needed to repay capital at bond maturity is deposited in the fund. In accounting terms, the assumption is that all debt will be fully repaid in twenty years; a ten-year bond must be renewed once before it can be completely funded. The fund currently holds $1.6 billion, against a total debt of $10 billion. It's a credit-strengthening strategy designed to reduce the risk of the province failing to pay back its creditors.

To protect its access to markets, Nova Scotia has set up an investor relations program that features brochures, fax letters, and telephone conferences with the Finance minister. "It's not only because we want to borrow again on these markets," explains McAloney. "Our paper is outstanding there. We owe it to investors to say: you put all that money into us. Thank you very much. We would like to tell you where we are and why it continues to be a very good investment."

Contrasting approaches

The federal and provincial government approaches to financing are radically different. Ottawa sticks to the Canadian market, follows a strict schedule, and sells its bonds at auction; the provinces venture onto all markets, at any time they wish, and sell their bonds through syndicates.

As their creditworthiness tends to be lower than the federal government's, several provinces might well encounter problems were they to issue bonds at auction in a bear market or in the face of political uncertainty. In theory, auctions are the more economical method, but the provinces believe that the greater safety of syndicated sales provides more than adequate compensation. And by building additional flexibility into the syndicate structure, they have successfully stimulated healthy competition among its members, Ontario leaning more toward creative tension than Quebec, a lower-rated borrower.

Heavy debt loads are a handicap — but they have also generated a sophisticated new expertise. Canada's public borrowers are well respected worldwide for the professional quality of their financing operations. Nova Scotia, slow to adjust to the new reality, has replaced its management team.

Some believe that the provinces would be less dependent on foreign creditors if they had pursued a more systematic presence on the Canadian market, following the example of the federal government. But Ottawa, with its higher-quality credit, has simply gobbled up all available Canadian savings and forced the provinces into exile, say others. Certainly the possibility of selling debt abroad has weakened the clout of Canadian financial institutions and investment dealers in provincial capitals. Thus far, the provinces have always managed to find a hospitable market, even when most lenders were giving them the cold shoulder. While a simultaneous closed door on all the markets cannot be ruled out, it does remain an unlikely prospect.

Foreign exchange risk-management methods vary from province to province, swinging all the way from Ontario, which tolerates no risk, to Nova Scotia, which once naively embraced risks of all kinds. The Quebec government's compromise solution fits in somewhere between the two. Quebec swaps only a portion of its foreign currency debt, and uses an elaborate model to manage all interest-rate and forex risks; each year, its theoretical losses or gains on foreign exchange are amortized until debt maturity. Protection, based on swaps, is costly. The question is: do the provinces want a full insurance policy, or are they prepared to take certain risks to bring down debt service costs? Moreover, the insurance policy is only as effective as the insurers are strong and diversified. Borrowers may ask themselves about the staying power of the chartered banks that act as counterparties. And as provincial creditworthiness is eroding, those provinces with low ratings are encountering greater difficulty in obtaining the desired amount of the insurance that swaps provide.

Finance department officials are aware of the need to stop credit-rating decline, and to polish their image in the institutional investment community. Even Ottawa has taken the plunge, setting up an investor relations program with liaison agents in New York, London, and Tokyo. But if the news is always bad, even the world's premier PR experts will be helpless to sell the bonds issued by our governments.

Chapter 10

CONCLUSION: FINDING SOLUTIONS

HALIFAX, JUNE 15–17, 1995

FOREIGN FORCES HAVE occupied this port city. Barricades have been set up; troops patrol the streets; traffic has been rerouted; all hotels within a hundred-kilometre radius have been requisitioned. And yet, Halifax is in a festive mood. Couples with kids in tow line the sidewalks hoping for a VIP sighting. It's the kind of event people remember for years to come. Down at the harbour, Montreal's Cirque du Soleil has set up its blue-and-yellow-striped big top. But the greatest contortionists and acrobats in town are not to be found in the circus ring; they're sitting around an oval conference table, reducing the gravest problems of the day to the lowest common denominator in jargon-laden communiqués.

Like most of the two thousand journalists covering the G7 summit, I watch the comings and goings of the political elite on one of the TV monitors scattered throughout the press room. The only people going anywhere are the cameramen and the photographers who film the impeccably lighted set-piece scenes staged just for them. The "serious" journalists are holed up deep in the belly of the conference centre, clicking away at their PCs, plowing through mountains of bumf and nodding through background briefings in which anonymous PR hacks plead that only their boss can break the political logjam. None of which stopped several of the most serious scribes from watching the France–South

Africa soccer match while Prime Minister Jean Chrétien read the final conference communiqué. The same TV screens also showed the war in Bosnia, Canadian soldiers held as hostages, and the hostage-taking at Budennovsk, perfectly timed by the Chechen rebels to spoil Russian President Boris Yeltsin's cameo appearance alongside the Seven.

The year before, at the Venice summit, the same group had agreed to discuss reform of international financial institutions, shorthand for the International Monetary Fund (IMF) and the World Bank. In the months that followed, three events revealed just how timely the subject was: the Mexican crisis of December 1994; the collapse of the Barings Bank in February 1995, and the incomprehensible weakness of the American dollar vis-à-vis the yen and the Deutschmark. Canada's Jean Chrétien, who, as summit host, has the responsibility for carrying through with the conference agenda, is worried about the "tequila effect": the danger that ripples from the peso crisis, which has shaken most of Latin America, might spread to the red-ink-saturated economies of the north. The Canadian government is concerned that traders have handcuffed it politically and put into question its credibility during the run-up to the recent budget. "We cannot simply expect those famous currency speculators to shut off their computer terminals, hang up their red suspenders, and get a life,"[1] he said. The Canadian prime minister would like to shift the balance of power away from the speculators and back toward political sovereignty. Markets discipline governments, as the saying goes — but who will discipline the markets?

Chrétien's clichés are out of date, as it happens. No one wears red suspenders any more. More important, when capital movements buffet a currency, says Kenneth S. Courtis, a Saskatchewan-born economist turned strategist for the Deutsche Bank in Asia, "it is not money that is driven by speculators. It is money that is driven by people prudently managing the risks to which they are exposed and moving away from economies unable to make adjustments."[2]

The close-to-the-vest conservatives who administer insurance company, pension fund, and mutual fund money are convinced that truly speculative behaviour would be to keep their investments in vulnerable currencies or in bond markets threatened by fiscal policies seen as irresponsible. In normal times, these investors display a wide variety of attitudes, reacting to a multifaceted reality in as many ways. But at critical moments they have reacted like sheep, and that's the kind of behaviour that can lead to excess.

That's not to say there is no pure speculation. When hedge funds feel a big wave building, they position their surfboards to ride the quick gains. Despite British Prime Minister John Major's sharp denial of any devaluation, speculator George Soros was said to have made as much as $1 billion betting on sterling devaluation in 1992. True, speculators can exacerbate the movement of capital; they might even be able to touch off such movement. But they cannot exploit a weakness that does not exist. While no one at the G7 conference is calling for limitations on capital mobility, there is growing concern that reactions are out of proportion to the events that cause them. The Mexican crisis provided an eloquent example.

The Mexican crisis

The 1994 crisis is totally unlike the 1982 version, when Mexico announced that climbing interest rates, which had been orchestrated by the United States Federal Reserve to wrestle inflation to the ground, meant that the country could no longer repay its debts. In 1982, the creditors were a consortium of foreign banks. Most had a stake in the country's economic development and were vulnerable to pressure from government regulatory agencies, which could bring pressure to bear to extract concessions. The upshot was the Brady Plan: Mexico restructured its debt and put its financial house in order.

In 1994, Mexico's debt stood well below Canada's, accounting for only one-third of GDP. This time around, most borrowing had taken place in the private sector. The government's error — a minor one at that — was to have dragged its feet, poorly managing a peso devaluation that had become unavoidable due to a serious current accounts deficit. When investors became aware that Mexico had exhausted its international foreign currency reserves, they began to doubt the government's ability to honour its *tesobonos*, Treasury bills denominated in U.S. dollars. Doubt became a flashing red light; investors decided not to renew short-term investments as they matured, triggering not a 1982-style solvency crisis but a crisis of confidence. Says Jeffrey Sachs, the American economist who acts as a consultant to several governments: "Adverse expectations about Mexico's financial conditions are proving self-fulfilling prophecies of doom."[3] Distrust quickly spread to the peso, then on to Mexican securities as a whole. Mexicans themselves were the first to sell, followed closely by foreign investors, who had rushed in to profit from Mexico's new-found strength on the heels of its membership in NAFTA. Unlike the banks involved in the first crisis, the thousands of institutional investors who had bought *tesobonos* could not be forced to keep on buying. "Hot money" burned a lot of fingers in Mexico.

Paul Volcker, chairman of the U.S. Federal Reserve during the 1982 Mexican crisis, says inadequate information and IMF weakness, two of the issues discussed at the Halifax summit, were not responsible for the second crisis. "The failure to me was more of a human nature: greed followed by fear. And this is not easily cured by G7 communiqués."[4] The peso sank like a stone, far deeper than any reasonable person could have expected. "The volatility of exchange rates is a major problem for the international financial system," Volcker admits. "Something should be done." But even this international finance heavyweight is unable to suggest any short-term solutions.

Volcker's only recommendation would be to restrict exchange rate fluctuation to within a bracket, as in Europe. Unfortunately, governments weakened by indebtedness are no longer able to turn their heavy monetary and fiscal-policy artillery on the speculators. A low-level tax on all international financial transactions, as suggested by economist James Tobin, would not resolve the problem. Such a tax would be almost impossible to police: traders could merely reroute transactions through offshore tax havens. As well, argues Volcker, the banks, which reap fat profits from foreign exchange volatility and from the sale of swaps and other hedges, would resist a European-style currency system. The banks manage a huge daily volume of currency trading estimated at $1,230 billion (US), more than twice the official foreign currency reserves of the G7 countries. Transactions involving the Canadian dollar involve a mere 3 percent of this total.

Remaking the world

The spectacular volume of currency trading has little relation to the needs of international trade. Nor is it purely the work of speculative transactions by hedge funds, which use currencies as full-fledged investment vehicles. There is only one reasonable explanation for it: the movement of capital from one country to another and the continuous risk management made necessary by investing and borrowing abroad. Five factors have fuelled the staggering upsurge of capital movement across national borders.

1. *Changes to the rules of the game*: The liberalization of markets in the 1980s abolished regulatory barriers to investment abroad, authorized new financial instruments, and stoked competition among financial intermediaries.
2. *Technological development*: New, advanced communication infrastructures and increased computer capacity have expanded transaction-processing capacity; they have also fostered the creation of increasingly sophisticated financial instruments.
3. *Structural development*: The expansion of exchanges that specialize in derivatives (futures and options), reinforced settlement mechanisms, more extensive coverage by credit-rating agencies, and the growth of financial news agencies (Reuters, Dow Jones, and Bloomberg) have all reduced the risks of investing abroad.
4. *The rise of institutional investing*: Institutions, particularly pension funds, manage an ever-growing portion of savings in the wealthier countries. These funds seek to diversify their portfolios with foreign investments and have built up the expertise to use the complex tools now available to them.
5. *The recycling of savings and trade surpluses*: Above and beyond the need to diversify investment, capital from countries with high savings rates or strong trade surpluses flows toward countries that are heavy borrowers, or that show attractive growth opportunities.

Recycling savings is big business. Total outstanding debt on the world's bond markets, consisting primarily of domestic markets, stands at $24,428 billion (US)[5]. Most capital movement takes place among these national markets. The NAFTA countries, for instance, borrow $1 billion (US) per working day from the rest of the world, half of it coming from Japan alone. The Euromarket (or international market) accounts for only 10 percent of all bond markets, but the proportion is climbing. In 1994, new issues reached $1,757 billion (US), 17 percent of which were globals. Transaction volume on the secondary market, as registered by international settlement agencies, rose by 29 percent to reach $24,400 billion (US). That same year, Canada and Sweden were the two largest players on the international market, to the tune of $20 billion (US) each, or one-fifth of all government issues. On the international market, the relative weight of currencies is shifting. In 1994, the value of yen issues gained one-third, those in U.S. dollars lost one-third, while those in Canadian dollars fell by two-thirds. Investors clearly prefer certain currencies to others.

Traders are changing their behaviour patterns, says the Bank for International Settlements, the Basel-based central bankers' private club. In 1994, notes the BIS in its annual report,[6] markets sharpened their scrutiny of the fundamentals — public indebtedness, long-term inflationary trends, current accounts deficits, and political uncertainty (a possible obstacle to implementing appropriate measures). In countries with the best performance, like Switzerland and Japan, rates rose more slowly than in countries with the worst performance, such as Italy, Sweden, and Canada. "All of this can only be seen as positive, providing, of course, that the judgments of the markets themselves are accurate. Unfortunately, though this is generally the case, recent events have demonstrated that it is not always so,"[7] reads a cautiously worded passage. "In the financial landscape that has arisen over the last two decades, it is indeed possible that extreme price variations have become more frequent, and that their impact has become wider."[8] Does this mean that "Canadian Club syndrome" will follow on the heels of the "tequila effect"? Whatever happens, we would be on our own, because "the capacity of the central banks to intervene cannot be compared with the volume of resources that the private sector can now put in play when it becomes aware of a distortion in the fundamentals,"[9] concludes the BIS, noting the abysmal failure of its concerted action of March 2–3, 1995, to halt the fall of the American dollar. "Whatever one may think of the power wielded by capital markets, this power is not about to weaken."[10] Thanks for the warning.

In a sense, very little in the preceding paragraph is really new. For centuries, the bankers have kept kings on a short leash. Canada has been dependent on foreign capital since its inception; the only thing that has changed is the extent of the dependency. Once a certain point has been reached, complexity nudges us over into a different system. International trade is as old as civilization itself. But the growth of trade has touched off a profound transformation: today, we speak of a global economy. The financial community is reaching a similar point in its development, but so far no one has come up with a sexy name. There can be little doubt that the new regime conceals systemic risks which we can intuit without fully understanding. The risks inherent in each instrument have been studied by experts, but we know little of the cumulative impact of these financial innovations, and in particular of the chain reactions that might be touched off in a crisis situation.

Unable to grasp all of the threads that make up the complex web, financiers fall back on the general theory of the portfolio, based on the negative correlations that can be observed between certain products or markets. Traditionally, when certain securities fall, others rise; a well-diversified portfolio minimizes total risk, while profiting from the high yield of certain investments that would be too daring if made by themselves. In 1994, the BIS observes, market volatility and synchronization increased. Are we witnessing an aberration — or a new trend? If all markets move in the same direction, and at the same time, in moments of crisis, then a policy of keeping all one's eggs in the same safe basket would appear the prudent one. Should this behaviour pattern become widespread, it would heavily penalize marginal, risky markets such as Canada. The size of the Canadian bond market alone will always relegate it to secondary status in the eyes of international investors. Is there any way to make it less risky? No need to adopt Luddite tactics, but we should treat the experiments concocted by the financial wizards with healthy scepticism. In that sense, the G7 Halifax communiqué, with its proposed solutions, conceals an admission of powerlessness, or an act of blind faith.

What we've learned

How is Canada faring today? After spending months exploring the back rooms and the corridors of the financial world, listening to and observing dozens of traders throughout the developed world, we can summarize as follows:

- Canada's overall reputation remains very positive.
- The principal risks associated with Canadian names are public indebtedness and constitutional uncertainty.
- Exchange rates play a key role in decision-making among the Europeans and the Japanese, because Canadian bond yield is measured in the investor's currency. Exchange rates are particularly sensitive to indebtedness and political uncertainty.
- Canada belongs to the dollar bloc. Americans have confidence in Canadian debt, particularly in U.S.-dollar bonds (Yankees), which they know well. European and Japanese perceptions of Canada are shaped by their analysis of the United States.
- Canadian bonds are seen by foreign investors as a substitute for American bonds. Canadian bonds are considered riskier because of debt, political uncertainty, and a small market; they therefore demand higher interest rates.
- International portfolio managers allocate Canadian investments an average weight of 3 percent. In practice, Canada's share varies between 0 and 10 percent, depending on whether managers are optimistic or pessimistic on the yield outlook.
- When it comes to credit ratings, European and Japanese institutions are demanding, but not individual investors. American institutions are less so, but they will adjust interest rates in accordance with ratings.
- Americans pay heed to relative values. They purchase bonds on the Yankee market when the spreads are wide in relation to historic averages (relative prices are then weak) and sell when differentials are tight (and relative prices are high). On the Canadian bond market, a view of the progress of the

241

Canadian dollar is added to this analysis.

- Doubts have been raised about the credibility of Canadian fiscal policies. Investor judgments are based on trends as observed in public accounts, and not on the projections of politicians. The 1995 federal budget, and those of several provinces, are viewed as a step in the right direction, but further steps are expected.

- Foreigners appreciate Canada's low inflation rate, but several years will be necessary in order to rebuild the Bank of Canada's credibility. They wish it would defend the international value of the Canadian dollar, particularly its exchange rate vis-à-vis the greenback.

- Recurrent constitutional uncertainty adds a variable premium to Canada's and Quebec's borrowing costs.

- The lively competition between investment dealers and banks to lead bond issues maximizes the borrowing capacity of public bodies. Canada's largest issuers are seen as quite sophisticated.

- Canadian financial institutions are naturally the largest bearers of Canadian bonds, and form something of a captive market. However, to diversify risk and increase yields, these institutions are placing a growing portion of Canadian savings abroad.

- Institutional investors in Canada choose bonds by relative value. Federal and provincial governments' weights are derived from the ScotiaMcLeod index, which in turn reflects the composition of the Canadian bond market.

- The federal government borrows primarily in Canada, in Canadian currency, while the provinces borrow heavily abroad, in foreign currencies. Some provinces, such as Ontario, are stricter than others, such as Nova Scotia and Quebec, in protecting themselves against foreign exchange risk.

- Among the credit-rating agencies, only Moody's and Standard & Poor's exert a real influence on Canadian and foreign investors. The two agencies evaluate a borrower's long-term ability to service debt by comparing its financial ratios with those of similar borrowers.

Drawing conclusions

Canada's debt is one of those topics about which reasonable people can reasonably disagree. A majority of the men and women I interviewed, both at home and abroad, spoke frankly, but it would be shortsighted to ignore several biases. Foreigners tend to couch their criticisms in polite terms; the investment dealers and bankers who earn substantial revenue as members of the syndicates that handle government debt are understandably loath to bite the hand that feeds them. At the other extreme, carried away by their political convictions, some Canadian investors have been known to paint an overly gloomy picture.

Now that we've established that there is no such thing as perfect objectivity, it's my turn to offer you my own personal views on the subject. But at this stage, you might as well draw your own conclusions: you have the same facts at your fingertips, the same contradictions, the same ambiguities.

In the end, this report on international financial markets carries a double message: there is good news, and bad news. It has a painful conclusion, and two warnings.

The good news
Canada is not tottering at the edge of a financial precipice. The country is not on the verge of sliding into a Mexican-style crisis, or of hitting the kind of wall that would force potential lenders to turn away. Canada's creditworthiness is still relatively high. The country enjoys a strong and diversified economy. A serious crisis, the kind that would plunge the county into turmoil, is not impossible, but it is improbable.

The bad news
Canada's fiscal situation is cause for concern. Public debt is far too heavy; national savings are inadequate. The country depends far too much on its foreign creditors. Access to the world savings pool is becoming more difficult as the quality of Canadian credit deteriorates; international markets are increasingly brutal and erratic in their allocation of capital.

The painful conclusion

Several more tough budgets will be needed to prod public finances back on course. Citizens will have to make sacrifices, and alter their concept of the role of the state.

First warning

Financial markets are not in favour of the Parti Québécois's goal of sovereignty, even if they acknowledge the long-term viability of an independent Quebec. Financiers are concerned about the uncertainty and the potential disturbances that would attend Quebec's secession, particularly with regard to servicing the debt and the Canadian dollar. From a strictly market point of view, indebtedness is a more serious problem than the uncertainty arising from Quebec's eventual independence. But the two factors in combination produce an unstable, explosive mix, which could breed extreme reactions. I will return to this subject in the epilogue.

Second warning

Textbooks on financial theory depict the relation of risk to yield as a smooth, upward curve: slightly greater risk means slightly greater yield. A marginally riskier borrower must pay marginally higher interest rates. But in the real life of markets, the curve is anything but smooth. At a certain point, which cannot be predicted, a small increase in risk radically transforms investor perceptions: it's the straw that breaks the camel's back. When this happens, a slightly greater risk can lead to sharply increased borrowing costs. Reality might have changed only slightly, but perceptions will have swung wildly. Cautious judgment is swept aside and violent, excessive corrections take place.

Vulnerability is greatest in small countries, where investors do not always notice the slow deterioration of their balance sheets. Increased disclosure of information, as suggested by the G7, is unlikely to change that. Even where the objective outlook for countries viewed as risks has improved, these countries will still be buffeted by external shocks. On the 1994 bear market, countries with red ink on their ledgers fared much worse than their penny-watching counterparts. Even the smallest detonator might touch off a downward spiral, where high-priced money clogs up debt service, gums the cogwheels of the economy, and discourages businesses that must invest to bolster their ability to compete. Markets react with fright, demanding even higher interest rates.

Bound hand and foot

The deficit and the debt have insinuated themselves into every nook and cranny of public life. Both Canada and Quebec are being held hostage. But by what — or whom? Is the culprit mass hysteria, an amalgam of individual interests disguised as national interests, the inescapable arithmetic of compound interest, foreign creditors, spending programs spiralling out of control, or a topsy-turvy economic strategy? The answer is not a simple one, for it involves some of each of these factors. The financiers are not the hostage takers; they never forced us to borrow their money. Our governments, with their shortsightedness and their lack of courage at a time when it would have been easier to say no, have bound us hand and foot — with our tacit agreement. We, as citizens, were all too happy to pay less than the full price for the services we enjoyed. It's time to recognize that the responsibilities are as public as our debt. Sacrificing a scapegoat would be less than useless.

All around us, the world of finance has undergone a sea change. Where bankers and industrialists once held sway, now pension fund managers and other institutional funds wield the power. These are people whose logic stands in total disregard of national sovereignty. Their objective, rational interests favour some policies, such as price stability, and oppose others, such as high debt levels. So much for the economy. But the tools used by the risk-management professionals have proven pathetically useless in grasping social dynamics — and in understanding political uncertainty. They hide behind a conservative, pseudo-objective ideology, convinced that they are always right about everything. Some are capable of more flexible thinking, but they also know that markets as a whole judge harshly, and that to go against them would be tantamount to financial suicide.

Investors shift their capital from place to place, seeking optimum prospects for yield and risk. All things being equal, Canada accounts for a mere 3 percent of a conventional international portfolio. Alas, things are rarely equal. In practice, Canada is in hot competition with an increasing number of countries for a slice of world savings. Fortunately, the number of countries perceived as safer than Canada for fixed income investment remains limited. What does remain to be seen is which investors will agree to lend us their money, which they have no obligation to do. As a rule, the worse the creditworthiness, the worse the lender. Better to owe money to a Swiss insurance company that buys our paper and forgets about it until maturity, than to a hedge fund that gives us a few days' worth of credit. Better to borrow in Canadian dollars than to tolerate the foreign exchange risk, or to pay the insurance premium that forms an integral part of the swap.

The debtor-creditor relationship is not a zero-sum game, where one side's win is the other side's loss. Both lost heavily in the Mexican crisis. Investors who placed their capital in Mexico came away feeling they'd been bushwhacked; Mexicans felt like survivors of a gang-rape. It need not have been this way; both parties could have come away convinced they'd come out on top. Remember that when interest rates decline, bringing relief for borrowers, bond values increase, which suits lenders.

Can we minimize our dependency, or can we transform it?

We can do both. Canadians stand to profit, via their retirement funds, from investment possibilities throughout the world. They will be all the richer in the long run. And if foreigners finance a (small) portion of our public debt and share the risks and the potential payback of more adventurous private projects, it can only work to our advantage. But it would be desirable if savings flows were closer to equilibrium. Despite the sizable drop in the current accounts deficit in 1994 and 1995, we should keep our feet solidly anchored on terra firma. Even if Canadians' overall savings were sufficient to meet the borrowing needs of the public and private sector, the country would still not be fully protected from the shock waves that ripple through the financial markets or from portfolio movements. On an open market, nothing can stop Canadians from increasing their investments abroad. Nothing can stop foreigners from dumping their Canadian paper for whatever reason, whether it is related to the situation in Canada or not. All we can do is hope that higher savings levels will build confidence and cushion the impact of market tremors.

So, encouraging savings is a part of the solution. In macroeconomic terms, saving means reducing indebtedness among all economic players.

The most obvious method is to reduce government deficits, but the same end could be attained if citizens decided to pay back the unpaid balance on their credit cards. We would accomplish the same thing, too, if corporations borrowed less to finance their investments, but that would reduce their capacity for growth and job creation.

Toward solutions

Bearing in mind Otto von Bismarck's dictum that politics is the "doctrine of the possible, the attainable . . . the art of the second best," let us look more closely at some of the ways that we can reduce our economic dependency and reinforce sovereignty. There is, of course, no simple, painless solution to the debt-management dilemma. Some of the proposed solutions are only partial ones; others lead to a dead end.

1. *Reform the international financial system (the G7 solution)*
   The G7 leaders meeting at Halifax agreed to bolster the IMF, to provide more financial information about individual countries, and to tighten regulations. But a far-reaching reform designed to reduce market volatility, such as a European-inspired semi-fixed exchange rate system, is not in the cards. There is no intellectual or political consensus on the necessity for change, and even less on what, specifically, to do. Progress is possible, but it's unlikely to pull Canada out of its financial nosedive.
2. *Practise benign neglect (the ostrich solution)*
   Keep a firm hand on the public purse strings, but without bringing in structural reforms. Despite the wailing of the prophets of doom, Canada is unlikely to hit the debt wall if it follows this course. But low-speed accidents will become more frequent, slowly destroying the economy.
3. *Restructure the debt (the magic-wand solution)*
   Accounting trickery to restructure the debt has been proposed (trading the debt for shares, redistributing it to individuals, reforming the RRSP system, etc.). These daring solutions look good on paper, but in practice they would run right up against

major political obstacles, and could lead to a crisis of confidence. In the past, such alternatives as the Brady Plan were adopted, but only as a last resort, when countries had reached the point of no return. Canada is not that desperate, yet.

4. *Bring home the debt (borrowing from Peter to pay Paul)*
The problem would not be so acute if Canada's public debt were held by its own citizens, as in Belgium or Italy. But in the long term, as long as savings are low, forcing Canadians to finance all the debt would oblige corporations to borrow abroad, if possible, or simply do without capital.

5. *Monetize the debt (the sneaky solution)*
Foreign investors worry that the Bank of Canada will simply speed up the presses and print money to pay down the debt, a move that would mean the end of the policy of price stability. If this happened, there would be a sell-off of Canadian bonds, the dollar would fall, and interest rates would soar. Inflation can only nibble away at debt if the markets don't expect it, but markets aren't to be taken in as easily as they were in the 1970s. The cost of higher interest rates would far outweigh the benefits of monetization. The Bank of Canada can influence short-term rates to a certain extent, but it cannot control long-term rates. Monetary policy can create some room to manoeuvre, but not enough to solve the debt problem. As deficit reduction measures began to bite, the Bank of Canada would have to be more accommodating and act to compensate for the contraction of the economy that would ensue.

6. *Bring down several tough budgets (the responsible solution)*
The deficits of all levels of public administration must be eliminated within three or four years if Canada is to be in a stronger position to face the next recession. Even if this happens, governments will not have fully recovered their ability to stimulate the economy — but they will be able to cope with the drop-off in tax revenues and the increase in transfer payments to individuals when a recession occurs. In the long term, the viable solution will be Keynesian: a small surplus during periods of growth and a modest deficit during recessions. The Maastricht Treaty criteria

— a maximum deficit of 3 percent of GDP and debt of 60 percent of GDP — could become tomorrow's international standards for responsible financial behaviour. The federal government has set a target of 3 percent in its 1996–97 budget, but for Canada as a whole, public debt still hovers near the 100-percent mark. It will take several years to bring the debt down to a safer level; the task of the hour is to turn the trend around.

·······················

Some of the remarks made by financiers that appear in this book struck me as reasonable; others I found shocking in their narrow-mindedness. But agree with them or not, their opinions carry weight — and shape behaviour patterns that have an impact on all of us, in our daily lives. Markets remind us that governments cannot ignore the laws of gravity; debt cannot be allowed to grow more rapidly than wealth.

We can argue at what point the debt becomes excessive just as we can argue about how many angels can dance on the head of a pin. But the time will come when the financial markets step in and settle the dispute — on their terms. All the signs are there to see. When finding lenders becomes a more and more complex task, when the terms of borrowing become costlier, when loan sharks take the place of distinguished bankers, a country is too deep in debt. We must come to grips with economic power and learn to understand how it works. Yet this need not signal the end of political debate. In fact, the political debate has just begun.

The Public Choice school of thought argues that the political system favours interest groups who have the most to gain in making demands on government, and in mobilizing to make their voices heard. Individual taxpayers tend to be passive to such demands, comforted in their rational belief that it costs less to satisfy the noisiest groups with a few extra dollars than to act to stop them. Public Choice concludes from this systemic imbalance that democracy leads to a bloated, invasive state that undermines liberties. Its solution is a minimal state and complete liberalization of market forces: a conclusion I cannot share. Churchill argued that democracy was the least bad of all political systems; likewise, the free-market economy is the least bad of all economic systems for creating wealth. Both have provided us with case histories of brilliant

249

accomplishments and disastrous failures. The two systems must continue to exist in a delicate balance.

At the other end of the ideological spectrum, some argue that today's monetary policy is itself the root of all evil, and that our problems could be solved if we were able to reform it. In *Shooting the Hippo*,[11] Linda McQuaig rightly points out that the high costs of the war on inflation waged by the Bank of Canada have been devastating, swelling government deficits. It is also true that keeping real interest rates high has triggered a transfer of wealth from borrowers to creditors. It can legitimately be asked whether the Bank of Canada was not acting more Catholic than the Pope — the U.S. Federal Reserve in the early 1990s.[12] But what's done is done; we cannot rewrite history. As for the future, McQuaig is wrong to suggest that the Bank of Canada should stimulate growth by forcing interest rates down. She forgets that the Canadian economy is an open one, that the government does not have a free hand in terms of policy. Today, to squander the price stability that was so painful to achieve would be irresponsible.

Eliminating deficits and reducing the debt cannot be ends in themselves. The ultimate aim of the economy is the creation of wealth and its redistribution, through employment for those who are able to work and through social programs for those who cannot. The challenge is to break the vicious circle of anemic employment growth, which inhibits revenue growth and swells government spending, the two factors that lead to higher deficits and debt service outlays that devour an ever-greater share of the budget. How can we turn the downward spiral around, promote job growth, reduce the cost of transfers to individuals, naturally increase tax-generated revenue (which in turn underwrites essential public services), eliminate the deficit, and, eventually, lower taxes? Growth itself, leading to a better balance between debt and the size of the economy, will alleviate the debt problem.

One thing seems certain: the classical strategy of priming the pump by deliberately inflating deficits no longer works. In fact, it encourages markets to incorporate a higher risk premium in interest rates. Using government funds to stimulate demand is a waste of money; in a country like Canada, imported goods account for a significant part of overall demand. In the face of world competition, Canadian corporations with full order books prefer investing in technology that not only reduces costs but eliminates jobs as well. Even increased job supply in growth industries will not mean that the unemployed can fill these positions.

This book does not offer a prescription. But it has become increasingly clear to me that the structural changes we need must not be purely negative, with the sole aim of reducing the cost of public services. The country's accounts cannot be straightened out without solid economic growth — unless, of course, we decide to reduce the state to its bare bones. Changes must be positive, growth-driven, focused on expanding wealth and employment. Large corporations restructure themselves, getting out of certain areas of business and radically transforming their operations while at the same time developing new growth strategies. The state must learn to do the same thing; it will always have a key role to play.

Growth strategies must be built around two related objectives that will have a positive impact on debt management. First, to reduce transfer payments and boost revenues, jobs must be created; then, to lower the current accounts deficit and lessen dependency on foreign capital, exports must be expanded.

Government action must concentrate on creating a climate for economic development, and not focus on specific industrial projects better left to the private sector. Experts agree that the state should invest in education, and in decentralized manpower training programs, in upgrading infrastructures, and in R&D. It should set tax policy to encourage savings. As guidelines, these concepts are well understood; we must find the best ways to put them into effect.

There is no miracle cure. Restructuring the state will call for pragmatism. Some experiments will succeed, others will not. The process will also require patience: structural changes produce results in the long term. Wherever possible, the new policies must meet certain criteria. They should focus on public goods, such as health and education; they should be economical in their use of resources and prod market forces into action; they should be flexible, decentralized, and be regularly evaluated and revised.

Reviving the political debate

This book has outlined the growing risk of the debt burden; it has shown that we must change course. A country's budget is like a supertanker: it takes a long time to turn around. And the markets know it. But even though they are prepared to be patient, they demand results. Efforts, excuses, hitches, and glitches are no longer sufficient to gain time and to forestall the inevitable. Notes former Bank of Canada governor John Crow: "Confidence is like oxygen — people often realize they need it when they do not have it, which is usually rather late."[13]

Turning the fiscal ship around means sacrifices. Legitimate interests, even those with solidly entrenched acquired rights, will be shaken, even pushed aside. But the need to put public finances on an even keel and keep them there need not mean swallowing the whole conservative political agenda. On the contrary, more than ever we need a vigorous political debate among all social groups and all viewpoints on what must be done.

Financiers and economists are making arguments, often valid ones, on a wide range of political issues. But in certain areas, such as public health, they are simply not experts, and other values must take precedence over cold cash. Other, hard realities are staring us in the face: too many young people are unemployed; the population is growing older; workers lack the qualifications to do their jobs. But the ever-expanding debt is gnawing away like a cancer at the government's ability to finance social programs; if it isn't soon halted, it will destroy these programs. The fight against deficit reduction is a losing battle. Society's progressive elements should instead be concentrating on how the job is to be done, on the question of priorities, and accept that they cannot defend every good cause, meet every need. We would be misleading ourselves if we believed that another solution would spare us the pain and the social tension. But we cannot escape.

Governments must walk a fine line between the constraints of the market and the claims of social groups. They will have no choice but to change their role; however, they cannot abdicate their responsibilities. In the final analysis, the decisions to raise or cut taxes, to shift the tax burden from one group to another, to reduce some expenditures while increasing others, are legitimate political choices.

Financial and fiscal constraints will be with us for several years to come; the political infighting will be fierce. Nothing could be more normal. Whatever measures are finally adopted must be the result of freely discussed choices that take as much account of the social and economic realities of the day as of the financial situation. This book has dealt with one aspect of the problem. I hope that my journey through the back rooms and corridors of the world of finance will help us make better-informed decisions. Information is what fuels markets; it is also vital to a functioning democracy. The kind of quality information that transmits the image of a shifting, complex reality is the foe of ideological quick-fixes. An understanding of the facts can help release creativity in the search for solutions. Shopworn ideological blinders or passing fashions must be set aside. Trading yesterday's ideologies for creative compromise does not mean we abandon our values, nor should it stop us from vigorously defending our interests.

If we are to reduce the debt, citizens accustomed to receiving more goods and services than they paid for must now accept that they will be receiving fewer — for the same money. The new state that will emerge will be tighter with its money, and aware of its limits. Its ambitions might be more modest, but it will still have tremendous clout.

AFTER
THE
REFERENDUM

MONTREAL, TUESDAY, OCTOBER 31, 1995

SO, WHICH WAY did you vote? I asked a fellow journalist the morning after. "50.6 percent No." He laughed, but there was a hint of sadness in his voice. It was an ambivalence that mirrored Quebec's. Most of us in the *La Presse* business section had cast our votes without any great enthusiasm for one side or the other, torn between the political siren song of the Yes, and the hard-nosed economic reasoning that whispered No. Throughout the referendum campaign we taunted, needled, joked, and held on to our sense of humour. Over the years, Quebeckers have learned to live with the great divide that runs right down the middle of their society and to keep it from breaking friendships.

My own job — covering the financial markets — wasn't exactly smooth sailing. The owner of *La Presse*, Paul Desmarais, is a committed federalist, and the paper's editorial page fought tooth and nail for his cause. In the newsroom, management's attitude was "Be neutral and stick to the facts." That's the way I saw it, too. Like every French-speaking journalist, I was well aware that half my readers were sitting on one side of the fence, the other half on the other side: I wanted both sides to read what I had to say. I'm as non-partisan as they come, but facts are never neutral. More inconveniently, some facts are not as factual as they look.

The business section at *La Presse* is a busy place — telephones ringing, people hurrying to and fro, desks crammed with computer screens and stacks of books, files, and papers. It's a newsroom. But like a trading room, it's driven by information, and the air is thick with adrenaline. Like an investment dealer, I'd spent my last few days chatting with the street, keeping track of prices. But as R-Day crept closer, the job got harder. Even experienced traders and veteran economists did not want to be quoted, not even about the weather. Earlier constitutional debates had seen the financial community get carried away, issuing extremist, partisan statements. Now the pendulum had swung to the other extreme. Behind closed doors, Quebec government ministers were indulging in some discreet arm-twisting to keep Canadian bankers and investment dealers in line. Who would want to risk a lucrative place on the province's financial syndicate, or turn their back on such an important chunk of its retail business? It was intimidation, and it worked. Only a few experts dared mention the economic consequences of a Yes vote, leaving the subject to Liberal Party politicians, with their limited credibility.

The Caisse steps in to support the dollar

Perhaps it was a consequence of PQ censorship, but it had all the symptoms of a case of mass hypnosis: traders swore to me they had seen the Virgin Mary's statue weep tears of blood! In a front-page story, the *Globe and Mail*[1] reported that the Quebec government, the Caisse de dépôt et placement du Québec, and Hydro-Québec had attempted to stabilize the price of the Canadian dollar and thus reassure nervous voters on the eve of the referendum. But no one knows better than currency traders that even the Bank of Canada, with its enormous reserves, could not possibly keep the loonie under control. Quebec Finance minister Jean Campeau issued a vehement denial. But still the market rumour mill churned on.

What happened is this: traders were short when the Caisse began to buy up Canadian dollars a week before the vote. The Caisse had been speculating on the dollar, just as it regularly does with foreign currency shifts.

256

Hydro-Québec had just wound up a small, routine transaction worth $50 million after converting a medium-term note placed in Europe. The Quebec Finance department, meanwhile, sat on its hands.

Whether the outcome was Yes or No, the Caisse planned to make a tidy profit. As the first part of a two-pronged strategy, Caisse traders bought a put option valid until November 1. Under the option, purchased at a cheap price during the second week of October, when a victory for the No side seemed certain, the Caisse could sell $500 million (US) worth of Canadian dollars at $1.40 (CA) (71.42 cents [US]). The exchange rate then stood at $1.33 (CA) (75.19 cents [US]).

One week prior to the referendum, the Caisse activated phase two of its strategy, buying $200 million (US) worth of Canadian dollars on the cash market at a rate close to $1.3750 (CA) (72.73 cents [US]) in $50–$70 million (US) increments on Tuesday, Wednesday, and Thursday. The original plan was to buy $250 million (US) worth of loonies, but the Caisse could not raise the money at the exchange rate it wanted.

The day after the No victory, the loonie jumped by three-quarters of a cent to $1.3450 (CA) (74.35 cents [US]). The Caisse promptly took the euphoria to market, selling the $200 million (US) worth of Canadian dollars for a profit of nearly $6 million (CA). The option, which had cost $300,000, was not exercised.[2]

Had the Yes side prevailed, the Caisse would have exercised its sell option. To be able to deliver the Canadian dollars at the agreed-upon rate of 71.42 cents (US), it would have used the dollars bought the previous week, picking up loonies at a bargain-basement panic rate to make up the difference. Shaped by its internal referendum forecast, the Caisse strategy was astute, with a strong, built-in probability of profit no matter the outcome. In the event, the Caisse's total profit was nearly $7 million (CA); in addition to the one-two punch, it had bought $50 million (CA) at the same time as the option, which it later resold at a higher price.

The Tuesday before the referendum, the dollar gained $\frac{23}{100}$ of a cent, even though the polls were pointing to a tight race. The upward swing was startling; the loonie had lost 1.6 cents (US) over the previous two days. Behind the dramatic turnaround was buying by the Caisse, some traders alleged. But there were other, more compelling causes. The Bank of Canada's bank rate had shot up by almost a full percentage point, making Treasury bills a much more attractive proposition for foreigners; the Canadian dollar had reached a significant resistance threshold; two traders told me that they had seen a New York–based hedge fund snap up ten-year Canadian bonds in $100-million (CA) tranches, at an attractive spread of 205 basis points. Another currency trader confirmed that he sold large amounts of Canadian dollars to European customers. The market itself was shallow, accentuating the impact of volume on prices. But like blind men trying to describe an elephant, some traders insisted that they knew exactly what had happened: the evil Caisse had manipulated the foreign exchange market for political purposes.

Is it fair to speculate on the foreign exchange market with the savings of tomorrow's pensioners? The answer is not a simple one. Ontario Teachers' never hedges the foreign exchange risk on its currency investments. Some would call that speculation; not so, others would claim, since the fund makes no attempt to predict foreign exchange fluctuations. The Caisse hedges 100 percent of its risks, and its speculative positions never have the indirect effect of bringing the hedging ratio below the 90-percent level. Some label this policy as extremely conservative; others criticize it as pretentious in its ambitions, however limited, to predict these same fluctuations. In Europe, Japan, and the United States, many of the great institutions we visited vary their hedge ratio to suit themselves. Who's right; who's wrong? Only the Shadow knows.

Two days after the referendum, Montreal's French-language TVA network broadcast an exclusive interview with Jacques Parizeau. Recorded a few hours before polls closed, and originally to be aired in January, the piece was shown after the Quebec premier's surprise resignation, which followed his controversial referendum-night statement blaming money and the ethnic vote for his defeat. Like a cat that has just swallowed a canary, Mr. Parizeau in the interview praised his own prescience and skill.

A strategy had been set up to counter the speculators, he revealed: "The important thing is for them to lose money. If they lose, they'll see where their interests lie. The important thing is how we manage the first day. If the people who want to play lose enough money, what happened last Monday will happen all over again; it will go right back up the next day." Hinting that the Caisse had immense liquidity on hand, he boasted:

"We are the co-defenders of the Canadian dollar. I have come to praise the Canadian dollar! I intend to support it alongside the Bank of Canada, the Caisse de dépôt, the federal Finance minister, the Quebec Finance minister. Everybody is supporting the glorious Canadian dollar! We shall never let it fall!"[3] English Canadians believed him; it was the first time Bay Street traders ever showed that kind of faith in the Premier's word. All of which goes to show that when things get tense, traders hear what they want to hear. More proof? Parizeau was rumoured to have deposited his personal savings in a Vermont bank!

A concerted plan for market intervention in the event of a Yes victory did exist. The Caisse had on hand more cash than usual. But the money could hardly have propped up the Canadian dollar; at best it might have maintained a semblance of order on the secondary market for Quebec government and Hydro-Québec bonds, while financing the borrowing needs of the province and the municipalities if market access were to be blocked for too long. None of this was out of keeping with the institution's policy. The Caisse would have bought $300 million (US) worth of Canadian dollars to exercise its put option — but it would not have been enough to salvage a floundering loonie.

The Caisse's cash assets consisted almost entirely of U.S. Treasuries, U.S.-dollar-denominated securities. Couldn't it have used the greenbacks to buy loonies in the hope of keeping prices up? Not a chance. That position had already been hedged against foreign exchange risk. Sale of U.S. Treasuries to buy Quebecs denominated in Canadian dollars would have had no effect on the loonie. By winding up the hedge, the Caisse would force the hedging bank to sell an identical quantity of Canadian dollars, cancelling out the upward effect of the purchase. In a word, the Caisse could not have supported the Canadian dollar, even if it had wanted to; in the event, it did not even try. What the Caisse did do was make money, which is its job. For all its post-referendum ambitions on the Quebec securities market, which is much smaller than the foreign exchange market, the Caisse's moderating influence could not have held back an upsurge in interest rates if the Yes side had won.

In the referendum campaign, as in all wars, truth was the first casualty. In the trading rooms, the battle was fought with rumour and counter-rumour, while on the hustings, the debate over the costs of transition vanished halfway through the campaign. Lucien Bouchard, leader of the Yes campaign, simply refused to discuss the issue.

All signs point to another referendum, with Quebeckers attempting once again to slice through the Gordian knot that binds them to Canada. The time to talk about the issues is now, before the barometer starts rising. In scrutinizing the way markets act and how their actions influence the fiscal situation, this book has posited the same constraints as existed immediately after the 1995 referendum. Of course, only a fortune-teller with a crystal ball could possibly foresee when or under what circumstances the next vote on Quebec's future will take place. My aim in these final pages is to pinpoint some of the underlying, long-term trends and shed some light on the factors that might emerge as crucial. These factors do not include loss or postponement of direct investment, the threatened exodus of part of the English-speaking population, the slow, hard bargaining that would be a prelude to joining NAFTA. Nor do they include the advantages of a more compact, friendlier state machinery. I have not touched on the political and cultural problems that have shaped our complex dilemma.

A roadblock across the highway to sovereignty

The highway to sovereignty, as former Quebec premier Jacques Parizeau called it, has a major roadblock: the public debt. Quebec can strain to move it out of the way, but it will put a strain on other Canadians, too.

The first referendum on Quebec sovereignty was held in 1980; since then, the terms of the independence debate have changed radically. Back then the federalists, who were the dominant force, declared that a sovereign Quebec was simply not an economically viable proposition. Today, respected economists for both camps argue over whether Quebec, as an independent state, would be a little richer or a little poorer in the long run.

Fifteen years ago, Quebeckers were worried about being cut off from the Canadian market. Today, a sovereign Quebec and Ottawa might not be able to agree on economic links with the rest of Canada, but thanks to

NAFTA, most trade would continue as usual. If these were the only issues, there would be no serious economic obstacle to Quebec independence. The real problem lies elsewhere.

Since 1980, Quebec's debt has risen from 17 percent to 44 percent of GDP. The Canadian debt, of which Quebec would have to shoulder its share, has soared from 16 percent to 73 percent of GDP. A burden of these dimensions means that both Quebec and Canada are less free to do as they wish.

In 1980, most people believed that only Quebec would suffer in the aftermath of a vote for independence. Today, it is clear that the costs of transition would be roughly the same across Canada.

Foreigners finance 40 percent of our public debt. They would eventually learn to live with an independent Quebec — and a shrunken Canada. But during the transition period they would prefer not to hold Canadian or Quebec bonds. With a few exceptions, Canadian investors appear to feel the same way.

Fleeing uncertainty

Investors hate uncertainty. Astonishingly, financiers, the people whose day-to-day work is risk management, are poorly prepared to deal with political risk. They might wield powerful computers and sophisticated models for analysing economic and financial statistics, but they are woefully unqualified to judge political developments that do not jibe with the laws of supply and demand. In the face of political risk, their first reflex is to leap headlong from blindness into paranoia, then run away.

But bailing out is easier said than done. Vendors must find buyers; not everyone can sell at the same time. Panic selling drives prices down and dries up liquidity. If this were to happen, all the cash in the Caisse would be nothing more than a drop in the bucket.

With such a scenario, the dollar would fall and interest rates would soar. By how much and for how long? Nobody knows for sure. What we do know is that international investors have become more selective. Movements of capital have become more violent.

Speculators would launch an attack on the Canadian dollar. The plummeting loonie would drag all financial instruments denominated in Canadian dollars down with it, starting with Government of Canada bonds. Canadian bonds denominated in foreign currencies would follow suit, but more slowly.

Ottawa would be hardest hit, since almost the entire federal debt is in Canadian dollars. Aside from the bonds held by the Caisse, most Quebec borrowing is in foreign currencies. In the short term, a foreign investor holding Canadian paper denominated in Canadian dollars would lose more money than someone holding Quebec bonds denominated in yen, or Ontario bonds in Deutschmarks.

But not all investors act the same way. Those who choose the long term prefer provincial bonds in foreign currencies; those who like short-term speculation buy Canada bonds or Treasury bills that they can buy and sell quickly, and in quantity.

Rain or shine, Ottawa issues each week billions of dollars' worth of T-bills and bonds. To attract buyers, it would have to offer much higher interest rates. If that didn't work, the federal government could borrow in American dollars, or call on other banks, and even the IMF, for help.

The provinces that have reduced or eliminated their deficits or have accelerated their new borrowing or debt-refinancing programs could afford to wait out the storm. Quebec could fall back on the Caisse de dépôt and a solid savings bond campaign. But if Quebeckers began to doubt that the Canadian dollar would continue to be legal tender, they might turn to U.S. Treasuries instead of "sovereignty bonds." We had a taste of things to come in the final days of the referendum campaign, as both federalist and sovereigntist Quebeckers moved millions of Canadian dollars into U.S. dollar accounts. Some money actually fled the country, but no one knows how much. For Quebec, the crunch would come soon enough, as the province attempted to persuade investors to buy bonds again.

Transition costs

The longer and the more intense the political crisis following a Yes vote, the more acute the financial crisis. The Quebec government's sovereignty law provided for a year of negotiations with Canada, perhaps longer. But the pressure to conclude an agreement rapidly would be overpowering. And to win back investor confidence, there would have to be agreement on sharing the federal debt, and on the currency to be used in a sovereign Quebec.

Governments will find the money they need during the transition period. But credit could be beyond the reach of most businesses and individuals. If interest rates were to rise for several months, the entire Canadian economy would slide into recession, complete with job losses and higher mortgage payments.

Playing with fire

Public debt traded in the form of government bonds is the bedrock of the capital market. The relationship is a dependent one, which makes the debt issue a dynamic one. Any uncertainty about how and when the debt will be repaid — and who will repay it — drives down the value of government bonds; any loss in bond values drives interest rates up. Any rise in rates increases the cost of financing the debt and slows down the economy. And any slowdown slashes government revenues and boosts transfer payments to individuals. The upshot is still-greater deficits and a heavier debt load. The debt could spiral out of control.

While facing a heavy debt load from day one, an independent Quebec would have to contend with significant transition costs in an atmosphere of political turbulence. These would include the cost of restructuring the civil service, and the indirect costs of economic slowdown. At least one, perhaps two years would have to pass before the savings from a slimmer, trimmer government would begin to kick in.

The relation between the debt load and the size of Quebec's and Canada's economies could undergo substantial changes, depending on the terms of an eventual debt-sharing arrangement between the two governments. The financial ratios of the two countries would be affected by whether Quebec assumes 17 percent of the debt, as the sovereigntists suggest, or 25 percent, the Reform Party figure. The 8-percent gap between the two negotiating positions represents the tidy sum of $37 billion, for an annual interest bill of roughly $3 billion. The $3-billion figure would be that much more, or less, for either the Quebec or the Ottawa deficit. The debt-sharing differential alone would account for 22 percent of Quebec's GDP, and 6 percent of Canada's (not including Quebec). A disagreement of that size is bound to make the New York bond-rating agencies look twice. The agencies themselves, which were sharply criticized for not having foreseen the Mexican debacle, have become more demanding.

A critical rating

Moody's and Standard & Poor's assessment of Quebec's finances after the transition phase would be a critical one. A downgrading would have much more serious consequences for Quebec than for Canada. Canada's AA rating indicates high quality, but for most international investors Quebec's A^4 lies at the lower limits of acceptability. And if Quebec's rating were to slip to BBB, a low mark for a developed sovereign state, the vast majority of foreign investors would refuse to touch Quebec bonds; many would feel obliged to sell. Of the twenty-six OECD countries, only three have a rating lower than AA: Iceland (A), Greece (BBB), and Turkey (B). Quebec would be the fourth.

A country cut off from the bond market would have to turn to the great international banks, who already lend to several Third World countries. Why not Quebec? Let's be frank: the banks would not lend the new sovereigntist government all it asked for, and in return, they would demand their pound of flesh. If sovereignty is to have any meaning, this would be the kind of extreme solution better left unexplored.

The costs of transition, combined with a tattered balance sheet, would make the danger of a BBB rating real indeed. The only way out would be a round of budget cuts far more draconian than in Ralph Klein's Alberta or Mike Harris's Ontario. But do the union leaders who backed the Parti Québécois have that kind of society in mind? The business community would hail a tough budget, but is their enthusiasm the kind it takes to build a country? The economists who argue that independence would make Quebec wealthier are counting on the surge of motivation and creative energy touched off by founding a country. But will the motivation and the energy be there when they are needed most?

Quebeckers can put Quebec's financial house in order or they can begin sharpening their knives for the final battle. But do they really have a choice? Whatever their political allegiance, Quebec's citizens have a shared interest in healthy public finances. The financial housecleaning is bound to spark conflicts and create new divisions, but when the house is in order, making a constitutional choice might be an easier task. A healthier bottom line would not eliminate transition costs, but it would cut them down to a more manageable size. All things considered, it would be less costly, and less risky, for Quebec to put its affairs in order before the next referendum, even though the federal system, with its labyrinth of overlapping jurisdictions, makes it a complicated and frustrating exercise.

What will the foreigners think?

The financial markets strolled into the referendum campaign with a mixture of nonchalance and confidence, convinced that the No side would win in a cakewalk. Curiously, in the past, traders have panicked at less. This time they badly misjudged probabilities, which only goes to prove what they already know: politics is unpredictable — and risky. But it would be a mistake to mistake their casual behaviour for indifference in the event of a Yes verdict.

Selig Sechzer, vice president of Alliance Capital, visited the Canadian Consulate in New York to watch the referendum results come in. "The markets are relieved, but upset that the question hasn't been settled," he told me later that evening, by telephone.

The next day I chatted with Adam Chester, London-based international bond market strategist for Yamaichi, the Japanese investment dealer. "Incredible," was how he described the referendum result; "the clouds of uncertainty are still there," he said. Investors are expecting Prime Minister Jean Chrétien to respond to Quebec's expectations, he added. Statements by Yes side leaders calling for another round left him stunned: "Is it rhetoric or is it real?" he asked.

Over a lunchtime sandwich, Charles Thompson seemed relieved: "We were substantially overweighted in Canadian bonds," the North American bond specialist at Barclay's Zoete Wedd told me, admitting to "a few sleep-less nights." Since the start of the year, Thompson had built up a position of several hundred million dollars in Canada bonds, expecting a victory by the federalist forces. An internal study produced by this subsidiary of a major British bank had an independent Quebec's rating falling to BBB, with the new country being forced to slice expenditures or raise taxes by 9 percent. A Yes would have cost Barclay's a pile of money. The No verdict made the bank a profit.

"I've really been scared shitless these days," Mike Rosborough admits. Rosborough is international portfolio director at Pimco, the largest fund manager in the United States. He has called me three times in the last two weeks for my slant on the referendum campaign. Altogether, we've spoken for more than an hour and a half. And I'm certain he talks about the same subject with plenty of other people. "This morning, the referendum made the front page of the *Orange County Register*, a daily paper in southern California," he told me. Last night he followed the vote tally closely. Rosborough did not want to say what his position in Canada bonds was, but he admitted it was "substantial." My guess is that it was well over $1 billion. The position had been built up from February to August, in anticipation of a No victory and lower government deficits. Now, in spite of the cliff-hanger, he hopes austerity will still head the agenda.

In New York, Ravi Bulchandani, Canada analyst at Morgan Stanley, believes that the narrow No victory "has reduced short-term risk a little bit, but has not eliminated it." Still, he feels that change will take place within the Canadian political system and that governments will bring down reasonable budgets, even if it might be more difficult to make progress.

The risk premium that goes hand in hand with political uncertainty may well lessen, but it is unlikely to vanish, and might reappear at any time. In the short term, Canadian bonds might be hampered as the risk problem continues to act as a brake on putting our financial house in order. In Quebec the worry is even greater; investors who compare figures can see that the province is isolated, adrift with its huge deficit.

Clearly, constitutional uncertainty cannot be allowed to continue indefinitely. It is costly and debilitating. But any attempt to stage a replay in the short term would be disastrous. The supreme commanders will have to let the troops take a breather. Respecting the October 30 vote also means giving the rest of Canada time to appreciate how crucial the issue really is, and to draw up a counterproposal, if it can.

This book makes no pretense of analysing the strengths and weaknesses of Canadian federalism. Summary judgments would be out of place. It is true that the markets lean heavily toward maintaining Canadian unity. But it is also true that for many citizens, choice of a country springs from values that transcend money matters. If Quebeckers wish to make the great leap, they would be well advised to do so on a balanced budget. If, on the other hand, they decide to remain in Canada, a serious financial housecleaning will stand them in good stead.

NOTES

INTRODUCTION

1. *La Presse*, December 8, 1993

2. Public accounts do not include health care expenditures, the Canada Pension Plan (CPP), or the Quebec Pension Plan (Régie des rentes du Québec); they do include money owed by governments to civil servants' pension funds.

3. Negotiable debt consists primarily of bonds and Treasury bills, and comprises some 80 percent of federal debt and 70 percent of provincial debt. It also includes securities purchased by the Canada Pension Plan, the Quebec Pension Plan, and public pension funds.

4. Moody's draws a distinction between provincial debt supported by tax revenue and debt supported by commercial revenue, as in the case of electric utilities, even if both are formally guaranteed by the province. But in the eyes of most foreign investors, electric utility debt is closely related to provincial creditworthiness.

5. Graham Allison, *Essence of Decision: Explaining the Cuban Missile Crisis* (Boston: Little Brown, 1971).

CHAPTER 1: THIRTY-SIX HOURS ON THE FINANCIAL MARKETS

1. Estimates have been taken from an international survey commissioned by the Bank for International Settlements in April 1995. Most exchange transactions are agreed upon today for a future date: the forward market accounts for 8 percent of transactions, the swap market for 53 percent.

2. The regulations mean that the overnight rate will remain within the operating range. Banks prefer not to borrow overnight funds at a rate higher than the high end of the range, knowing that the Bank of Canada will lend them money up to that point, i.e., the bank rate. Banks will not lend below the low end of the range, knowing that the Bank of Canada will pay more for its excess funds.

3. "The Bank of Canada's Operations on the Financial Markets," remarks by Tim E. Noël, Deputy Governor, Bank of Canada, to the Toronto Association for Business and Economics and the Treasury Management Association of Toronto, October 25, 1995.

4. Philip Coggan, "A market impossible to tame," *The Financial Times*, February 11–12, 1995, p. xvi.

5. Repos were widely used after the stock market crash of 1987 to inject temporary liquidity into the market and to bring interest rates down rapidly. A few weeks later, when damage appeared less acute than anticipated, the bank reversed course.

6. A decline in the value of the dollar increases the price of imports, which contributes to inflation. The impact on prices is more rapid than the impact on export volumes. In 1994, the danger seemed remote.

7. The developing countries that fell heavily into debt in the late 1970s had contracted debt in U.S. dollars. But their central banks could not print greenbacks, a privilege restricted to the U.S. Federal Reserve.

8. *Globe and Mail*, October 13, 1994, p. B1.

CHAPTER 3: MONEY FROM EUROPE

1. *Le Monde*, October 18, 1994.

2. *La Tribune*, October 18, 1994.

3. OECD and IMF macroeconomic policy surveillance surveys overlap. At the June 1995 G7 meeting in Halifax, leaders agreed to press the OECD to devote more research to structural policies.

4. *OECD Economic Outlook*, No. 56 (Paris: December 1994), p. 19.

5. François Leroux, *Marchés internationaux des capitaux*, 2nd edition (Sainte-Foy: Presses de l'Université du Québec HEC-CETAI, 1994), p. 10.

6. *Les Échos*, October 14–15, 1994.

7. William Dudley, *Canadian Economic Commentary* (London: Goldman Sachs, International Economics Research, October 14, 1994).

8. *L'Express*, October 27, pp. 36–41.

9. Pictet & Cie, Banquiers, *Marchés obligataires*, Geneva, Fall 1994, p. 19.

10. *Bilan*, October 1994, pp. 44–46.

11. *L'AGEFI*, October 19, 1994.

12. Credit Suisse, *The Global Asset Manager*, Zurich, Summer 1994, p. 25.

13. Credit Suisse, *International Business Monitor*, Zurich, September 1994, p. 30.

14. "Canada's Debt Dilemma," *Financial Times*, October 25, 1994.

CHAPTER 4: THE CITY

1. *Euromoney*, May 1993, pp. 30–36.

2. Eurobond market figures include so-called global financing, a portion of which is sold in Europe, the remainder being placed in the United States, in Japan, and on the Canadian market.

3. The Canadian ambassador to London holds the title of high commissioner.

4. *Euromoney*, October 1994, pp. 62–64.

CHAPTER 5: SHAKE-UP IN JAPAN

1. Iwata Yukihiro, "Canadian Finance Minister announces formation of G7 task force to prepare for the creation of emerging market assistance structure; Minister indicates he's determined to tackle reduction of Canada's deficit," *Nihon Keizai Shinbun*, February 6, 1995, p. 3.

2. David H. Sawyer and Todd G. Buchholz, *G7 Daily Briefing*, February 7, 1995, p. 1.

3. Canadian Embassy, Tokyo, "1994 Canadian Embassy Survey: Japanese Portfolio Investment in Canada."

4. Horaki Itoh, "Canada trying to reverse deficit increase trend; combined federal and provincial debts match GDP. Strong economy helps Finance minister remain upbeat as attention focuses on budget proposal," *Asahi Shinbun*, February 17, 1995, p. 12.

5. *Nihon Keizai Shinbun*, February 17, 1995, p. 2.

6. Canadian Embassy, Tokyo, "1994 Canadian Embassy Survey: Japanese Portfolio Investment in Canada."

CHAPTER 6: ADAM SMITH STRIKES BACK

1. On February 16, 1995, Moody's imposed a credit-watch, with negative outlook, on the Canadian government. The decision to downgrade the rating of its Canadian dollar debt from Aaa to Aa1, and of its foreign currency debt from Aa1 to Aa2, was announced on April 12, 1995.

2. "Canada Makes Right Turn," *The Wall Street Journal*, March 1, 1995, p. A16.

3. At $44.8 billion, the Caisse de dépôt et placement du Québec manages greater assets. However, the Caisse brings together several specialized public funds, including the Quebec government employees' pension fund ($16.2 billion), the Quebec Pension Plan ($14.4 billion), and the construction workers' pension fund. *Benefits Canada* ranks Ontario Teachers' as Canada's largest pension fund. See "The Top 100 Pension Funds," *Benefits Canada*, April 1995, pp. 41–53.

4. In economic theory, the marginal buyer is the person who lends the government the last dollar it needs. The interest rate he demands for the loan of this last dollar becomes the market rate, the price that ensures that capital supply equals government demand.

5. The $300-million issue brings the bond's total outstanding debt to $4.8 billion. This real yield paper matures on December 21, 2021. The interest coupon ensures holders a yield of 4.25 percent above the consumer price index for the preceding three months, with interest being calculated on the face value of the bond. Reger's higher yield — 4.587 percent — can be explained by the discount obtained on bond prices, which stood at $94.985 per $100 of face value. When an issue is reopened to increase its outstanding debt and thus its liquidity, the coupon rate will differ from the yield, since the market will have evolved since the initial issue.

6. The median yield, which divides pension funds into two equal-sized groups, offers a better point of comparison than average yield, which can be influenced by a handful of extreme performances. Quartiles, which divide funds into four equal groups, allow for a finer distinction. Those belonging to the first quartile perform substantially better than those in the last quartile. On the bond market, yield variations from one quartile to another are small; these variations are larger on the stock market.

7. The father of liberal capitalism, Adam Smith, in his *Wealth of Nations* (1776), maintains that businessmen, in seeking their own personal interest, work for the common good, as though guided by an "invisible hand."

CHAPTER 7: IN UNCLE SAM'S BACK YARD

1. *Business Week*, March 20, 1995, pp. 46–56.

2. Colin Nickerson, "Deep in Quebec's frozen heartland, independent fires burn," *Boston Globe*, March 20, 1995, p. 1.

3. Reuven Brenner, "Canadian Finances Look a Lot Like Accounting at Barings," *The Wall Street Journal*, March 24, 1995, p. A15.

4. Ravi Bulchandani, *Canadian Economic and Policy Outlook*, Morgan Stanley, March 1995.

CHAPTER 8: THE RATING GAME

1. Much interesting information can also be found in the prospectuses accompanying Quebec government and Hydro-Québec bond issues in the United States.

2. In stock-market jargon, the bull represents the optimist who believes the market will rise; the bear believes the market will fall.

3. S&P had put Mexico's foreign currency rating under surveillance, with negative outlook, on December 22, 1994.

4. Of the thirty-one countries to default on their foreign currency debt, S&P numbers thirty that have rescheduled bank debt, even though, legally speaking, the measure was freely agreed to by the banks.

5. Moody's analysts did not agree to an interview during my trip to New York, as Canada's ratings were under review at the time.

6. *The Economist*, July 15, 1995, p. 54.

CHAPTER 9: FOUR BORROWERS, FOUR STRATEGIES

1. Quoted in Peter Desbarats, *René Lévesque: A Canadian in Search of a Country* (Toronto: McClelland & Stewart, 1976).

2. See Yves Rabeau, *Les Subventions et le secteur de l'électricité au Québec*, working paper, Centre de recherche en gestion, Université de Québec à Montréal, November 1995.

3. For a description of federal government financing activities, see *Debt Operations Report* (Ottawa: Finance Department, December 1995), 52 pages.

4. More provincial debt is held by foreign hands, bringing the proportion of Canadian public debt financed by non-residents to 40 percent.

5. The 1995 figure differs from the 2 percent noted in the introduction, where 1994 statistics were used.

6. As of March 31, 1996, the percentage of the debt of Nova Scotia that is floating has increased to 17 percent and the net foreign currency exposure has been reduced to 55 percent; the province wants to bring it down to 20 percent. The budget tabled for fiscal year 1996–97 is balanced.

CHAPTER 10: CONCLUSION: FINDING SOLUTIONS

1. Speech to the Montreal Conference, June 14, 1995.

2. Speech to the Montreal Conference, June 13, 1995.

3. Jeffrey Sachs, Aaron Tornell, and Andres Velasco, "The Real Story," *The International Economy*, March/April 1995, p. 14.

4. Speech to the Montreal Conference, June 14, 1995.

5. Bank for International Settlements, *65th Annual Report*, April 1, 1994–March 31, 1995, Basel, June 12, 1995, 241 pages.

6. Ibid.

7. Ibid.

8. Ibid.

9. Ibid.

10. Ibid.

11. Linda McQuaig, *Shooting the Hippo* (Toronto: Viking Canada, 1995).

12. In May 1991, I published a series of articles critical of Bank of Canada Governor John Crow's monetary policies in *La Presse*.

13. John Crow, "The New World of International Finance: Implications for Business and Labor," in *Reform of the International Monetary System: Views from North America. North American Outlook*, Washington, National Planning Association, June 1995, vol. 5, no. 3, p. 22.

EPILOGUE: AFTER THE REFERENDUM

1. Andrew Wills and Greg Ip, "Quebec buying up dollars," *Globe and Mail*, October 25, 1995, p. A1.

2. The risk was that markets might remain unaffected by a Yes victory and that the Caisse would lose its $300,000 option.

3. Quoted in Mario Fontaine, "Le gouvernement péquiste avait préparé une stratégie pour contrer les speculateurs [PQ government strategy designed to block speculators]," *La Presse*, November 2, 1995, p. B5. See also Barrie McKenna and Allan Freeman, "Parizeau admits to war chest: Quebec Premier says multibillion-dollar fund amassed to prop up dollar in the even of a Yes win," *Globe and Mail*, November 3, 1995, p. B1.

4. To be more exact, Quebec's S&P rating is A+, Moody's, A2. In theory, the province's rating would have to slip a few notches, to A and A- for Standard & Poor's, A3 for Moody's, before hitting the BBB level. But such nuances do not affect the scenario presented here. Quebec's creditworthiness would still decline substantially.

GLOSSARY*

arbitrage
Simultaneous purchase and sale of securities to benefit from a difference in price between two related markets, products, or maturities.

arbitrageur
A professional who simultaneously buys and sells stocks or bonds with the intention of benefiting from price differentials between markets, products, or securities.

asset class
Group into which similar securities are classified; e.g., a portfolio's assets can be divided into shares, bonds, cash, foreign currency, and real estate — each can be considered a different class.

assets
A general term designating all property, claims, and values belonging to an individual or an enterprise.

bank rate
Rate set by the Bank of Canada for its loans to the chartered banks.

banker's acceptance
Short-term note of exchange guaranteed by a bank.

basis points
Units corresponding to one one-hundredth of 1 percent; i.e., a movement of one hundred basis points equals 1 percent.

bear
A market in which prices fall; or, a person who is pessimistic about market developments and speculates on a drop in values.

Belgian dentist
Symbol of tax evasion by European professionals.

benchmark issue
Bond used as reference for measuring yield spreads of other bonds of identical maturity; e.g., Government of Canada two-, three-, four-, ten- and thirty-year bonds are seen as benchmarks in the Canadian bond market.

bond
Debt security issued by a government or corporation, usually for a term of two to thirty years. Unlike savings bonds, bonds can be bought and sold on secondary markets at any time, but usually are not redeemable before maturity.

bond market
The secondary market in which government and corporate bonds are traded.

bull
A market in which prices rise; or, a person who is optimistic about market developments and speculates on a rise in values.

Bund
German government bond.

---

* Some of the terms listed in this glossary might have other meanings than those indicated here. Definitions have been simplified. For more detailed explanations see John Downes, *Dictionary of Finance and Investment Terms* (New York: Barron's Educational Series, 1991); P. H. Collin, *Dictionary of Banking and Finance* (London: Peter Collin Publishing, 1991); and David Crane, *The Canadian Dictionary of Business and Economics* (Toronto: Stoddart Publishing Co., 1993).

buy-back (*see also* **repo**)
Purchase of a security with a promise to resell at a later price and time; repo indicates sale of a security; buy-back, its purchase.

capital gain
Profit realized in selling an asset at a price higher than the purchase price.

capital market
A market where long-term capital (shares, bonds, etc.) is traded.

cash
Money on hand or on call, ready for use.

commercial paper
Short-term debt security issued by a company.

counterparty
An intermediary who buys or sells securities corresponding to a specific buy or sell order; counterparty risk is the risk that the buyer will not respect his commitment.

coupon (*see also* **yield**)
Detachable portion of a bond that entitles the holder to periodic interest; the coupon rate is the annual interest rate stipulated at the date of issue.

credit rating
Status bestowed by a rating agency, such as Standard & Poor's, which evaluates the ability of a lender to meet its obligations.

creditor
Person who is owed money.

currency trader
Professional who buys and sells foreign currencies.

current account
Portion of the balance of payments between countries, including the trade balance (international trade in merchandise) and invisibles (principally international tourism and income from cross-border investments).

derivative instrument, product
Financial instrument (options, futures, swaps, or a combination of the three) whose price is derived from one or more ordinary securities such as stocks, bonds, foreign currencies, or market indices.

distributing syndicate (*see* **issuing syndicate**)

Eurobond
Bond issued outside the country of origin and denominated in a Euro currency.

Eurocan
Canadian dollars held outside of Canada; the Eurocan is a Eurocurrency.

Eurocurrency
Money deposited outside its country of origin, often in Europe but not necessarily so.

fiscal policy
Manipulation of tax revenues and government expenditures to regulate global demand and influence employment levels.

fixed income
The portion of a portfolio's yield derived from securities that produce a steady income (i.e., bonds, Treasury bills, mortgages, cash), as opposed to variable yield instruments such as stocks.

foreign exchange risk
Risk arising from exchange rate fluctuations between different currencies.

forex
Foreign exchange.

forwards
Future contracts that are negotiated with a bank over the counter.

futures
Commitment to buy or to sell a security at a previously agreed-upon price and time; the contract can be negotiated on a public exchange (futures) or privately, through a financial institution (forwards).

gilt
United Kingdom bond.

gross domestic product (GDP)
Value of all goods and services produced
by a country in a given year.

hedge
To protect a given position, short or long,
by taking another position whose value
will fluctuate in the opposite direction.

hedge fund
Funds characterized by speculative
operations; their portfolio of risks is partially hedged by positions that move in
opposite directions.

hot money
Capital that moves rapidly from one country to another in search of better security
and short-term yields.

index (plural: **indexes** or **indices**)
Basket of securities used to represent a
financial market's overall performance.

institutional market
Market consisting of financial institutions
such as banks, insurance companies,
pension funds, fund managers, and trust
companies, as opposed to individuals.
(*see* **retail market**)

international reserves
A central bank's reserves of foreign currencies, gold, and Special Drawing Rights;
used to support domestic currency.

investment dealer
An intermediary who executes security
transactions on his own or his clients'
behalf.

issue
Totality of securities issued by a government or a corporation at a given time; or
distribution of these securities on the
primary market.

issuer
Government, government agency, or company that borrows by issuing bonds or
other paper.

issuing syndicate
Group of investment dealers and bankers
that assume the financial risks of a bond
issue (underwriting syndicate) and its
distribution (distributing syndicate); a
syndicate is headed by a lead manager or
co-leads.

leverage
Yield-multiplying effect produced by use
of borrowed funds rather than one's own
capital; leverage can multiply profits, but
also losses.

LIBOR
London Interbank Offered Rate; floating
interest rate for loans made in U.S. dollars; international rate at which banks
lend to one another.

liquidity
The ease with which a security can be
bought or sold; or, cash available for the
purchase of securities.

long, being
The position in which an investor holds
bonds or other financial instruments.

Maastricht Treaty
Agreement signed in 1992 by the members of the European Union establishing
the Economic and Monetary Union, under
which member states must respect certain convergence criteria, including a
maximum indebtedness of 60 percent and
a maximum deficit of 3 percent of GDP.

market maker
A dealer or establishment that continuously posts buy or sell prices for a security, thus helping ensure the security's
liquidity.

matching of maturities
For banks and insurance companies,
the act of coupling each element of a
liability with an asset of identical term,
so that the cost of funds remains less than
the yield throughout the term, and so that
liquidity is always sufficient when liability
comes due.

medium-term note (MTN)
Medium-term loan instrument issued in limited volume to meet the specific needs of a small group of investors.

merchant bank
European financial establishment that leads bond issues, advises corporations, manages portfolios, and invests its own capital in commercial ventures.

monetary policy
Use of monetary variables such as interest rates and the amount of money in circulation to regulate the economy; in Canada, the main objective of monetary policy is price stability.

monetize (debts)
Reduce government debt by printing more money; this fuels inflation and leads to currency depreciation.

money market
Market for short-term debt securities such as Treasury bills, bankers' acceptances, certificates of deposit, etc.

mutual fund
A pool of money invested in common by savers with a view to collective placement in securities, and managed by a third party.

name
Bond issuer, borrower; or, a borrower's creditworthiness.

national accounts
An economy's revenue and expenditure account; or, national revenue accounting system that measures such macroeconomic variables as GDP, balance of payments, savings, investments, etc.

open-market operation
Central bank intervention on the money market through sale or purchase of Treasury bills, or through repos/buybacks.

over-the-counter
The market(s) for securities not listed on a public exchange but traded directly by investment dealers and institutions; over-the-counter transactions are carried out by telephone or by computer.

overnight rate
Interest rate used by banks and investment dealers for short-term funds.

placement (*see also* **issue**)
To find buyers for securities being issued.

portfolio
Overall basket of securities held by an investor; a portfolio may be diversified or specialized.

primary market
Market consisting of first buyers of a newly issued security.

prime rate
Interest rates charged by banks to their best clients; the prime rate is used to peg all short-term interest rates that banks charge their clients.

private placement
Sale of a large number of securities to a limited number of institutions.

repo (*see also* **buy-back**)
Sale of a security with a promise to repurchase at a predetermined price and time; repo indicates sale of a security; buyback, its purchase.

retail market
Market consisting of individual investors.

savings bond
Debt security issued by the government, to individuals who lend it money; a savings bond can be redeemed for its face value at all times, but cannot be traded on secondary markets.

secondary market
Public market on which securities are traded after initial distribution, i.e., stock exchange, over-the-counter markets.

security
A tradable stock, bond, or Treasury bill.

share
A negotiable security representing a right of participation in the capital growth and profits of a corporation.

short, being
The position of someone who sold a security he doesn't own; this is typical when one is speculating on a future price drop; the short-seller hopes to purchase the security later at a lower price to cover his current position and take a profit.

spread
The difference between yields on comparable securities but issued by different borrowers.

strong hands
An investor who tends to hold bonds until maturity, or for a long time.

swap
Exchange of borrowings consisting of different maturities, currencies, or interest rates.

technical analysis
Method of market analysis based on the study of price fluctuations and operating volumes using graphs and charts.

tekkie
A person who favours or practises technical analysis.

trader
Professional who buys and sells securities.

Treasury bill (T-bill)
Short-term debt security issued by the state; Treasury bills are sold at a price below face value; the spread plays the role of interest.

underwriting syndicate (*see* issuing syndicate)

U.S. Treasury
American government bond.

when issued (WI)
Treasury bill to be issued at upcoming auction but traded in advance.

Yankee
U.S.-dollar bond issued by a foreign borrower on the American market.

yield
The total return on an investment; with bonds it comprises the coupon rate as well as changes in the face value (capital gains or losses) occurring in the secondary market. Yield rate at maturity (or actuarial return) is yield obtained if the bond is held until maturity.

yield curve
The graphic depiction of differing yields for different bond maturities or different interest-rate terms.

INDEX*

---

* Page numbers in boldface indicate information in boxes.